Dear Katharine Courageous:

The Letters of Sir Edward Grey to Katharine Lyttleton

Edited and
Introduced by Jeff Lipkes

Cover design: Kachergis Book Design
Cover photo: Katharine Lyttelton, Queen Mary University London Archives
Typesetting and index: Diane Collins

Dear Katharine Courageous

TABLE OF CONTENTS

ACKNOWLEDGEMENTS

I'm very grateful to the Queen Mary University London Archives for permission to print the letters from Edward Grey to Katharine Lyttelton in the Lyttelton Papers. I would especially like to thank archivist Lorraine Screene for her assistance when I read the letters at the Mile End campus and to Lorraine and to Victoria Platt for photocopying the correspondence last fall and locating and scanning pictures of the Lyttelton family.

Archivists and staff at the following institutions were unfailingly kind and helpful: the British Library, the Bodleian Library, Cambridge University Library, Churchill College Cambridge, Durham University, the National Archives, the National Archives of Scotland, the National Library of Scotland, the Times International Archive, Winchester College, and, in the U.S., the Hoover Library of Stanford, the New York Public Library, and the Fales Library of NYU.

Apart from Lorraine, Colin Harris of the Bodleian, Ian Dawson of the Royal Society for Protection of Birds, Maria Castrillo of the NLS, and Nick Mayes of the TIA especially extended themselves, and Suzanne Foster of Winchester College graciously took me on a tour of the buildings and grounds.

I appreciate as well the following public archives for sending photocopies or scans: the Devon County Archives, Duke University, The Royal Society for the Preservation of Birds, University of Newcastle, and the Harry Crowe Ransome Center.

I'm grateful to individuals who permitted me to consult papers in their possession or corresponded with me or spoke with me about Grey. Hugo Vickers was particularly helpful, letting me look at letters from Pamela Grey and other material and introducing me to Dame Frances Campbell-Preston, a granddaughter of Katharine Lyttelton, who kindly shared recollections of her grandparents and of Grey himself. The late Michael Foote saw the former Foreign Secretary briefly when he was a schoolboy at Winchester, and sent me an amusing account of the episode. Carolyn Dakers introduced me to the Francis Dineleys, who permitted me to look at early letters from Pamela in their possession, rescued from Clouds, and sent a photocopy of one. I'm grateful as well to the Earl of Wemyss, who allowed me to look at material relating to Pamela, and who kindly showed me around the storied Stanway. I must thank also the holders of other private papers who permitted me access to them: the Duke of Westminster for letters from Pamela to George and Sybell Wyndham in the Grosvenor Papers at the Easton Estate Archives, Cheshire, and the Marquess of Lansdowne for access to letters between Grey and Lord Edmond Fitzmaurice. I'm especially grateful to the archivist at Bowood, Kate Fielden, for transcribing and taking notes on these letters.

I'd like to thank the historians who corresponded with me about Grey: Jim Covert, Cameron Hazelhurst, who generously offered to read sections of *The Lamps Go Out*, Gordon Martel, Keith Neilson, and Keith Robbins. I'm glad also for the chance to have spoken with Zara Steiner at Cambridge and with Mike Waterhouse at Winchester.

Individuals with connections to Grey also corresponded with me about him: Sir William Curtis, the grandson of his youngest sister, Agatha-Ann Graves, the widow of his oldest sister's grandson, who wrote me extensively about the family, and Richard Graves, nephew and biographer of the poet, a nephew of the oldest sister, Alice Graves. Cecilia Chance, grand-niece of Dorothy

Grey, very kindly photocopied for me the part of her great-grand-mother's diary that was devoted to Dorothy. I appreciate being introduced to her by her nephew Anthony Heaton-Armstrong. I'm particularly indebted to Alice Graves' great-grandson Adrian, who hosted me in Essex and showed me some of the Greyiana in his possession, including the Foreign Secretary's fishing tackle and his garter, as well as family photos, and later sent me a memoir by his father, Christopher Graves. Janet Babbitt, a conjectural grand-daughter, spoke with me by phone about her search for records of her mother and grandmother, and conjectural grand-son Hans-Joachim Heller generously shared the interesting documents in his possession.

Bruce Kinzer read the introduction and made some helpful comments. My greatest debt to any individual is to Pat Brockway, author of *Sir Edward Grey: More Than a Politician*, focusing on Grey at Winchester and in Hampshire, and her husband Derek. Pat accompanied me along the route Grey used to take from Winchester to Itchen Abbas, where she has restored the site of Cottage, and then, with Derek, we did part of the legendary walk the Foreign Secretary and Teddy Roosevelt took in the New Forest in June, 1910. Pat has a great fund of knowledge about Grey, and has been immensely helpful. She has read the entire introduction, asked some provocative questions, and saved me from some errors.

My apologies to any individuals I may have overlooked.

☙

The place from which Grey wrote each letter is indicated before the date, except when he used blank stationery and didn't note his location.

I have omitted some sentences, and a few letters, which only discuss plans for meetings or travel arrangements, and are otherwise of no interest, and have very occasionally modernized Grey's punctuation, if the sentence was otherwise not immediately intelligible. I've dispensed with the salutations and closings after they settle into "My Dearest Katharine" and "Yours ever, Edward Grey," apart from a few jocular greetings.

Though Grey refers to his close friend Edward Tennant as "Eddie," both his wife and his sister always wrote the name "Eddy," and this is the version I've used in the introduction.

Not knowing one's readers, one always runs the risk of saying too little or too much in footnotes, and I'm sure I've done both, though I expect I've erred more on the side of the latter. In particular, places that will be familiar to British readers are identified for the benefit of Americans who may not be.

ILLUSTRATION CREDITS

Illustrations appear between pages 120 and 121.

Quotations are from the text, unless noted in parentheses; full citations are in the notes. My thanks to Adrian Graves for permitting me to use family photographs in his possession, to Queen Mary University London Archives, and to the National Portrait Gallery, London.

1. Louise Creighton, *Dorothy Grey* (C. Chance, *The Widdrington Women*, 84)
2. Adrian Graves
3. Adrian Graves (L. Creighton, *Dorothy Grey*, 112)
4. Adrian Graves
5. Adrian Graves (G. Trevelyan, *Grey of Fallodon*, 43)
6. L. Creighton, *Dorothy Grey*
7. L. Creighton, *Dorothy Grey*
8. National Portrait Gallery, London (first two lines of "Non Nobis Domine" by Harry Cust)
9. National Portrait Gallery, London (H. Asquith, *Letters to Venetia Stanley*, 269)
10. National Portrait Gallery, London
11. Adrian Graves (S. Gordon, *Edward Grey of Fallodon and his Birds*, 5)
12. Adrian Graves
13. L. Creighton, *Dorothy Grey* (final sestet of a sonnet by Dorothy Grey, p. 61)
14. through 20. Queen Mary University London Archives

ABBREVIATIONS

The papers are always those of the recipient of the letter, unless otherwise indicated.

BL: British Library
Bodleian: Bodleian Library Archives, Oxford University
CUL: Cambridge University Archives
Durham: University of Durham Archives
Grosvenor: Grosvenor Papers, Eaton Estate Archives, Cheshire
NA: National Archives, Kew
NAS: National Archives of Scotland
Newcastle: University of Newcastle Archives
NLS: National Library of Scotland

INTRODUCTION

People who know nothing else about Sir Edward Grey (1862–1933), the longest-serving British Foreign Secretary (from December 1905 to December 1916), are familiar with his uncharacteristically fatidic observation on the eve of the First World War: "The lamps are going out all over Europe; we shall not see them lit again in our lifetime."[1]

The remark was made at dusk on August 3rd, 1914. At a little after 7:00 a.m. that morning, the Belgian government had rejected an ultimatum demanding that German troops be permitted to pass through the country. Kaiser and *Reichskanzler* were reminded of their nation's solemn pledge to respect Belgium's neutrality, and were told that the Belgian Army would resist the invasion.[2]

Rising at a little after 3:00 that afternoon in the House of Commons, Grey had given a speech that had shifted sentiment among members.[3] A majority, in the Cabinet as well as

---

1 E. Grey, *Twenty-Five Years*, v. 2 (London, 1925), 20; J. A. Spender, *Life, Journalism, and Politics*, v. 2 (New York, 1927), 14–15. Journalists sometimes substitute "lights" for "lamps." It has more resonance. Even more frequently, writers–including Grey's second biographer–assume the lamps the Foreign Secretary observed were going out.(K. Robbins, *Sir Edward Grey* (London, 1971), xiii.) In fact, they were coming on. Grey had more imagination than he's sometimes credited with.

2 By the terms of the Treaty of London of 1839, Berlin was obliged to observe and to defend the country's neutrality, the Empire having assumed Prussia's commitment. Despite pious disclaimers in the German note, King Albert and the majority of his ministers recognized that Belgium would become a satellite, if not a German province, after a successful war.

3 *Parliamentary Debates*, 5th series, LXV, 1809–1827, reprinted in P. Knaplund (ed.) *Speeches on Foreign Affairs by Sir Edward Grey, 1904–1914* (London, 1931), 297–315.

the House, may still have supported British neutrality before he spoke. This was not the case afterward. Grey pointedly refrained from mentioning repeated German and Austrian rejections of British proposals for a negotiated settlement, and, with characteristic scrupulousness, did not even refer to the insulting bid for British neutrality that German Chancellor Theobald Bethmann Hollweg had made the day before. Instead, he stressed the country's moral obligation to defend the northern coast of France from the German Fleet. He and the Prime Minister both seem to have hoped that naval action was all that would be required of the U.K. in the coming war.[1] Then, at some length, he made the case that it was in Britain's vital interest to preserve Belgium's neutrality.[2]

Now he and the country were waiting for the first shots to be fired, presumably in the vicinity of the Liège forts. There would be a British ultimatum to Berlin the next day, but everyone assumed it would be ignored.

The Foreign Secretary was standing at his office window, looking across St. James Park to the Mall. It was around 9:00 p.m. The street lights flickered on. Grey's friend J. A. Spender, editor of the *Westminster Gazette*, was beside him, and it was to Spender that he addressed the remark. Grey later recalled that the lamps were "being lit," but they'd been electric for over a decade, and came on without the benefit of a lamplighter.

---

1 "For us, with a powerful Fleet, which we believe able to protect our commerce, to protect our shores, and to protect our interests, if we are engaged in war, we shall suffer but little more than we shall suffer if we stand aside."(Knaplund, 311.) H. Asquith to V. Stanley, 2 August 1914, in M. and E. Brock, *H. H. Asquith: Letters to Venetia Stanley* (Oxford, 1982), 145–7.
2 The speech was considered all the more effective for its dispassion. "Grey made a most remarkable speech—about an hour long—for the most part almost conversational in tone & with some of his usual ragged ends; but extraordinarily well reasoned & tactful & really *cogent*—so much so that our extreme peace-lovers were for the moment reduced to silence; tho' they will soon find their tongues again."(H. Asquith to V. Stanley, 3 August 1914, *Ibid.*, 148.

The lamps never came back on. About 16.5 million soldiers[1] and civilians lost their lives in the conflict,[2] but historians cannot even estimate to the nearest 10 million how many individuals were killed as an indirect result of the war, for the triumph of National Socialism and Communism are inconceivable without it. We are still living with the war's consequences a century later.

⁓

If someone knows anything else about Sir Edward apart from the "lamps" quote, it's likely that the Foreign Secretary was regarded by friend and foe alike–save for German propagandists during the war–as an exceptionally honest, straightforward, sincere, and trustworthy individual, a man of his word. "Lies and intrigue are equally repugnant to him," wrote the last pre-war German Ambassador to London, Prince Max Lichnowsky.[3]

If a third thing is known about Grey, it is surely his love of the countryside, and his preference for fishing and bird-watching to politics. In fact, he is remembered today by some individuals primarily for his contributions to ornithology and for his nature writing. His *Fly Fishing* (1899) and *The Charm of Birds* (1927) are regarded as classics, and the Edward Grey Center for Ornithology at Oxford, founded in 1937, commemorates Grey the naturalist. The Foreign Secretary recalled for Katharine Lyttelton how he used to look longingly out the window while cramming for his exams at Balliol, wishing he could exchange places with the gardener, who was trundling by with his wheelbarrow.[4] On the hustings and attending sessions of the House and Cabinet meet-

---

1 The great majority of these were not, of course, professional soldiers, but young men conscripted into the armies of the warring countries, except for the original British Expeditionary Force and the men who volunteered during the first year and a half of the war.

2 Totals are notoriously difficult to estimate (figures for the Ottoman Empire in particular are unreliable), but there were approximately 9.7 million military deaths, including from accidents and disease (but excluding the Spanish flu pandemic), and as many as 6.8 million civilian fatalities, about 950,000 of which were combat-related.

3 M. Lichnowsky, *Heading for the Abyss* (London, 1928), 68.

4 E. Grey to K. Lyttelton, 12 July 1908.

ings, or writing despatches and letters at the Foreign Office, he also often seemed to wish he were elsewhere–pulling trout from the Itchen or salmon from the Spey, or feeding the ducks beside the ponds at Fallodon.

While there is something charming about the notion of the gentleman politician, a throwback to the eighteenth century, this picture of Grey has for decades provided ammunition for critics. Not only was he insular, incurious, and unambitious, but he lacked the seriousness, the professionalism, required of a Foreign Secretary in the tumultuous years before the outbreak of the First World War, and particularly during the crisis of July 1914. He was an amateur, a dilettante, who permitted the country to drift into war while he went fishing.

The first biography of Grey, by the Oxford historian George Trevelyan,[1] did much to reinforce this impression of the Foreign Secretary. And because it was so well-written, it enshrined the image of the upright, utterly candid, but disengaged Whig patrician, who, but for the call of duty, would have happily immersed himself in rural pleasures.

Keith Robbins, thirty-one when his biography of Grey was published thirty-four years later, in 1971, found Trevelyan's book "suffused with a rather oppressive sentimentality." Robbins' book is also well-written, as well as thoroughly researched. There's a reason that, in the eighty years following Grey's death, only two full-length biographies of the Foreign Secretary appeared. But Robbins' is a political biography and the "rough places" Trevelyan made "smoother" and the "puzzles" that he neglected have mostly to do with Sir Edward's career, not his private life.[2] One gets a better sense of the man himself from Trevelyan's book–Grey's profound

1 *Grey of Fallodon* (London, 1937)
2 Robbins, xiv.

feeling of loss after his first wife's death, his flashes of schoolboy humor, his appreciation not only of the Northumberland and Hampshire countryside, but of books and people.

For Trevelyan, Grey was above all a tragic figure, "one whom Fortune loved and hated out of the common measure."[1] Grey's first wife, Dorothy, was killed when she was thrown from an open carriage after her horse shied. His second wife, Pamela, died of a heart attack after just six years of marriage. One brother, George, was killed by a lion in Kenya, a second, Charlie, by a buffalo in Tanganikya. His beloved ancestral home Fallodon was destroyed by fire in 1917; his fishing cottage in Hampshire burned to the ground in 1923.

Grey was exceptionally close to both wives. His relationship with the reclusive Dorothy was especially intimate.[2]

Grey was very fond of both brothers, and Cottage and Fallodon were sacred places.

In 1914 Grey's eyesight began to deteriorate rapidly. By 1916 he was nearly blind. For so passionate a naturalist, someone who was so keen an observer of birds and so avid a fisherman, this was a terrible blow. As Trevelyan puts it, "It was an irony that tested the unconquerable sanity of his spirit, to be set free at last,[3] too late; the leisure he had longed for was his, and the bounty of nature's loveliness was spread before him, invisible... He returned to his birds but he could no longer see them; to his books, but

---

1 Trevelyan, vi.
2 "I shall feel the need of friends," Grey wrote to Haldane after Dorothy's death, "a thing I never felt while I had her love every day and could give all mine to her."(E. Grey to R. Haldane, 4 February 1906, Haldane Letters in Rosebery Papers, NLS). The arrival of friends seemed "like the interruption of a honeymoon."(E. Grey to K. Lyttelton, 14 August 1908.) There is a whiff of *egoisme à deux* in Dorothy's letters, especially during bleak moments in London: "The strongest hatred we feel now," she wrote in 1893, "is of people, any people; they are all horrid and there is no health in them; they are mean and selfish."(L. Creighton, *Dorothy Grey* (London, 1907), 199–200.) The chirping of starlings is "so much nicer and more mysterious and pure than the jabbering of people."(Creighton, 200.) Both, though, had close friends and admirers.
3 Grey had resigned with Asquith on December 6, 1916. He officially submitted the seals of office on December 10.

he could no longer read them."[1] "It is a living death," Grey told a friend of his last years, Seton Gordon.[2]

But the tragedy that will always be associated with Grey is, inevitably, the outbreak of World War I. The Foreign Secretary was preeminently a man of peace. He had organized and chaired the conference that resolved disputes arising from the first Balkan War, and offered to do the same for the far less thorny disagreements that were the pretext for the third Balkan War, World War I. The offer was rejected by the German Chancellor, as were other suggestions for a negotiated settlement of the crisis.

Late in the afternoon on August 3, when he was congratulated by Sir Arthur Nicolson, the Permanent Under-Secretary, after his speech to the House, Grey didn't reply. "He moved to the center of the room and raised his hands with clenched fists above his head," Nicolson recalled. "He brought his fists with a crash upon the table. 'I hate war,' he groaned, 'I hate war.'"[3]

After the outbreak of hostilities, he lay awake at night wondering if there were anything more he could he might have said or written during the preceding years to have prevented the conflict.[4] He concluded that there was little he could have done. Not all historians have agreed with him.

Anyone reading Grey's letters to Katharine Lyttelton, or to his other confidantes, will see at once how bitterly he resented being trapped in London by his office. If the July Crisis had been amicably resolved, if he had not lost the people and homes he most loved, he would still be a tragic figure for the sacrifices he made. Again, one has to read his letters, and *Cottage Book* and *Fly Fishing*, to appreciate what he gave up to go to the Foreign Office

1 Trevelyan, 384, vi.
2 S. Gordon, *Edward Grey of Fallodon and his Birds* (London, 1937), 19.
3 H. Nicolson, *Portrait of a Diplomatist* (Boston, 1930), 306.
4 E. Grey, *Twenty-Five Years*, v. 2, 48.

each morning and sit on the front bench, to attend Cabinets when Parliament was in session, and give speeches when it adjourned.

It wasn't merely that he enjoyed nature. He had a heightened capacity to observe birds and wildlife, and derived something more intense and transcendent from watching and listening than mere pleasure. Trevelyan believed he had a "genius" for observation and, blessed with the additional gift of being able to share what he saw and felt with others, he helped thousands "to enjoy the purest and most lasting joys of mind and heart."[1] What makes Grey's misery in office tragic is the knowledge, by the spring of 1914, that in remaining Foreign Secretary, he was sacrificing his eyesight.

Why did he not fling open the cage door then or earlier? He was not pinioned, as Trevelyan points out, any more than the Fallodon ducks. The Regius Professor goes on to suggest that Grey derived real satisfaction from directing the nation's foreign policy: "the exercise of great talents on great affairs gave him more intellectual pleasure during his working hours than he records in his private letters, perhaps more than he was conscious of himself."[2]

Except for the final phrase, this may have been true. But there were other motives that his friend and biographer ignored or chose not to mention. Grey very much wanted to see the Liberals enact the reforms to which they had pledged themselves. The need in particular to ameliorate the conditions of the working class and rural poor, and to grant unions some of the power to which they aspired, was much more acute in 1906 than when the Liberals had last held office over a decade earlier. But Grey did not trust any of his colleagues to preside over British foreign policy. One can't help but feel he would not have minded so much had Lord Lansdowne, his Conservative predecessor, returned to office. But he no more wished to see Harcourt or Bryce in his place than to

---

1 Trevelyan, vii.
2 *Ibid.* Subsequent historians have tended to agree that he protested too much. Grey himself conceded that work was a great solace in the months after Dorothy's death.

see Balfour or Bonar Law installed in 10 Downing Street. So it was not merely the case that he found the transacting of Foreign Office business intellectually stimulating. His Liberal colleagues (with the possible exceptions of Asquith, Haldane, Crewe, and, to a lesser degree, Morley and McKenna, and, later, Churchill) admirable as they might be in other respects, were, to put it baldly, too naïve, too insular, too insensitive to the complexities of the domestic politics of the continental Powers, and too indifferent to the requirements of India and the Empire.[1]

If Trevelyan did not conceal from readers Grey's misery in office, he drew a veil around his subject's private life. This is not what Grey himself would have wanted. Writing to Maud Selborne, he observed, "a man's biography unless it tells what things made him happy, in what thoughts he found the means of bearing grief and what his relations with women were, is nearly useless; and the telling of these things is necessarily intimate: it is of no use telling about them, they must be told in the man's intimate private letters."[2] But all of Grey's correspondence was destroyed–including letters his second wife Pamela had wished to publish. It was likely Grey's oldest sister, Alice Graves, who burned the letters. It was certainly she who chose Trevelyan. He was selected not only for his "real love and immense admiration for Edward," but for his "delicacy of feeling." The project, she trusted, would be "safe in his hands."[3] Trevelyan was asked to submit copies of each chapter

1 This has to be qualified further with regard to other colleagues. For a fuller discussion, see Part II of *The Lamps Go Out*.
2 E. Grey to M. Selborne, 17 June 1917. Bodleian. Selborne, Salisbury's daughter, was the wife of Grey's friend and former fag-master at Winchester, William Palmer.
3 A. Graves to F. Barton, 28 April 1934. Bodleian. There is no direct evidence that Alice Graves destroyed Grey's papers; she does report doing so in any surviving correspondence. But she was with him at the time of his death, and seems the most likely suspect. Pamela made a selection of her correspondence with Grey shortly after they were married and asked her friend the crime novelist Marie Belloc Lowndes to edit it. Edward then decided that he did not wish the letters to appear during his lifetime, and Pamela enlisted the novelist Anne Douglas Sidgwick to bring out an edition after his death, if she didn't survive him. (M. Lowndes, *A Passing World* (London, 1948), 185–6.)

to Graves. She was "quite delighted" with the book, she told a friend. Trevelyan's "delicacy of feeling and his discretion are perfect. ...I do not think we could have chosen a better biographer."[1]

Graves' confidence was not misplaced. In a characteristic example of his delicacy and discretion, Grey's biographer neatly excised references to his subject's poor health and financial worries in a letter to Katharine Lyttelton that he quotes on page 387. The omitted passages are in italics: *"I am now comfortable-no sickness and hardly ever pain or even discomfort, but I am not fit for a day's work yet. After 5 o'clock I do little but read gently and rest on the sofa. It is comfortable but* there is so much to be done and enjoyed with a library inside and one's own house and home *and I feel that my weakness wastes it.* On coming outside I see whole vistas of enjoyment if the war were over *and if I were sure of money enough to live here...* [2] In another letter to Katharine later in the year, Trevelyan omits Edward's mildly ironic conclusion: "I am sure I can do no good by talking: and I am disposed to think Lloyd George is doing well, considering all the difficulties he has to face; *but I admit I have little else but his own speeches to go by...*"[3]

At some point Grey wrote, or at least began, an autobiography, apart from his political testament, *Twenty-Five Years*. This disappeared after Trevelyan consulted it, as did a journal Grey kept in the mid-1880s. We have only a few quotations from each in *Grey of Fallodon*.

A very few of their letters to each other are preserved at the National Archives of Scotland, with comments on them that suggest Pamela expected they would be read by others.

1 A. Graves to F. Barton, 8 January 1936, Bodleian. Trevelyan was, of course, constrained as well by the fact that a number of Grey's friends and colleagues were still alive. There are moments when the biography seems almost to be addressed to the former. "I find it intensely interesting," Trevelyan told his daughter after he began work on the book. "It is a great consolation to live most of the day thinking about him."(G. Trevelyan to M. Moorman, 23 September 1935, U. of Newcastle.)

2 E. Grey to K. Lyttelton, 5 February 1917. The reader is even shielded from the bad news that the Fallodon ponds are frozen. *"After sparing Fallodon all January the frost has at last come north and my ponds are frozen.* There is some snow but not enough to make the fields pure white..."

3 E. Grey to K. Lyttelton, 1 June 1917. Grey adds: "except something I heard from a good and unbiased opinion last month."

The discreet official biographer naturally did not mention that Grey had acceded to his first wife's request during their honeymoon that they abstain from sexual intercourse, and honored the request for the twenty years of their marriage. Nor did he mention the Foreign Secretary's long extra-martial affair with Pamela Glenconner, probably begun at least four years after Dorothy's death and apparently carried on with his friend Eddy Glenconner's consent. Indeed, Trevelyan virtually ignored Grey's second wife. Though she and Dorothy had gotten on well, they were quite unalike, save for their love of the outdoors, and Grey's friends seem to have chosen one or the other. Few had nice things to say about both. Robbins also appears to have had as little time for Pamela as did Trevelyan, and makes no mention of the affair between her and Grey.

Britain and the world are very different places than they were in 1971, and it's no surprise that Grey's most recent biographer, Michael Waterhouse, has taken off in the opposite direction.[1] Naturally, he describes the *marriage blanc* and the *menage à trois*. (The insular Foreign Secretary's sexual relationships were so exotic that there are no English words for them.) But Waterhouse believes the affair with Pamela Tennant, as she was then called, commenced very early, before 1900, when Dorothy was still alive, and that his best friend's wife bore him at least one son. Not only was Grey's relationship with Katharine Lyttelton an intimate one, Waterhouse suggests, but the Foreign Secretary also engaged in several one-night stands or brief flings as well, at least two of which resulted in additional illegitimate children.[2] These claims are discussed in the Appendix, "Sex and the Foreign Secretary."

Readers can make up their own minds about the relationship with Lyttelton. I don't believe there is sufficient evidence in the letters to support the notion that she and Grey were sleeping

---

1 M. Waterhouse, *Edwardian Requiem* (London, 2013).
2 *Ibid.*, 44–47, 94–96, 256–257.

together. Indeed, there are many lines that suggest this was not the case. One is not likely to write the following to one's mistress:

> I could to another woman now give more kindness, more patience, more understanding, more unselfish sympathy than ever before; only I couldn't give the love to anyone but Dorothy. There is more to give than ever before, but to no one but her could I give it all; I give some things to friends and take all gratefully that they can give to me, but only in such a way that if Dorothy came again I could give all to her with undivided love.[1]

Lines that sound suggestive out of context are immediately followed by sentences or phrases that make them seem less so. "It is after midnight and I am only writing to tell you that I have been thinking of you," Edward writes to Katharine on 31 July 1910, but then adds, "I have just been reading two or three of Dorothy's letters written to me in this month in 1903: every now and then I find something written to me which makes me feel it is worth having lived and which makes me feel very grateful. Don't think, however, that I am not grateful also to some living friends, both because she liked them and because they have been kind to me since." "I hunger to see you," he writes on 15 February 1911, but this is followed by "–the number of friends who knew and loved both Dorothy and George is not so very many, though each had many friends who loved them especially well."

If there is no evidence of a sexual relationship between Edward and Katharine, there are signs in the earlier letters that he may subconsciously have desired one. After first giving Katharine an update on Dorothy's health and then telling her how much he looked forward to seeing her at Fallodon, he adds coquettishly: "You will no doubt observe that his letter has now said two distinct things: I wonder whether you will have any decided instinct as to which of the two is the chief reason for my writing. I am

---

1 E. Grey to K. Lyttelton, 8 October 1908.

not sure that I know, though one came into my mind before the other."[1] Then, ten months later, speaking of the feelings that the Sudan campaign has elicited, he writes:

> it is so good to be stirred by something big, and nothing does this better than great work with some risk about it. Don't you feel already how all the trivial things are losing their hold? All the horrible little worries and busy-nesses and planning, which creep upon one in numbers and cling and cluster upon the spirit and drain its energy and make it anaemic and weak–all these cannot stand the throbbing of a pulse which is stirred, and fall from one and shrink and perish on the ground, and you feel that you are standing erect and strong and clean.

He says later that he feels a "glowing sympathy" for her, not another "sort, which is like a limp figure climbing out of a weedy pool dripping…"[2]

In March, 1905, Edward told Katharine, "I live in a whirl of trains and speeches and weekends in the North; sometimes I imagine I am Chairman of a Railway, sometimes that I am an M.P., sometimes that I am married, sometimes that I am not…"[3] His previous letter was signed "yours sickly," after he had joked about the differences between home-sick, sea-sick, and love-sick.[4]

If the letters do not reveal any clandestine relationships, they also don't disclose much that is new about the foreign policy questions Grey grappled with during his eleven years in office, nor, in particular, his thoughts during the July Crisis. There are some piquant observations about the Kaiser, the Czar, and their

---

1 E. Grey to K. Lyttelton, 6 August 1897.
2 E. Grey to K. Lyttelton, 20 June 1898.
3 E. Grey to K. Lyttelton, 22 March 1905.
4 E. Grey to K. Lyttelton, 30 May 1904.

ministers, and Grey's Cabinet colleagues and critics. But no secrets are unveiled.

What the letters do reveal, though, is a Grey who has not quite been captured by his three biographers. "Interesting" was for Edward a very high term of praise, and his letters to Katharine Lyttelton are interesting. There is wit and whimsy, not just schoolboy jokes. Grey emerges as someone wise, shrewd, and humane, as well as amusing, someone well read and with a prodigious memory. His observations still speak to us. They will resonate with everyone who loves the outdoors and solitude. Those coping with an overpowering grief, with a strong distaste for their work, or with approaching blindness may find them especially poignant. But others not so afflicted may discover they have become kinder, more courageous, and more observant for having read Grey's letters.

EDWARD GREY

Sir Edward Grey was born in London on April 25, 1862, the first child of Captain, later Colonel, George Henry Grey and the former Harriet Pearson. The Greys could trace their ancestry back to the Conquest,[1] but it was only comparatively recently that the Northumberland branch of the family had become politically prominent.

Grey's great-great grandfather, Charles, the first Earl, a general under George II and George III, had been ennobled for his exploits against the French in North America and on the continent. His eldest son, also called Charles, headed the Whig ministry that passed the Great Reform Bill in 1832. Edward, however, was descended from the first Earl's youngest son, George. Shipped off to sea at age eleven, despite his pleas to be permitted to continue his education, George Grey became a devout Evangelical—something not likely to have happened had he gone to Oxford. He married the daughter of the wealthy brewer and anti-slavery campaigner Samuel Whitbread. Awarded a baronetcy after directing the Portsmouth Naval Yard for many years, he sent his only son to Oriel, then the most intellectually distinguished of the Oxford

---

1 The family claimed descent from Rollo, chamberlain to Robert, Duke of Normandy, and grandfather of William the Conqueror, Rollo's daughter Arletta having been Robert's mistress. Rollo's son or grandson Anschitel De Croy crossed the Channel with William and was rewarded with "Divers lands in the County of Oxford and Elsewhere." "De Croy" became de Grey and Grey. (E. Hepple (ed.), *The Milfield MS* (London, 1856), 11.)

colleges. Young George (1799–1882), Grey's grandfather, shared his parents' piety: troubled by an "ever-present sense of sin," he felt himself unworthy of becoming a clergyman, as his father had wished, switched to law, was called to the bar, and entered Parliament. Handsome and eloquent, trusted and admired by the House, he became Home Secretary in 1846, and served with distinction in that office for seventeen of the next twenty years. "Really Prime Minister in all internal affairs," according to Lord Granville, Sir George, more than any individual, was responsible for the fact that 1848 did not play out in Britain as it did on the continent.[1]

To the Home Secretary's disappointment, his only son, still another George, had no political ambitions. He joined the army against his father's wishes—it was not a reputable profession—and served in India and the Crimea before being named first equerry to the wayward Prince of Wales, for whom it was hoped he would set a good example. His oldest son saw little of him. Colonel Grey was frequently at Windsor, Balmoral, and Sandringham, and Edward was sent off to school at age nine. Two years later, George Grey died of septic pneumonia. In his autobiography, Edward Grey says nothing about his father's influence on his mind and character, only that "he liked all country life and country pursuits" and was affable and handsome, "always in good spirits, with that sort of manner which made him exceedingly popular with both men and women." However, "he had no

---

1 His fellow M.P.s were appreciative. After the Home Secretary addressed Parliament on the evening of the Great Chartist March, "he sat down in the midst of the applause which greeted him from all parts of the House and which I never remember equaled on any other occasion."(M. Creighton, *Memoir of Sir George Grey, Bart.* (Newcastle, 1884), 72.) Grey inspired great trust and devotion. "No colleague ever created in me deeper feelings of attachment and of admiration than Sir George Grey," said one former Cabinet Minister. "I have regarded his public and private character with respect and admiration, mixed with personal affection, such as I have felt for few other men," declared another colleague. "A man of nobler nature, a man more worthy at once of love and respect I have never known," said a third. (*Ibid.*, 103.)

intellectual interests and did not care for reading or any discussion such as politics."[1]

Edward's mother was no more influential. She came from a Shropshire family of small landowners, soldiers, and clergymen. In his autobiography, Grey wrote only about how accommodating she was. His mother "was one of the gentlest of human beings. She shrank even from argument and in order to make life go smoothly was always prepared to efface herself."[2] Grey's later confidante Louise Creighton, after moving to Embleton from Oxford, hoped to be her friend, but found her "rather dull and commonplace."[3]

Fortunately, after Colonel Grey's death at age thirty-nine, two surrogate fathers stepped into the breach, Edward's grandfather and Sir George's friend Mandell Creighton, then rector of Embleton. Both did much to shape Grey's character and beliefs.

Though a devout Evangelical, the former Home Secretary was a vigilant defender of religious freedom and toleration. He had worked to limit the jurisdiction of ecclesiastical courts and had opposed the Anglican monopoly in Ireland, defending the grant to the Catholic university at Maynooth.[4] Two maxims from his commonplace book nicely illustrate a conscience simultaneously Evangelical and Whig: "There are few things so helpful to our growth in grace as concerning ourselves actively for the souls of others." "A man is not tolerant till he is tolerant of the intolerance of others."[5]

---

1 *Autobiography*, cited by Trevelyan, 9. A sole exception: shortly after the outbreak of the Franco-Prussian war, George Grey asked his son which side he favored. The eight-year-old boy had not given any thought to the question, but because he was partial to a game called "German," a form of dominoes, he said Prussia. Edward's father was not pleased. He had fought beside the French in the Crimea.(E. Grey, *Twenty-Five Years* (London, 1925), v. 1, xxii.)

2 Trevelyan, 10.

3 L. Creighton (J. Covert, ed.), *Memoir of a Victorian Woman* (Bloomington, 1994), 66–7.

4 "I do not think we are precluded by our duty to God from contributing to the support of tenets which we may think erroneous."(M. Creighton, 48–9.)

5 M. Creighton, 120.

"My grandfather," Grey recalled, "was very religious, but his nature was such that he brought sunshine wherever he was." (Sir George would have winced at the post-Victorian "but.") "In any problem he would ask one question—what was right—and follow it without hesitation... When once he had said, 'That is wrong,' or 'That is not right,' he had no wish to say anything more about it, or anything about the person who did it. We all felt…his presence as a blessing."[1]

To the dismay of his wife, Mandell Creighton (1843–1901), tiring of Oxford and wanting more time to write, applied for the living at Embleton, which was at the disposal of Merton College, where he was a fellow. Abandoning their circle of University luminaries,[2] the Creightons moved to Northumberland and soon became good friends with their Fallodon neighbors. When Edward appeared to be in danger of not passing his Moderations with honors, Creighton offered to tutor him over the summer.

"When they meet in after years, students talk about their tutors, not their books," Creighton wrote, and, despite his great erudition and his ability to make the past come alive for students,

---

1 *Autobiography*, cited by Trevelyan, 13–14.
2 Creighton, the son of a self-made businessman from Carlisle, capped a brilliant career as an undergraduate—two firsts, presidency of the Union, sundry prizes—with the Merton fellowship. In addition to his remarkable erudition, he possessed "common sense in a degree which amounts to genius," wrote his favorite tutor, the philosopher Edward Caird.(J. Covert, *A Victorian Marriage* (London, 2000), 45.) He impressed as well the other Oxford legends under whom he studied, Jowett and Green, Mark Pattison, Stubbs, and Bryce. The Creightons' circle also included the Paters, the Max Müllers, the T. H. Greens, Andrew Lang, George Saintsbury, Frederic Harrison, and J. R. Green. Friends were puzzled that the witty and irreverent Creighton was never troubled by doubts about Christian dogma. He was selectively uninquisitive, finding Darwin not of "sufficient interest" to warrant the time.(Covert, 52.) Creighton went on to hold the Dixie Professorship at Cambridge, was the founding editor of the *English Historical Review*, and was appointed Bishop of Peterborough and then of London, and would likely have become Archbishop of Canterbury had he not died at age fifty-seven. As with Sir George Grey, even allowing for eulogistic excesses, the glowing encomia he received after his death—from a wide range of admirers—are revealing. "The more I think of Dr. Creighton's death, the greater seems the loss," wrote Beatrice Webb. "Every day brings a new revelation of one's affections for him as a human being." Lord Rosebery called him "perhaps the most alert and universal intelligence that existed in this island at the time of his death." For Mrs. Humphry Ward, his death was a like a catastrophe, "as if some great tree fallen." "It is certainly rare to find so much intellectual force and so high a standard of conduct combined in one man," concluded an obituarist in the *Quarterly Review*.(Covert, 292).

molding character rather than imparting knowledge was always his first object. One of the things he tried to teach was intellectual humility.[1] "The important thing," he urged, "is to know what you know and to know what you do not know."[2] "Give an opinion about the things you know, but refuse to give an opinion about the things of which you know nothing." Another favorite maxim: "Self-satisfaction is the death of the mind, as truly as it is the death of the soul." "I never knew any one who did anything worth doing without taking a great deal of trouble."[3]

"Would you doubt the word of a Wykehamist?" Edward Grey is supposed to have asked, and many critics have assumed that both his strengths and weaknesses as Foreign Minister derived from the ethos he imbibed at Winchester and at Balliol, "*le fair-play*" of the former and the high-minded idealism of the latter. But Sir George Grey and Mandell Creighton were more responsible for his high-minded outlook, and they implanted a more venerable and demanding Victorian credo.

"He was a very remarkable man," Grey wrote of Creighton in his lost autobiography.[4] He kept a bust of his mentor at Fallodon.[5] "I want to have it in the library," he told the friend who sent it to him, "where I can see it constantly and be intimate with it; and I have put it there... It is difficult to get a place where it shall always be seen and be an intimate thing and yet be in the best light."[6] A year before the outbreak of war, in the midst of problems foreign

---

1 This opinion would get him into trouble with Lord Acton after he expressed it in the preface to volumes 3 and 4 of his *History of the Papacy*. Acton's rebuke is famous: "If the thing be criminal, then the authority permitting it bears the guilt... You say that people in authority are not to be snubbed or sneered at from our pinnacle of conscious rectitude. I really don't know whether you exempt them because of their rank, or of their success and power, or of their date... Historical responsibility has to make up for the want of legal responsibility. Power tends to corrupt, and absolute power corrupts absolutely. Great men are almost always bad..."(L. Strachey, *Portraits in Miniature and Other Essays* (London, 1931), 214.)
2 M. Creighton (L. Creighton, ed.), *Counsels for the Young* (London, 1905), 147.
3 *Ibid.*, 148, 149, 72.
4 Trevelyan, 22.
5 Now in Holy Trinity Church, Embleton
6 E. Grey to E. Tennant, 9 September 1909. Glenconner Papers, NAS.

and domestic, he wrote wistfully to Louise Creighton, "I have thought sometimes of my grandfather and the Bishop and of how I should like to have talked to them."[1]

∾

Grey was already fourteen when he was transferred by his grandfather to Winchester. He'd attended a small school in Yorkshire, Northallerton, and then Temple Grove in Richmond. Grey had done well there, being head of school during some terms, but had no real taste for scholarship, he later confessed. It was the competitive spirit that moved him to excel. At Winchester this was extinguished. He had been placed in the highest class to which students were admitted upon entrance, moved up quickly, and looked forward to entering "Sixth Book" at the end of term. But this was against the school's tradition. However, instead of merely being informed of this, Grey was made to stand up for an hour in front of class while the master fired question after question. The shaken fifteen-year-old was then placed near the bottom of the class. After this ordeal, he "was a changed being," he recalled, and "from that moment ceased to do any work ... Desire to succeed had been my motive. I was not allowed to succeed, and the motive was gone."[2] It would not return until after he left Balliol.

However, over time he became a Wykehamist: "the ways of the place, its traditions, and the country in which it is set, were all getting a hold upon my heart."[3] But it was the latter, the water meadows and the Itchen, that most deeply impressed him, not the captain's hand on his shoulder and the voice urging "Play up! play up! and play the game!" He participated only desultorily in team sports, but became a keen fisherman. Once, in fact, his fishing disrupted a cricket match. He'd hooked a very large trout, and half the students who'd been assembled for the match rushed

---

1 E. Grey to L. Creighton, 1 June 1913. Creighton Papers, Bodleian.
2 *Autobiography*, cited by Trevelyan, 14–15.
3 *Ibid.*, 15.

over to look. The captain had to threaten them to return to their places.[1]

∽

Balliol had become famous by the end the nineteenth century as the nursery of statesman, a reputation Benjamin Jowett had worked assiduously to cultivate for over three decades.[2] But Edward himself, though he admired the Master, was less susceptible than others to his exhortations. In January 1884 he was "rusticated."[3] With Creighton's assistance, Grey had received a Second in Classical Moderations, but Creighton had since moved to Cambridge. Still, inspired by a personal plea from the Master, Grey switched from Greats to Jurisprudence, which he thought would be easier, and scraped by with a Third.[4]

After the exam, Grey might have retired to Fallodon and devoted himself entirely to his ducks—he began collecting them when he was sent down—and to bird-watching and fishing. Instead, he began on his own to read voraciously. "Last June," he wrote in a diary he began keeping,

> I had hardly formed one political idea; now ideas have formed and are forming daily. Then I knew no Political Economy: now I have even got glimmerings of original ideas on it. In June I cared little for Music and not at all

---

1 *Ibid.*, 19

2 Very briefly and baldly, Jowett, the son of an Evangelical furrier, after engaging in polemics with High and Low Churchman as spokesman for the skeptical Broad Church, infuriating both—and getting into serious trouble—with his injunction that the Bible "was to be read just like any other book," shifted tack, distilling from Plato, with infusions of German idealism, a refined, quasi-Christian ethos that proved an addictive brew for two generations of bright young men from good—and not so good—families. (Jowett's predecessor had had the novel idea of offering scholarships based on academic merit.) The second Prime Minister Grey served under was one of these. So was Grey's predecessor as Foreign Secretary.

3 "Sir Edward Grey, having been repeatedly admonished for idleness, and having shown himself entirely ignorant of the work set him in vacation as a condition of residence, was sent down...," Jowett wrote in the Balliol minute-book. (Trevelyan, 24.)

4 Grey later maintained that he never received an undergraduate degree, having failed to pass the compulsory "Divinity Schools."(S. Gordon, *Sir Edward Grey of Fallodon and his Birds* (London, 1937), 3.

for Poetry, Nature or Art: now I have strong feelings about them all. I have dipped into Ruskin with great pleasure, and I have read and even committed to memory a good deal of poetry. I have enjoyed a good deal of sport but it has become a recreation, and the consuming interest I felt in it is now employed in carving my way into Politics, Social Problems, moral philosophy and culture. Oh! If I could only progress every year by such strides as this![1]

This journal, like his autobiography, was destroyed or lost, and we have only the following brief inventory of Grey's reading: "Meanwhile the tale of books read continues daily: Vergil [sic], Tennyson, Wordsworth, Mill's Political Economy, Milton, More's Utopia, George Eliot's Life, Progress and Poverty, Seeley's Expansion of England." If he commented further on any of the books, we have no record.[2]

However, from statements Grey made and positions he adopted over the next several years, it's possible to infer the influence of at least two of these books, Mill and Seeley. Though he never embraced the "single tax," it would not be surprising if the eager autodidact was impressed by Henry George as well, as were so many others in the '80s.

Seeley's *Expansion of England,* when it appeared in 1883, caused nearly as much of a sensation as George's book.[3] It's an exhilarating attack on the great theme of 19th century historians of modern Britain: that the nation's history is the story of the slow but steady growth of constitutional liberty, Protestantism fronting for Liberalism until it found its legs. For Seeley, the real story from the 16th century to the present was England's triumph in the great contest for overseas colonies, besting its four European rivals. Wars fought in the name of religion in the 17th century

---

1 cited by Trevelyan, 32.
2 *Ibid.,* 33.
3 Grey's friend H. A. L. Fisher doubted that "any historical work has exercised so great an influence over the general political thinking of a nation," and that judgment has been seconded by other historians.(D. Wormell, *Sir John Seeley and the Uses of History* (Cambridge, 1979), 154, 155.)

were actually waged in pursuit of commercial interests in North America and Southeast Asia, and the confusing sequence of wars between England and France in the 18th was really part of a single contest for the possession of India and the New World. French assistance to the rebel colonists and even Napoleon's conquest of Europe were attempts to avenge earlier losses to England.

Seeley was no advocate of imperialism, as is sometimes believed. The expansion he celebrates is the spread of native stock. The subjection of peoples of different races and cultures, he clearly sees, will lead to difficulties, and he is concerned about the vulnerability of the Empire. But having read and absorbed Seeley, Grey would never join forces with the Radicals on colonial questions, and would especially value maintaining good relations with the "white" colonies and with the United States. He would be sensitive to the long struggle against the French, revived in the 1890s, and be anxious to dampen hostile feelings on both sides.

But if one book may have helped make him a more "conservative" Liberal, another may have helped make him more radical than most of the party, and, along with a series of newspaper articles, helped convince him to remain a Liberal when so many individuals of his background fled to the Unionists. This was Mill's *Principles of Political Economy*.

For Mill, as for his classical economic predecessors, value was determined by cost of production, and there were three "factors of production," land, labor, and capital, which were rewarded by rent, wages, and profits, respectively. Mill's departure, to oversimplify, was to focus not on how productivity was to be maximized, but on how the "shares" accruing to each might be made more equitable. Though there were iron laws of production, the laws governing "distribution," he claimed, were more flexible. As Jevons clearly saw, Mill's warm heart led him to fudge the inexorable logic of Ricardian economics, as it did that of Benthamite ethics and Hartleyean associationalist psychology.

Mill's successors generalized economic rent—all goods were subject to diminishing returns—but for the Saint of Rationalism, land-owners, largely aristocrats, alone benefitted from the fact that, as population increased and dubious marginal land was resorted to, the price of food soared and the value of their property rose without any effort on their part: landowners "enriched themselves even in their sleep," reducing real wages and profits in a zero-sum game.

The solution, for Mill, was, along with birth control (through abstinence, of course), co-ownership of factories—called "co-operation"—and small holdings for agricultural workers—"peasant proprietorship." Factory workers would thus earn profits and agricultural workers rent. There was little the government could do to facilitate "co-operation," but he believed it could and should take an active role in the redistribution of land. After all,

> no man made the land. It is the original inheritance of the
> whole species. Its appropriation is wholly a question of
> general expediency. When private property in land is not
> expedient, it is unjust... The state is at liberty to deal with
> landed property as the general interests of the community
> may require.[1]

Any aspiring politician would have turned to Book V of the Principles, "On the Influence of Government," and here Mill stressed again that the concept of a "nightwatchman" state—only protecting against force and fraud—was obsolete. In particular, the government was entitled to tax the "unearned increment" that accrued to landowners: the increase in the value of the land that owed nothing to their efforts. He was perfectly confident this could be assessed.

---

1 *Principles of Political Economy*, Book II, Ch. II, Sec. 6.(W. Ashley (ed.) (London, 1909), 233, 234)

10

Other arguments perhaps appealed to Grey, particularly Mill's passionate case for the government to preserve the nation's uncultivated land.[1]

Grey's reading of Mill almost cost him his seat during his first election campaign. "Albert,"[2] he confided to his diary, "came to see me at the Treasury," where Grey was working for the Chancellor of the Exchequer, Hugh Childers. He "says my chances for North Northumberland are ruined by my unsound Radical views as to fixity of tenure and fair rents."[3] But given "the accumulation of evil of hundreds of years of bad land system, I believe I am...on the right track." He later asked his cousin, "Have you ever read any account of Belgian peasant proprietorship? It has undoubtedly done great things."[4] This was the favorite example of Mill's, described at length.[5]

Perhaps the best evidence for Mill's influence is Grey's only publication before the 1920s, apart from *Fly Fishing* (1899)—*Rural Land*[6] He advocated, he declared, changes for which "the name of revolution will, perhaps, be more appropriate than that of reform." Local authorities were to be established, elected by manhood suffrage, and "given large powers of acquiring land compulsorily by purchase for public purposes..." He makes the very Millite argument that "first among the advantages" would be "moral rather than material ones." "Pride in possession" would lead to "keen personal interest in the forces of nature," and would "restore a vigorous tone of mind." The creation of local bodies

---

1 "It is not good for man to be kept perforce at all times in the presence of his species. Solitude...is essential to any depth of meditation or of character; and solitude in the presence of natural beauty and grandeur, is the cradle of thoughts and aspiration which are not only good for the individual, but which society could ill do without."(*Ibid.*, 750.)

2 his cousin, Albert Grey of Howick

3 Trevelyan, 33. These were two of the "Three Fs" agitated for by the Irish Land League. Other relatives were also anxious about Edward's radicalism, including his own mother.(Robbins, 20–21, 23.)

4 E. Grey to A. Grey, 27 June 1885, Durham University.

5 Book II, Ch. VI, sec. 5 (Ashley, 271–5.)

6 London, 1892, published by the Eighty Club. Grey was a vice-president and Sidney Webb sat on the executive committee. A few speeches were published by Liberal Party associations. Grey also refers to Mill several times in his letters, and mentions him in *The Charm of Birds* (p. 146)

wielding great powers will also reinvigorate the electorate, and spur capable men to devote time to public service. Among the material advantages would be better, cheaper, and more plentiful supplies of milk, eggs, vegetables, and fruit. Landowners normally extract high rents for allotment land, located around villages. This is "distinctly a part of that 'unearned increment' of which all reformers just now are in hot pursuit..." The land will be taken over by public authorities, rents will be set by the parish council, and fixity of tenure and compensation for improvements granted.[1]

The shrewd Cabinet diarist Charles Hobhouse recognized that Grey was "more radical than is commonly supposed."[2] Arthur Balfour concurred: the Foreign Secretary was "a curious combination of the old-fashioned Whig and the Socialist."[3] Grey went so far as to threaten to resign when the Cabinet opted for a more moderate solution to the House of Lords question than he favored.[4] When the Miners Federation called out its members in March 1911 and the strike threatened to paralyze the country, it was Grey who took the leading role in negotiations, and eventually effected a compromise. On all domestic questions, including women's suffrage, he remained the stalwart Millite Radical he had become in 1885.

A series of articles by Mill's erstwhile disciple John Morley in the *Pall Mall Gazette* is also credited with keeping Grey a Gladstonian Liberal after 1886, when so many members of his class defected. Morley made the case that coercion would never succeed in Ireland, and that some form of autonomy would have to be conceded.[5] But it was his Radical views on land as well as his

---

1 *Rural Land,* 3,5,6, 11.
2 E. David (ed.), *Inside Asquith's Cabinet* (New York, 1977), 121
3 Trevelyan., 192.
4 He wanted a democratically elected Chamber; the majority in the Cabinet was content with restricting the powers of the Lords.
5 Characteristically, his loyalty to the Grand Old Man did not mean that Grey always took the party line on Ireland. He was one of a handful of Liberals who crossed the floor to vote with Conservatives in favor of Balfour's Irish Land Act, which he was convinced would improve tenants'

conviction that granting autonomy to Ireland would strengthen rather than weaken the bonds between the two islands that kept him from joining the Unionists.

The decision was very important for Grey's career. Old, established families were thin on the ground in the Liberal Party by the beginning of the twentieth century. Undoubtedly, Grey owed his rapid rise in the party—and his being the only serious contender for Foreign Secretary when the Liberals finally returned to power—to his gifts as a speaker and to general admiration for his sterling character—the directness, simplicity, and candor inevitably mentioned by contemporaries. But it would be a mistake to underestimate the importance of his social position at a time when deference to rank was still the rule. The Greys, as mentioned, could trace their roots to the Conquest. The lineage of the few aristocrats and gentry in the Liberal Cabinet of 1905 were otherwise mostly dubious.[1] The Foreign Secretary in particular was expected to be an aristocrat. The ambassadors and ministers he received were, with the exception of the French and Americans, usually counts, at the very least. The Secretary conferred with the Sovereign and met visiting royalty.[2] When Grey initially refused the Foreign Office in December 1905, there was virtually no one else to whom the incoming Prime Minister Henry Campbell-Bannerman could offer the position.[3]

The author inevitably associated with Grey is not, of course, Seeley or Mill, but William Wordsworth. However, as the letters to Katharine Lyttelton reveal, the notion that Grey was infatuated

---

rights in Ireland.

1 Earl Carrington and, especially, the Earl of Elgin were the two exceptions, but they were minor figures in the Cabinet.

2 Three previous holders of the office had not sat in the House of Lords: Canning, Palmerston, who had an Irish title, and Lord John Russell. Castlereagh and Lord Stanley also took office prior to their elevation to the Upper House. However, all, with the exception of Canning, were the sons of peers.

3 He offered the Foreign Secretaryship to Lord Elgin, who declined, and then, in desperation, to Grey's relative Lord Cromer, not even a Liberal, who also turned him down.

with Wordsworth to the exclusion of all other writers is hardly accurate.[1] Wordsworth was nevertheless of paramount importance. He articulated Grey's *lebensphilosophie*. In doing so, he simply expressed Edward's own inner feelings. He is a "special poet," Grey wrote, because "as we read him, we constantly find ourselves saying, 'I know that I have felt that.' And sometimes he reveals to us what we have not been previously conscious of, so that we say, 'I have felt that without knowing it.'

> Thus, to those of us who have the same sort of suscepti-
> bility that Wordsworth had to all the aspects of natural
> beauty, his poetry becomes something not to be measured
> merely by poetic merit, but something which reproduces,
> interprets, and reveals to us our own experiences, and
> is therefore not like something outside appealing to our
> admiration, but like something which is akin to us, part of
> ourselves, part of our lives.[2]

And these exalted experiences in the countryside, Grey believed, following Wordsworth, offered intimations of immortality. "To be out of doors with a heart that watches and receives is to be, if not on holy ground in the same sense as a Church, at any rate in the presence of much that is not limited to this world."[3] He told the Vicar of Embleton, R. B. Dawson, that he regarded "the growing knowledge of the life of nature as a preparation for life to come, when a man will find his true place if he has learnt to love beauty here."[4] As Grey's first wife Dorothy breezily put it: "it is nice to have one's pleasures made into a religion."[5]

---

1 He quotes as frequently from a number of other poets (George Herbert, Goethe, Keats, Tennyson, Browning), and he was clearly a voracious reader of novels, even in office. For a number of years, he had a copy of Gibbon by his bedside at Fallodon, along with Thackeray, and would resume re-reading it when he returned.
2 E. Grey, *Fallodon Papers* (Boston, 1926), 148.
3 E. Grey to L. Creighton, 9 February 1908, Bodleian. The sentence quotes part of the final two lines of "The Tables Turned."
4 Trevelyan, 62.
5 L. Creighton, *Dorothy Grey* (London, 1907), 201.

Wordsworthian pantheism was in no way amoral. Nature had stirred the poet's conscience. Wordsworth, said Grey, had "an almost abnormal indifference to human censure; he is never depressed by blame nor elated by praise, but constantly worked up by his susceptibility to the outward aspects of Nature."[1] A famous example from his boyhood in the autobiographical *Prelude* is the way in which a peak looming above a bare ridge as he rowed toward it smote his conscience, after he had stolen some woodcocks.

No more than with Wordsworth himself did the exalted moods lead Grey to quietism. Grey's independent course of reading after Balliol convinced him to take up politics, or reinforced that impulse. In order to gain some experience, he wrote to his second cousin, Lord Northbrook, then First Lord of the Admiralty, who secured him a position with another Baring relative, Sir Evelyn, later the Earl of Cromer.[2] The Controller General of Egypt was in London for a conference, and Grey became his unpaid secretary during this time. Having performed well, he was able to move to another unpaid position at the Treasury. Here, he felt, he acquired "business habits."[3] Grey had strong feelings about the continued disenfranchisement of the rural lower classes in the counties, and was invited to address a meeting at Alnwick on the subject. He consulted Creighton, who told him that the most important thing when giving a speech was to prepare a clear and definitive ending, and having reached it, to sit down. "Remember that it is better for people to say 'I am sorry that it is over,' than 'I am glad it is over.'"[4] Creighton helped him with his speech, and suggested he deliver it in a simple, straight-forward, conversational manner,

---

1 *Falllodon Papers*, 151.
2 Northbrook was Sir George Grey's nephew, the son of his sister, and Evelyn was the earl's first cousin.
3 Trevelyan, 31.
4 L. Creighton, *Life and Letters of Mandell Creighton*, v. 1 (London, 1904), 202–3.

eschewing rhetorical flourishes and dramatic gestures. This would be Grey's platform style for the rest of his career.

The speech was well-received, and the twenty-two-year-old was invited to stand for a new constituency in Berwick-upon-Tweed. Northern Northumberland had been the bailiwick of the Percys for thirty years, but Grey defeated the son of the 6th Duke and entered Parliament in 1884.

❧

He had broken off his campaign briefly in October to marry Dorothy Widdrington.

Though they'd met in London, she had grown up only sixteen miles from Fallodon, at Newton-on-the-Moor. The two families didn't socialize. The Widdringtons, though unconventional—"Fitz" was an artist, and the couple were avid travelers—were Tories.

Dorothy was the oldest of four children, but grew up a solitary, fiercely independent child, who preferred walking by herself through the woods and over the moors to acquiring the skills—"parlour tricks," she called them—expected of a girl who would debut in London and be presented at court. "There's a great fuss made in this house over manners," she complained to her governess.[1] Mandell Creighton seemed to be the only person who understood and appreciated her: "He made me believe that I mattered... He helped me believe in myself. He talked to me like an equal about real things," she recalled. "He taught me to think."[2] "I have thought a great deal about you since I saw you," he wrote in one letter. "I think that I shall always be a little afraid of you. You are so strong and so reserved that you seem to be another sort of creature to ordinary folks."[3] Dorothy's mother resented and mistrusted Creighton's attentions: "There is a terrible intimacy

---

1 *Dorothy Grey*, 4.
2 *Ibid.*, 11.
3 *Ibid.*, 16.

between you and him I don't half like—he is distinctly rude to me and takes every opportunity of talking to you—alone—these Priests!...O how it intensifies my mistrust of priests!"[1] Though attractive as a young woman, in a demure, un-English way, with widely set brown eyes and a small, bow-shaped mouth, Dorothy bridled at the attentions of would-be suitors. Any man who became "sentimental" was instantly cut.[2] She confided to her friend Constance Herbert that she hated all the men she met, and would likely never marry. She would become a nurse and support herself. She was quite frosty with Grey, too, initially,[3] but they soon found they had much in common: chiefly their great affection for and gratitude toward Creighton, but also their interest in books—both had begun reading voraciously, if unsystematically—and their love of the Northumberland countryside. In nature she felt calm and complete. Not surprisingly, she hated "this horrid London" when she first went down to be presented at St. James, and the antipathy grew with passing years.[4] But despite her attraction to Grey, Dorothy resisted the idea of marriage: "I feel wildly rebellious sometimes at the thought of my lost freedom," she confided to Creighton.[5]

When the couple returned to Fallodon after the wedding at Newton-on-Moor—Grey had to resume campaigning—there was an unpleasant surprise for the groom. After initial attempts at lovemaking—or, perhaps, before—Dorothy informed Edward that she had "an aversion to the physical side of marriage."[6] According to Grey's second wife, Edward was surprisingly

---

1 C. Chance, *The Widdrington Women* (Andover, UK), 2010, 87.
2 "You were cold as ice and most repellant to men in your manners, never seeming to care for one of them save as things to dance with," wrote her mother. "But they admired you and I think were piqued, for they came back and hovered about, but got less than nothing for their pains." (C. Widdrington, Diary, Frances Dorothy Widdrington, 12. Cecilia Widdrington kept diaries for each of her four children, and addressed them in her entries.)
3 "Ed Grey seemed rather inclined to be nice to you—but certainly not you to him," her mother observed.(Diary, p. 14.)
4 *Dorothy Grey*, 10–11.
5 *Ibid.*, 20–21.
6 Marie Belloc Lowndes, *A Passing World* (London, 1948), 174. A popular crime novelist and the

understanding. He straight away consented to a *marriage blanc*, suggesting that henceforth "they should live together like brother and sister." At some point Dorothy reconsidered, and proposed that they should consummate their marriage, or resume sexual relations, if they had already made love. Grey, however, declined the offer. He insisted "that they were both happy and satisfied with the life they had agreed on leading."[1]

A friend encountering them at their fishing cottage recalled that they looked "like two happy boys."[2] Ronald Munro Ferguson remembered Dorothy as "an extraordinarily good man's companion, so self-reliant and helpful that out in the country one felt with her like being in company with another man."[3]

Life in the country came to center on an isolated cabin they purchased at Itchen Abbas (called simply "Cottage"), about four miles up the river from where Grey had fished as a boy at Winchester. Fallodon was too great a distance from London to allow for convenient escape. The Greys came each weekend from early March through summer, and sometimes well into fall, leaving from Waterloo station before dawn on Saturday morning and returning Sunday evening. Only a few special friends were ever invited to Cottage, and then usually when the Greys weren't there, and the couple avoided villagers and neighbors. "No outsider was allowed to disturb their peace," wrote Louise Creighton.[4]

They kept to themselves as much as possible in London as well. Dorothy continued to hate the city as intensely as she loved the country. The affectations of the people with whom she was obliged to associate were as offensive as the dirt, squalor, and noise. When Grey served as Parliamentary Under-Secretary for Foreign Affairs in the Liberal government of 1892–5, the couple had to spend

---

sister of Hillaire Belloc, Lowndes was a close friend of Grey's second wife.
1 *Ibid*, 175.
2 *Dorothy Grey*, 74.
3 *Ibid.*, 114.
4 *Ibid.*, 41.

much more time in the capital. Dorothy's comments on the city were particularly bitter. "I can't rest in this London," she wrote her brother-in-law in 1893. "It falls on one like a black darkness, its impurities, its conventionalities, its crowdedness and its filth... We come out of the bright sun and keen smells of autumn into fog and stinks. How can we praise God and keep our hearts up?" "The strongest hatred we feel now is of people, any people; they are all horrid and there is no health in them; they are mean and selfish." The chirping of starlings is "so much nicer and more mysterious and pure than the jabbering of people."[1] "I believe," she declared after three years of marriage, "we have arrived at the state when we have got all the good out of people that we shall ever get."[2] She avoided parties. "I have discovered that if you don't go and say nothing about it, nobody every finds it out."[3]

Yet Dorothy was not a recluse. She had a small circle of close friends who revered her. They admired her candor and her unconventional responses to books and ideas. Without being in any way a brilliant conversationalist, her insights struck friends as refreshing and penetrating. According to Ethel Arnold,

> "It was one of the peculiar features of one's relations with her that whereas one seemed in one sense to have known her always, so utterly frank, straightforward and simple was her attitude towards those she cared for, in another sense it was a never-ending source of surprise that one knew her at all. With all her frankness, amounting at times to brusquerie...there was always a certain elusiveness about her, a something wild and untamed, from which came her sense of kinship with all the wild, shy creatures she loved so well...."[4]

---

1 *Ibid.*, 199–200.
2 *Ibid.*, 37.
3 *Ibid.*, 31.
4 *Ibid.*, 79.

Among her admirers were discriminating politicians—Rosebery, Morley, and Haldane—and the writers W. H. Hudson, who became a good friend, W. E. Henley, and H. J. Newbolt. Hudson was particularly enchanted by her. "It was a rare pleasure, a surprise, to find one in her world who did not use the customary phrases, who was of so original a mind, so transparently honest, as to make it a mental refreshment to converse with her. But my chief pleasure was in the discovery that she herself was a native, so to speak, of my world."[1] "She said things more real than one often heard from people," summarized one friend.[2]

Unsurprisingly, not everyone was taken with her. Even friends acknowledged that she could be "cold and abrupt" with people she didn't know, and rude to those who did not share her tastes. She could be "'punitive' and 'tempestuous,'" Louise Creighton conceded. "She would not always listen; she was often prejudiced, almost contentious; too passionate in her likes and dislikes to be always tolerant and discerning." "I can't even be civil to people I don't like," Dorothy confessed.[3] To the novelist Marie Belloc Lownes, she seemed "extremely self-absorbed."[4] To Albert, Lord Grey, she was "farouche"[5] and "hard and selfish."[6] She coldly rejected everyone who "did not agree with the chaste atmosphere of the Temple in which she was determined to hide herself from the world."[7] Beatrice Webb found her "a fastidious aristocrat, intensely critical of anyone to whom work is the principal part of life..."[8] Acquaintances were sometimes put off by her dislike of children. "She did not know what to say to them, and seemed positively terrified in their presence. Neither did she appear to care

1 Trevelyan, 45.
2 *Dorothy Grey*, 108.
3 *Ibid.*, 109, 162, 166.
4 *A Passing World*, 175.
5 A. Grey to E. Pease, 17 June 1907, Grey Papers, Durham.
6 A. Grey to E. Pease, 5 June 1907.
7 *Ibid.*
8 Robbins, 106.

much to talk with her friends about their children, and one felt almost instinctively that the whole subject had better be ignored."[1]

Dorothy's indifference to family extended to her own relatives. The rebellious teenager never reconciled with her parents. Friends were surprised at how callous her feelings were toward the Widdringtons, even after her father went blind. Albert Grey was especially appalled.[2] Louise Creighton's memoir recounts no visits home, and there seem to have been no exchanges of letters. Dorothy's mother and siblings are never mentioned by name. Friends were scandalized by the omission.

Without children, without the responsibilities of a political hostess, what did Dorothy do when she was not exulting in nature? She was an avid reader, sometimes engrossed in four books at once. She especially revered George Meredith. Others might think him obscure and his humor rebarbative.[3] "I don't find him so," she said. "I don't pretend to be cleverer than other people, but I seem always to know what he means. I don't even have to think about it. He speaks my native language, in fact."[4] "It seems to me that a great part of what understanding of humans I have has been got through George Meredith."[5]

---

1 *Dorothy Grey*, 169.

2 She had severed relations, he wrote, with a man who was "clear, proud, cultured, big-hearted, affectionate...a beautiful old Venetian noble," and with her sister Ida, a girl "who was the incarnation of the mountain stream and the heather, but whose big-hearted sympathy with every lad of rollicking high spirits" offended Dorothy. (A. Grey to E. Pease, 17 June 1907, Durham.) Dorothy stopped speaking with her sister after a disastrous visit Ida paid the Greys in London. (She unwisely flirted with Haldane, and modeled her behavior on the abhorrent Margot Asquith.) Dorothy had always been rude to her father, who never addressed her in public, "not liking people to notice your rough reply."(Diary, 13.) Fitz took her hunting and discussed literature with her, but received "never a pleasant word—only sour looks."(Diary, 14.)

3 "As a writer," Oscar Wilde famously remarked about Meredith, "he has mastered everything except language; as a novelist he can do everything except tell a story; as an artist, he is everything except articulate."(L. Stevenson, *The Ordeal of George Meredith* (New York, 1953), 273.)

4 *Dorothy Grey*, 139.

5 *Ibid.*, 144.

She enjoyed essays and collections of letters; among her favorites were those of Bacon and Lamb, and the diaries and letters of Boswell and Edward FitzGerald. She read French and admired Montaigne, La Rochefoucauld, and Sainte-Beuve. Diderot, however, was too racy. "There is a lot of filth" in *Rameau's Nephew*, she wrote.[1] She read some history but preferred, unsurprisingly, books on nature, particularly the works of W. H. Hudson, who immortalized Cottage in *Hampshire Days*.

As a young woman, Dorothy had wanted desperately to do good. What did she accomplish as the wife of an influential landowner and rising political star? Infected by a friend's enthusiasm for a project to board workhouse children in the homes of villagers, Dorothy "tried to form a committee" in 1896 to arrange for the transfer of children, but was unable to find a secretary, and the project languished for three years. The first child was selected only in 1900. Dorothy herself did the choosing, and, armed with "lots of chocolate and buns," accompanied the child to Embleton. "What this meant only those who knew how little Dorothy naturally cared for children, and how shy she was with them, can fully appreciate."[2] No children were lodged at Fallodon, of course.[3]

Dorothy had once hoped to become a nurse. Her other major philanthropic venture consisted of helping to organize a visiting nurses association. Again, the impulse came from someone else, the vicar's wife. This time a secretary was located more quickly. The two nurses Dorothy's committee supervised stayed in the cottages of women who were ill and did housekeeping for the family, as well as care for the patient. Dorothy, of course, did not visit the homes of the incapacitated women, nor supervise the nurses, but wrote supportive letters to the secretary who did.

---

1 *Ibid.*, 144.
2 *Ibid.*, 119.
3 Dorothy did occasionally invite women from the village to stay at Fallodon for rest cures.

Political work, naturally, was uncongenial. "She could never speak in public, and the nervous effort of even the few words needed from the chair was distressingly great." And, not surprisingly, "her sensitive nerves were much tried by committee meetings."[1] The Greys did not host political dinners, but this did not prevent her from scolding a Liberal peer: "You are behaving very badly; you are not doing your duty at all. What do you mean by not entertaining?"[2]

∽

On the morning of February 1, 1906, when Dorothy wished to go out for a drive, she was warned by the head groom that the horse was unusually nervous and might bolt. She insisted on going out nonetheless. The horse shied and the left wheel of the dog cart hit a stump, overturned, and Dorothy was thrown to he ground.[3] She was carried unconscious into the schoolhouse in the village of Ellingham, and a telegram was sent to her husband. He received it as he entered a meeting of the Committee of Imperial Defense, after lunching with John Morley. Grey caught the overnight express north.

Dorothy was still unconscious when he arrived. She had fractured the base of her skull. There was only a small chance she might recover, Edward was told. Then Dorothy regained movement of her arm and leg, which had been paralyzed. But in the early hours of February 4, she died without regaining consciousness. Edward had already ordered his black overcoat and trousers to be sent north.

---

1 *Ibid.*, 131, 132.
2 *Ibid.*, 133.
3 "The Death of Lady Grey" *Times*, 7 February 1906. A dog cart had a separate compartment facing the rear. An under-gardener at Fallodon, Thomas Henderson, was sitting in this space. Uninjured, he kept the horse from kicking Dorothy and fetched a doctor.

Dorothy Grey was cremated, according to her wishes, and her ashes were placed under the sitka tree she and Edward had planted together at Fallodon.[1]

✑

"Pray for me," Dorothy had written to several friends when her husband was named Foreign Secretary.[2] "There is a lot of flummery about the Foreign Office," she told Ella Pease, "and I try not to think about how badly I shall do my small part of the work. But I shall try very hard."[3] Would Grey have remained in office for eleven years if she had lived? Trevelyan thought not. "There is little doubt that if she had lived, the mere fact that she was there, even if not her direct advice, would always have been a pull to draw him back out of office; whereas the misery and vacancy caused by her death made him, year after year, welcome the most exacting work as the surest relief."[4] Dorothy had Graves Disease, and experienced debilitating symptoms between 1896 and 1900. If these episodes had recurred, this would have increased the temptation to resign.

Grey himself was not so sure he would have left office. "It is not possible, in reviewing my work afterwards, to look back and say, 'Here if she had lived, I should have taken another decision,'..."[5] But it's difficult not to agree with Trevelyan. Given Grey's devotion to his wife and her misery in London, and her aversion to the

1 P. Brockway, *Sir Edward Grey* (Winchester, 2010), 64. Edward's ashes were buried beside hers after his death. Cremation had been legal in Britain for twenty years, but was still unusual. Louise Creighton, believing she would have to witness the immolation of her friend's body, dreaded the funeral. (Covert, *Victorian Marriage*, 308.)

2 E. Grey to K. Lyttelton, 31 July 1910.

3 *Dorothy Grey*, 184.

4 Trevelyan, 116. After his wife's death, Grey offered his resignation to Campbell Bannerman, but added that for himself "the best chance is to work & to begin at once."(Robbins, 153.) F.O papers were sent to him on February 7, and he wrote to Louise Creighton two weeks later, "My plan is to go on working in the belief that some life and spirit will come back in time. Meanwhile I do the work and the days pass slowly, but they pass." (E. Grey to L. Creighton, 22 February 1906, Bodleian.)

5 *Twenty-Five Years,* v. 1, 97.

duties required of the wife of a diplomat, it's difficult to believe he'd have remained at his post for eleven years.

She may have continued to exert an influence on his public life. In *Twenty-Five Years*, Dorothy is praised not for her unconditional love and support, but for inspiring her husband to live up to the exacting standards they shared.[1] Her death may have increased his resolve to adhere to those standards. When Grey addressed Parliament on August 3rd 1914—swaying the House with his reasonableness and transparent honesty—he felt Dorothy's presence by his side.[2]

∽

Trevelyan called Dorothy Grey "ultra-virginal."[3] No one would have used that term to describe Pamela Wyndham. In the most famous group portrait of the age, John Singer Sargent's *The Wyndham Sisters,* dubbed "The Three Graces" by the Prince of Wales when he viewed it at the Royal Academy in 1900, Pamela, the youngest and prettiest of the Graces, stares boldly at the viewer; her sisters' gazes are averted. She is sprawled on the sofa in a seductive pose, her white tulle and lace gown clinging to her body, one arm extended, the other poised gracefully on a pillow.

In the Wyndham home, pride of place in the drawing room was given to another painting of Pamela, a full length portrait by Ellis Roberts. Then as now, upper and middle-class parents not infrequently indulged their oldest son and their youngest daughter, and Madeline and Percy Wyndham were no exceptions.[4]

---

1 "For twenty years I had had the upholding support, inestimable in its value especially to a man in public life, of constant companionship at home with one to whom nothing small or mean was tolerable." (*Ibid.*, 28.) What she had to say, he added, was never "commonplace or second-hand, never the outcome of conventional or party or class thought."

2 S. Lowndes (ed.), *Diaries and Letters of Marie Belloc Lowndes* (London, 1971), 168. It was the first time this had happened since her death.

3 Trevelyan, 43.

4 The background of each was unconventional. Madeleine was the granddaughter of the Irish revolutionary leader Lord Edward Fitzgerald and Pamela Sims, herself probably the illegitimate daughter of Stéphanie Félicité Brulart, Comtess de Genlis, and Louis-Philippe Joseph, duc d'Orléans, later Philippe Egalité. (The new name did not save him from the guillotine.) Percy was the grandson

The spoiled eldest son was George.[1] He exercised a fascination for his generation out of all proportion to his achievements in both politics and literature.[2] Pamela early on had shown a talent for writing, and she was egged on by George, who called her "Dulcamara." He plied her with advice on subject matter—she should write about Pamela Sims and Lord Edward Fitzgerald—and about the process of writing, and subjected her poems to long-winded critiques.[3] Dulcamara worshiped her brother,[4] but didn't take his advice that she write about her great-grandparents. Pamela preferred writing about her children rather than her ancestors, and eventually published three books about them. To the extent that she is remembered as an author, it is for the second of these.[5] But among aficionados of the Souls, the intrigu-

---

of the eccentric third Earl of Egremont, wealthy art collector and patron of Turner, who had not bothered marrying his mistress of many years, the daughter of the librarian of Westminster Abbey. (The earldom thus passed to a nephew, though Percy's father was given Petworth, where the earl had built a studio for Turner, whose shimmering sunrises and sunsets looking across the estate's park rank among his masterpieces.) The Wyndhams themselves were avid collectors, and Madeleine a competent graphic artist and enamel-worker. Clouds, their avant-garde Wiltshire home, was itself a work of art.

1 When he went off with his regiment to the Sudan, Percy wrote, "My own dearest dearest boy, I must say once how deeply deeply I love you. I cannot express how I feel that my whole being is filled with eager tender love for you my darling. One cannot say this speaking but I should never forgive myself if I had not told you..."(J. Mackail and Wyndham, G., *The Life and Letters of George Wyndham*, v. 1 (London, 1925), 29.) As a young boy, he was encouraged by his father to hold forth on political and literary subjects. "Hush, George is going to speak," Percy would admonish guests. "Until the end of his life," his brother wrote, still innocent of Freud in 1925, Madeline and George "were like lovers and his heart was her home." (*Ibid.*, 22.)

2 He was "outrageously handsome, like some prince in the Arabian Nights," a friend recalled. "His good looks were of a kind to take one's breath away," wrote another. (*Ibid.*, 28.) He was a brilliant talker, if sometimes loquacious and diffuse, and a man of large and infectious enthusiasms. Invariably described as a romantic, he published only a few short essays and introductions. A protégé of Balfour's, he was appointed Chief Secretary of State for Ireland, but was forced to resign after a nervous breakdown following revelations about negotiations his secretary had conducted with the Irish Reform Association. He did not win the confidence of his colleagues ("Damn that fellow, he pirouettes like a dancing master," said one Tory backbencher), nor his Prime Minister ("I don't like poets"). (M. Egremont, *The Cousins* (London, 1977), 196 7.)

3 Mackail, v. 2, 321–4.

4 "Darling George," she wrote him, after she'd been married a dozen years, "I feel I never see you, and want to very much. How are you, my beloved; sometimes the thought of you, and all you are to me, and have been, comes over me like a big wave."(P. Tennant to G. Wyndham, n.d., but post-1906, Grosvenor Papers.)

5 *The Sayings of the Children* (1918). *The Children and the Pictures* (1907) was also popular, and those fond of Edwardian verse may enjoy *Windlestraw* (1905).

26

ing group of aristocrats with literary tastes who flourished in the 1880s and early '90s—and in whom there was a brief revival of interest a century later—Pamela is much better known for her affair with Harry Cust.

Henry John Cockayne Cust was the rival of George Wyndham in seductive good looks, and his superior in conversion.[1] Already smitten with Pamela, he made the mistake of sleeping with his shy, intellectual cousin Emmeline (Nina) Welby-Gregory, the cousin also of Katharine Lyttelton. Nina believed she was pregnant. Cust had already fathered at least one illegitimate child,[2] and Balfour, Nestor and *padrone* of the Souls, decreed he must marry his cousin. Only now did he realize how much in love he was with Pamela. When Nina had a miscarriage, or discovered she was not pregnant after all, Cust's misery turned to rage. Writing to George Wyndham's wife Sibell, his confidante, he vowed

> Except by English law I am not one bit married save to Pamela only... As I am spiritually Pamela's I am legally someone else's: the rest of life and all that pure if earthly joy of intimacy...belongs of right to Pamela, and if I may not give it to her none other shall ever have it...[3]

A broken heart occasionally inspires memorable verse. Cust's "Non Nobis Domine"—"our poem," Pamela called it—would be anthologized (anonymously) for decades in The *Oxford Book of Verse*.

---

1 "He was the unchallenged leader of the dinner-table. Quip, retort, repartee, quotation, allusion, epigram, jest—all flashed with lightning-like speed from that active workshop, his brain," wrote George Curzon.(J. Abdy and Gere, C., *The Souls* (London, 1984), 72.) "Cust was the best talker of his day," declared Charles Whibley. (*Ibid.*, 75.) At Eton he had been reckoned by one master as a more probable future prime minister than Rosebery or Curzon.(R. Storrs, *Orientations* (London, 1937), 27.) Another Balfour protégé, he was elected an M.P. for a division in Lincolnshire in 1890, but, by all accounts, was more intent on pursuing women than his political career. With his piercing blue eyes, curly blond hair, and finely chiseled features, it was more frequently he who was pursued, though, as someone noted, the women did not have to run very far or very fast. (J. Robertson Scott, *The Story of the Pall Mall Gazette*. (London, 1950), 386.)
2 Diana Manners. Margaret Thatcher's mother was rumored to have been another of his offspring.
3 Egremont, 163–4.

Pamela appeared to share Harry's conviction that in God's eyes, if not the law's, they were indeed married, and continued to exchange letters and gifts with him. The indulgent parents were appalled. Pamela was sent off to India and then to Italy. Here a meeting was arranged with Eddy Tennant, the diffident thirty-five-year-old son of the fifth richest man in Europe.[1] Eddy would become one of Edward Grey's closest friends.[2] On a balcony overlooking Florence, Eddy proposed and Pamela accepted.[3] She still loved Harry Cust. Pamela kept his picture in her sitting room and every New Year's Day she would reread Harry's letters, tears streaming down her cheeks.[4] On her visits to Clouds, she would stand in the hallway and rehearse their parting interview, she wrote her sister eleven years after Harry's death.[5]

Even while she was still pining for Harry in India, other thoughts were on Pamela's mind. "I wish," she wrote her sister-in-law, "it wasn't impossible to have a Baby without having a husband—I wish it weren't wrong even—for sometimes I feel I would willingly go to the bad—just to have a Baby of my own, to love."[6] The contrast between Grey's wives could hardly have been starker. Eddy Tennant, if he didn't satisfy Pamela intellectually

---

1 His father, Sir Charles Tennant, "the Bart," had inherited the chemical conglomerate founded by Eddy's great-grandfather, who had used a recently patented process to manufacture a bleaching powder for linen, replacing chlorine, which had noxious side effects. Byproducts proved immensely profitable and the Bart used revenue from what had become the world's largest chemical empire to speculate successfully in railroads, property in Australia, sulphur mines in Spain, and gold mines in North Africa and India.

2 The Bart was a major contributor to the Liberal Party, and two likely met at a soiree at his Grosvenor Square home.

3 "Did Auntie Pansie arx him to marry her, or did the man arx her?" inquired her seven-year-old niece Cynthia Charteris, later Asquith. (M. Elcho to A. Balfour, Spring 1895, J. Ridley and Percy, C. *The Letters of Arthur Balfour and Lady Elcho* (London, 1992), 124.)

4 P. Glenconner to S. Wyndham, 25 January 1912, Grosvenor Papers.

5 "Whatever I was doing," he had told her, "whatever I did, sad, mad, and bad, I always said to myself, 'I have got Pamela, like a star in a cupboard to come back to.'"(S. Blow, *Broken Blood* (London, 1987), 165.) After their marriages, Cust continued to send her affectionate notes and snippets of poetry. ("Now—& Then!/Here is Spring,/Late on the Wing,/& Where are you,/Child of Blue,/And when?") (*Ibid.*, 136.). She told the tragic tale to her oldest son, who cherished the legend and quoted "Non Nobis" and other Cust poems in letters to her from the front. (P. Glenconner, *Edward Wyndham Tennant* (London, 1919), 270.)

6 P. Wyndham to S. Wyndham, 28 January 1894, Grosvenor Papers.

or emotionally, at least provided her with children on which to lavish her affections. "She loved them," wrote Osbert Sitwell, "it seemed to me, in a French and not an English way; she wished to be with her children throughout the day—the last thing, as a rule, that an English parent of her kind would desire."[1]

Naturally, the indulged children did not turn out well, by and large, but upper-class mothers reading Pamela's books were taken with the idea of spending more time in the nursery, dispensing with the awkward "children's hour" at the end of the day, and carefully noting down, as Pamela had, all the amusing and endearing observations their children made. Pamela took her brood on caravan trips around Wiltshire, built them a two-storey cylindrical tower to play in, and gave each a garden plot.

Shortly before her death Dorothy had selected a house on Queen Anne's Gate, number 3, for the couple to lease while Edward served as Foreign Secretary—a five-minute walk to the Foreign Office across the southeast corner of St. James' Park. The Tennants lived at the other end of the street, 34 Queen Anne's Gate. Grey began dining with them frequently after work.

At some point, apparently with Eddy's blessing, or at least indifference,[2] the relationship between the Foreign Secretary and Pamela Tennant became an intimate one.

The effervescent daughters of Sir Charles Tennant were unlike their stolid and prosaic brothers, especially the brassy Margot, the "electric charge" of the Souls.[3] After hesitating for two years,

---

1 O. Sitwell, *Laughter in the Next Room* (London, 1949), 97. Pamela "preferred to lead an entirely country life, surrounded by her children,"—despite her "exceptional sense of humor," "delightful cultivation of mind," and "brilliant powers of conversation," recalled her good friend Marie Belloc Lownes, who also attributed this to her French blood. "She was quite unlike an Englishwoman." (*Passing World*, 180, 181.) This seems to have been the universal explanation for individuals who were fond of their children or parents, and had Gallic ancestors. Grey's predecessor, a descendant of Talleyrand, was also accused of un-English sentimentality toward his family.

2 He told guests at a dinner party that "he had never felt jealous in his life, and could not conceive what jealousy was like." (*Passing World*, 181.) To everyone's surprise, Pamela then burst into tears and left the table. She walked back and forth in the garden, sobbing loudly.

3 Margot was nonetheless very fond of Eddy, and liked the fact that he invariably would go home early from the parties he chaperoned her to, leaving her a copy of the house key.

Margot, in 1894, had married the Home Secretary, H. H. Asquith, a widower with five children. The relationship between the two sisters-in-law was a rocky one,[1] but they saw each other frequently. From a couple of sly references in Asquith's letters to Venetia Stanley, one can infer that by 1914 the affair seems to have been common knowledge among Grey's close friends. "Edward Grey came to see me to talk over the military situation," the Prime Minister told his girlfriend in September of that year. "He is in better spirits than he was, and Margot elicited from him at tea time that our Pamela was arriving to take her usual part in his weekly rest cure."[2] In a letter of 29 November, he noted that "meanwhile E. G. is taking a Sunday off—he left on Friday, I need not say for Wilsford."[3]

Some writers, including Grey's most recent biographer, have speculated the affair began much earlier, when Dorothy was alive, and that it resulted in at least one of the Tennants' children. The most likely candidate was David Tennant, born in 1902, who, says Waterhouse, with his "dark, masculine good looks, thin lips and strong nose," bears "a striking resemblance to Grey."[4]

Pamela was introduced to Grey during the election campaign of autumn 1900, when he spoke on behalf of Eddy at Innerleithen.[5] The couples first got together socially some time later, on a visit to Scotland, Pamela recalled after Dorothy's death. No date is

---

1 "Pamela Tennant arrives this evening," wrote Raymond Asquith to a friend. "It will be interesting to see how she and Margot get on: the allegory she wrote in which Margot figures as a princess in a glass house, herself as a beetle beloved by God, and my father as a muscovy duck, has made things a little strained."(J. Jollife, *Raymond Asquith: Life and Letters,* 108.)

2 H. Asquith to V. Stanley, 20 September 1914, in M. Brock and Brock, E. (eds.) H. H. Asquith, *Letters to Venetia Stanley* (Oxford, 1982), 249. Three weeks later, he remarked on Pamela "keeping a watchful eye on E G," at a dinner with Churchill, and added that "I'm afraid she is rather losing her look of distinction." (*Ibid.,* 269).

3 *Ibid.,* 324. This was the Jacobean manor house Eddy had purchased and remodeled for his wife.

4 Waterhouse, 95. There are other candidates for David's paternity, including the architect Detmar Blow and Ivor Guest.(Blow, 132–3.) According to Blow's grandson, the architect found the relationship with Pamela exhausting, and would snuff out his candle when he heard her footsteps coming down the hall. Blow's son would marry Pamela's granddaughter.

5 She reported to her father that he was "one of the nicest people in the world, cultivated, clever & amusing."(P. Wyndham to Percy Wyndham, 9 October 1900. (Francis Dineley papers.)

given, but Louise Creighton calls her a friend of Dorothy's latter years.[1] The first reference Grey makes to her in a letter to Eddy Tennant comes in December 1903, when he writes, "I do wish you and your wife would pay us a visit."[2] Not until 1907 does he refer to her as "Pamela," and his first surviving letter to her dates from August 1910. A year later there was a little flirtatiousness: "I have enjoyed the shooting and the hills," he told her after a visit to Glen, "but without that or any outside thing it is always a pleasure to be in your house and in your presence."[3] Later in the year, he wrote "I wonder how much you know of the pleasure you gave me on Friday. I was feeling so tired and flat that I half shrank from you coming, but I knew I should like to see you. Are you not more than Mary Queen of Scots beautiful!"[4] But only in 1913 was gallantry succeeded by some of the jauntiness and intimacy of Grey's letters to Katharine Lyttelton. "You ought to be gorsed, but I haven't been out alone [and] am not sure that when I am on a visit I feel superior enough to gorse you." In the same letter he told Pamela how, on a previous visit thirty-seven years earlier (he wrote from the Selbornes') he left behind a knife, and then, this morning, he lost his present knife ("a much poorer affair") among the blankets, adding, "You know how things get lost in bed." In the closing sentence, he said, "Don't forget that you are coming to lunch on Wednesday—it will be at 1:45. I know you wrote down KS for that evening, but I am not sure that you wrote down the lunch, which is a different sort of engagement and not so nice, though very helpful to me," and in a postscript, asked if Pamela "would like a KS evening on Friday as well as Wednesday."[5] An unconsciously revealing slip (perhaps), came in a letter a year later

---

1 *Dorothy Grey*, 110.
2 E. Grey to E. Tennant, 1 Dec. 1903, NAS.
3 E. Grey to P. Glenconer, 22 August 1911, Waterhouse, 255.
4 *Ibid.*, 256.
5 E. Grey to P. Glenconner, 23 March 1913, NAS. In brackets afterward Pamela adds, "K.S. means a 'knitting-supper'—when he reads aloud. P.G." This may be true, and gorse may have an equally innocent meaning, but it's clear the correspondents were at this point very close.

to Eddy, where he wrote, "I carried (this means convey by car, not in my arms) Pamela and Stephen to the zoo on Sunday."[1] Meanwhile, Grey's letters to Katharine Lyttelton were not quite so frequent and so playful after 1911.

Whenever the "rest cure" commenced, Grey made Pamela an honest woman on June 4, 1922, a year and a half after Eddy's death. Pamela delayed accepting Grey's proposal for the sake of the "boys," ages 18 to 23.[2]

His marriage to Pamela appears to have been a great source of happiness for the former Foreign Secretary. Posterity has reason to be grateful, too. Grey had written only one slim book, *Fly Fishing* (1899) and the pamphlet *Rural Land* (1892) before his second marriage, apart from entries in *The Cottage Book* (privately published in 1909). He records his debt to Pamela in the dedication to *Twenty-Five Years* (1925):

> This book has been written in intervals of quiet at home in the country during the last two years. There my wife read over to me that portion of the MS. that I had written each day. In this way the form and expression of the original draft were often greatly improved by her suggestion or criticism. Without her constant help and the encouragement the work would never have been done.[3]

There is no reason to doubt his claims. He had been out of office six years when he embarked on the account of his tenure as Foreign Secretary. Marriage with Pamela, the author or editor of fourteen books, inspired a burst of literary activity. In addition to his political memoir, he wrote *Fallodon Papers* (1926) and *The Charm of Birds* (1927). After his wife died, he published nothing more.[4]

---

1 E. Grey to E. Glenconner, 17 February 1914, NAS.
2 E. Grey to L. Creighton, 8 Nov 1921, Bodleian.
3 To Pamela herself, he wrote, "It becomes very clear to me that but for you *Twenty-Five Years* would never have been written. It is due to things and influences you brought, much rarer even than your material help, and which could have come from no one else." (*Passing World*, 186.)
4 "To write a book, one must feel happy," he told his friend Seton Gordon near the end of his life. (Gordon, 12.)

Pamela no doubt made the six years of their marriage a happy time in more conventional ways. She provided something like the close companionship he'd experienced in his first marriage. She accompanied her nearly blind husband around the grounds of Fallodon as he listened to the birds and fed his ducks, and read to him in the evening.

In one respect the marriage was a disappointment. Pamela was unable to bear him a child. This is hardly surprising: she was fifty-one when they married. Nonetheless, she had become pregnant six years earlier,[1] and after a few months of marriage was again expecting a child. But on a drive to a political meeting she had a miscarriage. Pamela intensely disliked automobiles. If she was in fact riding in a brougham, it would have been the second time Grey was bereaved by a horse-drawn vehicle. "The lack of a child...remained a bitter grief," according to Marie Lowndes, to whom he confirmed the story.[2]

The liaison with Pamela may have affected his relationship with other politicians. It might have drawn him closer to Asquith, long privy to the affair and now a quasi-brother-in-law. There are no surviving letters on the subject in the correspondence between Balfour and Lady Elcho, but the former Prime Minister may also have known that Grey was the non-platonic lover of his own quasi-platonic lover's sister, and thus something of a brother-in-law to him as well—one more illustration, if one were needed, of the close-knit, inbred world inhabited by political elites before the First World War.

There were minor downsides inevitably. Pamela was famously unpunctual. Grey's daughter-in-law, the actress Hermione Baddeley, recalled how she would "flutter back and forth while

---

1 This appears to have been a quixotic effort to persuade her son, then at the front, to accept a staff position in order to alleviate her anxieties. This he did, but the child was stillborn. Characteristically, Pamela wrote a four-page poem to "Hester": "Flower of the Field." ("O Mother's milk, that idly flows,/And no soft lips to gather it.")
2 *A Passing World*, 175.

he waited, looking at his watch, ready to leave. 'I'm just going to be two minutes,' she would cry; then ten minutes later: 'Just another minute!' 'Darling,' Lord Grey would wearily say, 'I do wish you'd stop 'justing' and get into the car.'"[1] Her extravagance was sometimes embarrassing. On one occasion she is supposed to have walked into a pet shop in Edinburgh, purchased all the birds in the store, and ordered them delivered to Holyrood Park, where they were liberated.[2] She was not "a citizen of the world," her sister-in-law Margot concluded. "The death of a half-tamed canary would be more to her than the loss of a whole regiment."[3] No doubt there are times when she was emotionally draining.

She imagined herself a "reasonable woman," but was "violently and enchantingly prejudiced," recalled Osbert Sitwell.[4] Her jealousy was notorious. According to Lowndes, she "took a passionate dislike to any man or woman who was loved by those she herself loved."[5] And she had a vile temper. A friend observed that her outbursts would never be tolerated today, though she would sometimes dig her nails into her wrist to prevent herself from being rude.[6] But it's unlikely she displayed this side of her character to Grey.

The real travails were her children. They seemed intent on pioneering novel forms of deviant behavior.[7] The man who had pored over diplomatic correspondence every day for eleven years, had adjusted nuances in his own dispatches, parried the queries of ambassadors, had scrutinized the clauses of old treaties and negotiated new ones, now found himself worrying about his step-chil-

---

1 H. Baddeley, *The Unsinkable Hermione Baddeley* (London, 1984), 47.
2 Blow, 171–2. Conversely, she is supposed to have ordered all the cockerels in Wilford village killed, because one kept her awake at night.
3 Blow, 131.
4 Sitwell, 98.
5 *A Passing World,* 180. She referred to her oldest and favorite son's girlfriends as "the hell-kittens."
6 Sitwell, 98.
7 Stephen was flamboyantly homosexual at a time when this was scandalous. Clare divorced three times when this was no less unusual. David also achieved the trifecta. Clare wanted nothing to do with her children, and her oldest daughter, like so many offspring two generations later, was shuttled between her paternal grandparents and the Greys.

dren appearing on the front page of the *Daily Mail.* This is not the way things were supposed to have turned out. Pamela, to her many fond readers, had seemed the most loving and supportive mother in England.

From July 1898 to shortly before his death, except for his years as Foreign Secretary, Grey sat on the board of directors of the North Eastern Railway.[1] But it is for his recreations[2] that he would still be remembered today had he never entered politics. *Fly Fishing* and *The Charm of Birds* are classics in their genres.[3] Grey had the great gift of being able to communicate his passion for fishing and birding to non-enthusiasts, to enable them to to appreciate the pleasures he enjoyed so keenly.[4]

Love of fishing, Grey believed, was innate, while birding was an acquired pleasure. "The keenest anglers are born and not made," he wrote. "The passion is latent in them from the beginning, and

1 The fourth largest railroad in the country, headquartered in York, the NER had over 30,000 employees. When he was named Chairman in 1904, it operated 1,670 miles of track, and carried 55 million passengers and also 55 million tons of freight per year, generating revenues of 9.3 million pounds. The company was the first to recognize unions, and Grey's membership on the board required him to oversee collective bargaining. He became familiar with working conditions and with relations between workers and management in the other major lines and in related industries. The position also paid handsomely. Grey initially earned 400 pounds a year as a board member. When he was appointed Chairman, this rose to 2000 pounds. "I have ordered a new tea-table and some extra bulbs," Dorothy exulted. "It's rather a fine salary you know... Just the sort of thing to manure one's expenses in a terrible way. It may be that we shall want one of the better sort of Grosvenor Road houses even." For his part, Grey found the work "agreeable and interesting," while it left him "plenty of leisure." In his last years, he seems to have been grateful for the duties it required of him, as well as the income.(Dorothy Grey, 136; Grey, *Twenty-Five Years,* v. 1, 57; Robbins, 102–4; Waterhouse, 69, 101–2.)

2 Only bird-watching was, for the English, a "recreation;" fishing, insofar as it involved killing something, was a "sport." Apart from being a superb fly-fisherman, Grey was also an outstanding tennis player, winning the Queen's Cup five times between 1889 and 1898, and the coveted Gold Racket of Lord's Club in 1896, when he was Amateur Champion of the U.K. (Trevelyan, 49.)

3 When Grey during his last years referred to "my book," he meant *The Charm of Birds,* not *Twenty-Five Years.* (Seton Gordon, 9.)

4 He was aware of just how hard this was: "It would be delightful to write about pleasures, if by doing so one could impart them to others... Unfortunately, nothing is more difficult...and it is only some unconscious egotism which ever prompts us to suppose that it might be easy. The insuperable difficulty lies in the nature of people and things. We do not all care for the same pleasures and do not want to hear about those of other people." (*Fly Fishing,* 4.)

is revealed sooner or later according to opportunity."[1] He first became aware of it at age seven, when, watching trout swimming in a small burn, he suddenly felt "an overpowering desire to fish, which gave no rest till some very primitive tackle was given me. With this and some worms, many afternoons were spent in vain."[2]

There were three things, he believed, that made fly-fishing "the very crown and consummation of the pleasure of angling."[3] The first was the "sense of high art in inducing fish to take for food something which is composed of feathers and materials that have...no resemblance to any edible thing whatever." This seemed more sporting than using a worm, prawn, or minnow. Second, with fly-fishing, except when using large salmon flies, the angler feels very little weight on the line until the fish takes the fly. The contrast between feeling nothing and then the sudden tug of the fish was exhilarating. Finally was the "effort and skill of casting." One was, in a sense, hunting with a rod and reel, watching for the rise while concealing oneself from the trout, then attempting to cast a bit in front of the fish, so the fly drifts over it and appears animate.[4] There are three kinds of fly-fishing: wet fly-fishing, dry fly-fishing, and salmon fishing. All have their distinct pleasures and it would be pointless, Grey says, to make invidious comparisons. In simple but vivid and evocative prose, he describes each.

Fishing, Grey felt, helped develop one's character. It fostered the "habit of attention and observation" and also taught "self-control."[5]

Grey's letters to Eddy Tennant reveal how much fishing meant to him. "Thank you very much for the salmon. I could have cried as I looked at it: as one in hell might cry at a message from

---

1 *Ibid.*, 87.
2 *Ibid.*
3 *Fallodon Papers*, 130.
4 *Ibid.*, 131–2.
5 *Fly Fishing*, 10–11. "If an angler is really keen, he will have many struggles with himself in early days. The greater the keenness the more bitter the disappointment, and the more highly nerves have been strung by excitement the more likely are we to collapse under disaster." Self-control is required as well "to withstand the small exasperations." (*Ibid.*, 11)

Paradise," he wrote at the end of February, 1912. A year later he confessed, "I am happy in the thought of being able to say 'Next week if all goes well I shall get away and catch a salmon.' No words can describe how I long for a holiday." And the following March, he wrote, "I do not expect to be prevented from getting to the Spey on April 8; but I tremble lest some political scare may prevent my starting for the Cassley next week: if so I don't know how I shall bear the disappointment."[1]

⁖

If fishing was a passion, bird-watching was something like friendship. And it was certainly not an innate predisposition. Grey recalled being asked by his father to listen to the little birds chirping outside the open library window at Fallodon, "'You wouldn't like to kill them, would you?' he asked; and I, somewhat reluctantly, said 'no,' because I knew this to be the answer expected and even required..." In fact, had he "a weapon of precision, nothing wild and animate, not even little birds, would be safe."[2] Until he left Oxford, he could identify some of the common birds, but knew only two songs, the robin's and a second that was either a blackbird's or a thrush's—he couldn't distinguish between the two. Around the time he began reading so voraciously, his interest in birds was also kindled. When he was sent down in 1884, he purchased his first five pair of waterfowl. Soon he was an ardent bird-watcher and the owner of a large and secure sanctuary.

For Grey, there were four "remarkable and attractive natural qualities" about birds that gave pleasure to observers: their ability to fly, their plumage, their eggs and nests, and their songs. If it was the latter he found most attractive, he was particularly fascinated by the differences among species in respect to all four attributes.[3]

---

1 E. Grey to E. Glenconner, 22 February 1912, 30 March 1913, and 24 March 1914, NAS.
2 *The Charm of Birds*, 2.
3 *Fallodon Papers*, 27–38.

37

He devotes most of the first seven chapters of *The Charm of Birds* to singing, which he believed was sometimes a spontaneous expression of joy.[1] The lark, peewit, and the curlew—with its "long, vibrating whistle" ("one can almost hear the air vibrating with the blessed sound") are among the most animated singers, along with the "churing" nightjar.[2] For musical quality, though, the nightingale, the song-thrush, and starling were the aviary prima donnas. The greatest performer, however, he felt was the blackbird. "To me there is something in it that I can best describe as intimacy. The songs of other birds please or delight us, but that of the blackbird seems to make a direct appeal to us and stirs some inward emotion."[3]

Just as fishing helped cultivate desirable traits, so the behavior of birds was an inspiration. Almost all British birds—save the discreditable cuckoo and three other species—are monogamous. Birds "have positive enjoyment in each other's society," and are distressed if they are separated.[4] But it was the relationship between himself and some of his birds that seems to have most delighted and moved him. Grey took great pleasure in taming unpinioned birds. Male robins, especially in winter, when they were hungry, could be trained to take worms out of his hand in a few days. Robins are territorial and each tame bird would accompany Grey to the border of its territory, and then withdraw.[5] It was his ducks that were most attached to him, and he to

---

1 *Ibid.*, 42.
2 *The Charm of Birds*, 186, 188.
3 *Ibid.*, 34. Grey's opinion was seconded by Teddy Roosevelt on the celebrated bird walk the two took in the Itchen Valley and New Forest on June 10, 1910. (*Fallodon Papers*, 70.)
4 *The Charm of Birds*, 139. In one case, when a female red-crested pochard was injured and Grey had her put out of her misery, the unpinioned male, instead of mating with another female, flew around restlessly for two weeks, then disappeared "as if he had gone on an endless search of the world for the mate he had lost...," evidence of "the great natural affection which exists amongst birds of a highly developed and intelligent species." The relationship "is one of real domestic happiness, not confined to the breeding season." (*Fallodon Papers*, 118–119.) Grey regretted that none of his step-children took to bird-watching, nor to fishing. But one of Katharine Lyttelton's daughters did, and the Foreign Secretary took pains to encourage her. (E. Grey to K. Lyttelton, 7 June 1907.)
5 *Fallodon Papers*, 44.

38

them. In his last years, nearly totally blind, he still took pleasure in sitting on his bench by the large pond at Fallodon and feeding them from his hand.

⸎

Not surprisingly, most of Grey's closest friends were fishing companions. Of these, only Sydney Buxton and Jack Tennant were colleagues.[1] The great names associated with the Foreign Secretary were, particularly after 1905, more political allies than friends. He was never on a first name basis with Henry Asquith— or even with Herbert Asquith, as he was called before Margot rechristened him after they married. Haldane he addressed as "Richard." But once they were in office, they saw little of each other socially. They were both, of course, inundated with work. But Haldane had been very close to Dorothy, and didn't care for Pamela.[2] Nor was he on good terms with the Lytteltons.[3] A turning point may have come right after Dorothy's death. Grey asked Haldane up for the funeral, but then disinvited him, telling him he wanted the company of one friend of his and Dorothy's only, and this was Louise Creighton.[4] When Grey was named Chancellor of Oxford University in 1928, Haldane scandalized some of the former Foreign Secretary's friends by his disparaging

---

1 Buxton (1853–1934) served as Postmaster General and President of the Board of Trade, before being named Governor General of South Africa in 1914. Tennant (1865–1935) was appointed Parliamentary Secretary to the Board of Trade after his brother-in-law became Prime Minister, joining the Cabinet, as Secretary for Scotland, only in 1916. Grey was grateful that Tennant never talked shop while they fished: Jack, he reported, gave "no sign…that he remembered being a member of the government or even of Parliament." (E. Grey to E. Tennant, 12 Sept 1910, NAS.) Eddy Tennant was a fellow-M.P for four years, until he lost his seat in 1910 and was created Baron Glenconner.
2 *A Passing World,* 176.
3 There were tensions between the Secretary of State for War and the first Chief of the General Staff over army reforms.
4 This, and their close friendship over the next months, had the unfortunate consequence of leading Creighton to hope that Grey would propose.(*Memoir,* 142, n. 22; confirmed by email from James Covert, 13 January 2010.)

39

remarks about Grey's intellect.[1] And when the portly Hegelian died later that year, Grey remarked only that "another chapter of very close association with my life has had 'finis' written to it." In the previous sentence, he had just praised Vernon Watney, who had also died in August, as someone who "had a rare and peculiar gift for intimacy, confidence, and affections. He was my most intimate friend and his death is a great grief and loss to me."[2]

Judging by Edward's letters to Katharine, the Cabinet member he felt closest to was John Morley. Morley was the one colleague who intimidated him slightly; "Honest John's" great erudition, but also his prickliness, made Grey a little ambivalent about inviting him up to Fallodon.[3] The fact that he was good friends with Morley, and with Lewis "Lulu" Harcourt, says something about the breadth of Grey's sympathies.[4] They, along with Robert Reid, Lord Loreburn, were the Cabinet Ministers most hostile to his policies, once Churchill and Lloyd George abandoned their roles as "economists"—insisting on cuts in naval and military spending Grey felt were dangerous and would reduce his leverage with Germany. In 1910, Grey scolded his friend Henry Newbolt at some length for writing a letter to the *Times* in which the poet had made invidious comparisons between the Foreign Secretary and his colleagues.[5]

But Asquith and Haldane are linked with Grey for good reason. From the time Asquith joined the two others in Parliament in 1886, they formed what the much put upon Liberal leader

1 H. Newbolt, *Later Life* (London, 1942), 356–7, cited by Robbins, 369.

2 E. Grey to K. Lyttelton, 9 September 1928, p.)

3 "I am thinking of asking J. M. to come here for a weekend when I am alone; but it is rather a bold thing of me to do." (E. Grey to K. Lyttelton, 1 October 1905); Grey had spent an invigorating weekend at Flowermead, Morley's Wimbledon home, the previous September. (E. Grey to K. Lyttelton, 8 September 1908.)

4 Grey spent several shooting weekends at Nuneham House. The only dream of his on record was set there.

5 E. Grey to H. Newbolt, 16 December 1910, Newbolt Papers, Bodleian.

Henry Campbell-Bannerman[1] called "the Triumvirate."[2] In the ten years of opposition before 1905, they led a small but influential minority advocating policies foreign and domestic at odds with the Gladstonian principles shared by most of their colleagues and the Party's rank and file.

The young M.P.s had two mentors, Arthur Acland (1847–1926) and Archibald Phillip Primrose, the 5th Earl of Rosebery (1847–1929).[3] The pair could hardly have been more unalike. Acland, though from a venerable and wealthy family in Devonshire,[4] was modest and self-effacing, a tireless committee member, conference attendee, article writer, and university extension lecturer. Grey already knew the slight, reedy reformer, fifteen years his senior, when "the little clergyman," as he was called from childhood, became Mandel Creighton's curate at Embleton.[5] Acland encouraged Grey's radicalism on the Land Question, but was himself more interested in the co-operative movement and educational reform—extending opportunities for education to the working classes.

If Grey was inspired by the scholarly Acland, he became the disciple of Rosebery. The Scottish earl exercised a fascination for the future Foreign Secretary and for so many of his generation that is not easy to appreciate today.[6] He was eloquent and

---

1 after 1896

2 He referred to them derisively as "Master Grey" and "Master Asquith" and "Schopenhauer." A fourth Musketeer was Ronald Munro-Ferguson (1860–1934), later Viscount Novar, M.P. for Leith Burgs, and the staunchest Roseberyite of the group.

3 When Foreign Secretary, Grey would express his gratitude by appointing the sons of each, successively, as his Parliamentary Undersecretary.

4 He would become the 13th baronet; the title dated from 1644.

5 The future bishop's sunny insouciance in matters theological did not rub off, and Acland experienced a classic mid-Victorian crisis of faith, finding, like so many other intellectuals, a surrogate religion in social reform. Inevitably, he wound up at Balliol, where he became a close friend of T. H. Green and attracted his own circle of disciples.

6 He was something like a rock star. The tumult when his daughter married Lord Crewe at Westminster Abbey in April 1899 led one paper to say that he "had attained the prestige of Royalty itself." Police blocked traffic in Parliament Square and the crowd in the Abbey was packed so densely it was feared some spectators would be crushed or suffocate. "Peggy's wedding grew into a popular demonstration," wrote her disapproving grandmother.(L. McKinstry, *Rosebery: Statesman in Turmoil* (London, 2005), 414.)

41

charismatic, and, apart from his celebrity status with the general public, commanded the fierce loyalty of advanced Liberals. His reserve, his distaste for politics, appeared to endear him all the more to Grey, if not to the other Triumvirs.[1]

The ugly fight between Sir William Harcourt and Rosebery for the leadership of the party is sometimes represented as being waged over the question as to whether the party should move to the left or to the right. Rosebery in fact wanted the Party to move in both directions at once.[2] Imperialism required social reform, and the Empire ought to benefit all classes, not just the aristocrats for whom, Radicals still believed, it was a form of out-door relief.[3] "The Imperialism," as Rosebery said in his famous Chesterfield speech in 1901, "that, grasping after territory, ignores the conditions of an Imperial race, is a blind, futile, and doomed Imperialism."[4] An uneducated, ill-housed, malnourished, drunken population would be unable to defend the Empire. To alleviate these iniquities a stronger, more efficient and interventionist government was required. The traditional watchword of the Gladstonians, "retrenchment," was outmoded. Roseberyites had no patience with either the "flyblown phylacteries" of the Newcastle Program—a shopping list of Nonconformist crotchets[5]—nor with Gladstone's monomaniacal obsession with Irish Home Rule, which doomed the Liberals to permanent opposition.

1 Rosebery resigned the party's leadership in 1896, a year after the Liberals left office, ostensibly to "plow his own furrow." He coquettishly refused leave the sidelines, though he made several feigns. In 1902, Grey was still describing himself as "a strong Roseberyite," and when Campbell-Bannerman formed his government in December 1905, resented that his former mentor had not been invited to join the Cabinet, though it was a given he would have declined any offer. (E. Grey to H. Newbolt, 3 Jan 1902, Bodleian.)
2 Of course the clash of personalities was important. Within a few months of Gladstone's resignation, the bluff, abrasive Harcourt and the hyper-sensitive and fastidious Rosebery were not on speaking terms.
3 In the words of James Mill.
4 B. Semel, *Imperialism and Social Reform* (Cambridge, 1960), 63.
5 The Programme called also for reforms with which Grey was more in sympathy, a land tax, employer's liability for accidents, payment of MPs, etc. The disparaging characterization came also from Rosebery's Chesterfield speech.

Though the Roseberyites proudly called themselves Liberal Imperialists,[1] they were, in the language of the day, "consolidationists" rather than "expansionists." Nonetheless, Rosebery believed that, given the scramble for Africa, territory that might one day be of value in defending Egypt and India ought to "pegged out." In particular this meant that Uganda, site of the headwaters of the Nile, should come permanently under British control. When Gladstone, after asking Rosebery to serve as Foreign Secretary when he took office in 1892, appointed Grey to be his Parliamentary Under-Secretary, Edward defended in the House the Portal Commission that he and Rosebery excepted would confirm this point of view.[2] The Parliamentary Under-Secretary also laid down what became known as "the Grey doctrine," when questioned about a possible French expedition to the upper Nile.

"Such an expedition," he declared on March 28, 1895,

> under secret instructions, right from the other side of
> Africa, into a territory over which our claims have been
> known for so long, would not be merely an inconsistent
> and unexpected act, but it must be perfectly well known to
> the French Government that it would be an unfriendly act,
> and would be so viewed by England.[3]

Though the language was diplomatic, it was regarded as a warning shot across the bow, and it alarmed some Cabinet members and some of the same Liberal backbenchers who would attack Grey after 1907. It would be cited when Kitchener confronted the French at Fashoda in 1898. Rosebery warmly approved.[4]

---

1 The noun has become so charged with negative associations—historians for decades have been reticent about using it—that it comes as a surprise that the name was not thrust upon the group by their enemies, like "Whig" and "Tory."
2 Gladstone had the opposite impression, and in fact Portal expressed reservations about holding Uganda.
3 *Parliamentary Debates,* 1895, v. 32, 404. cited by Robbins, 51. Grey made the declaration on the spot, having been advised by Kimberley, who had succeeded Rosebery in 1894 when the latter had become P.M., to speak firmly only about the Niger, not the Nile.(*Twenty-Five Years,* v. 1, 18; G. Martel, *Imperial Diplomacy* (London, 1986), 237–8.)
4 E. Grey to Rosebery, 30 March 1895, NLS.

Grey, however, did not inherit his mentor's Francophobia and Germanophilia.[1]

The Triumvirate seemed destined for high office in a future government. There was some question, though, as to whether it would be a Liberal government. Asquith, the party's most adroit debater, admired for his common sense as much as his intellect, was a loyalist. Both in 1892 and 1905, he was quick to abandon his co-conspirators when they had agreed among themselves not to accept office unless they were all offered Cabinet posts (in 1892) or unless Campbell Bannerman relinquished his leadership position in the House (1905). Even in a series of articles in the *Spectator* before he entered Parliament, he revealed himself as something of a trimmer, and he appeared to have had one eye on 10 Downing Street long before 1908. While he exuded the "effortless superiority" Balliol inculcated, his phrase, Jowett's Platonism and T. H. Green's Idealism soon ceased to fire his imagination, and by the time he achieved high office probably mattered to him not much more than the sermons he had listened to so raptly at Rehobeth chapel as a boy. His hedonism inevitably eroded his attachment to principles as well, just as it blunted his forensic talents.[2]

Haldane, however, was an idealist in both senses—a visionary and a neo-Hegelian—and an inveterate schemer.[3] Grey faithfully followed him as he conspired with high-minded Whigs, intelligent Conservatives (with the exception of Balfour, these were almost exclusively, for the Limps, Liberal Unionists), and prag-

---

1 Grey's appointment is usually represented as a bolt from the blue. He had shown little interest in other countries, and had written and spoken only on domestic issues. Rosebery had been asked to be Foreign Secretary when Gladstone wrote to Grey, but had characteristically refused to commit himself, and it would not be surprising if the Prime Minister wished to entice the indecisive earl by offering him a loyal disciple as his Under-Secretary. Or Rosebery himself may have suggested Grey. Nor is it surprising that, since the conduct of foreign affairs was then essentially the diplomatic defense of the Empire, Grey warmed to the task.

2 Balfour claimed "that he had never known anyone so absorbed in his own comforts as Asquith was habitually."(David (ed.), 83.)

3 This did not prevent him from being a connoisseur of food, wine, and cigars, though not of women.

matic socialists to lay the foundations for a coalition that would enact the social reforms he envisioned. He was a tireless organizer of political clubs. While secretary of the Eighties Club[1], he founded the Articles Club, which held an annual dinner to which leading lights from across the political spectrum, and from literature and journalism, were invited. Then Haldane became the moving spirit behind the Liberal League, the organization dedicated to promoting Liberal Imperialism. Still later, with Sidney Webb, he helped establish the Co-efficients, the self-appointed "Brains Trust or General Staff" of the "Party of Efficiency."[2] "Efficiency" became the slogan of the Limps.[3]

Haldane had studied at Heidelberg after graduating from Edinburgh, Rosebery was a Germanophile, and admiration for the Reich was widespread among advanced thinkers. The German education system, both the universities and the primary and secondary schools, and the social welfare system inaugurated by Bismarck, seemed as superior to their British counterparts as Idealism did to Utilitarianism. Muddling through would no longer suffice. The British would have to raise their game.

It happened that in South Africa a very Germanic Englishman was hard at work, and the Limps held up as an exemplar of efficiency the Balliol-trained Alfred Milner. Relations between the two wings of the Party would be poisoned by the Boer War, as much as were Anglo-German relations. The ill-will it generated survived until 1914.

---

1 named after the great Liberal victory of that year, and headed by Grey's cousin Albert

2 The quote is from Leo Amery. (G. Searle, *The Quest for National Efficiency* (Berkeley, 1971), 151.) The Club's original members, in addition to Grey and Haldane, included Sidney Webb, Bertrand Russell, H. G. Wells, Leo Maxse, and Leo Amery, and the leading theorist of the New Imperialism, the pioneer geographer Halford Mackinder.(*Ibid.*, 150; Semmel, 166–76.) But the club came to grief over Tariff Reform—would the Empire survive without erecting tariff walls around it? For a brief time, Grey was half-converted to this position.(Semmel, 170.)

3 Campbell-Bannerman was not impressed: the term was "pure claptrap. Efficiency as a watchword! Who is against it? This all mere rechauffé of Mr. Sidney Webb, who is evidently the chief instructor of the whole faction."(J. Spender, *The Life of the Right Hon. Sir Henry Campbell-Bannerman*, v. 2 (London, 1923), 14.)

By May 1899, the High Commissioner had decided that the threat posed by the Transvaal Republic, enriched by the discovery of gold, both to British security[1] and to British prestige[2] required that London's sovereignty be reasserted, and that the best means was another short war—given the Boers' reluctance to enfranchise the Uitlanders. These were foreigners, at least 75% British, who had moved to Transvaal after the discovery of gold in 1886. The bone of contention was over how many years of residency would be required before they were permitted to vote. Foreign-born males outnumbered Boer voters, so this was a critical issue. (The ratios were reversed, ironically, in the two British colonies, where Boers outnumbered English.) "You want our country," Kruger told Milner.[3] At the beginning of May 1899, Milner sent to London a melodramatic telegram describing the Uitlanders as helots, inflaming public opinion. He was inflexible at the Blomfontein Conference with Kruger, which began at the end of the month, and the talks were broken off.

But to the relief of the Cabinet, which had prepared an ultimatum of its own, it was the Boers who precipitated the war, handing the British resident in Pretoria a stiff note on October 10, 1899, demanding the withdrawal of all British forces from the Transvaal border, and the return to Britain of troops en route. When this was rejected, Boer armies invaded Natal and the Cape Colony, the two British colonies.

This created a dilemma for the Liberals. For the party's left wing, the Uitlanders were dubious characters, riff-raff cynically

---

1 What frightened the British was the prospect of losing the naval base at Cape Town and the Simon Town coaling station, vital for the defense of India, if Cape Colony and Natal were dominated by Pretoria, with its pro-German sympathies.
2 This was itself considered important for reasons of security in India, a country of 270,000,000 with a government whose armed forces consisted of fewer than 75,000 British.
3 I. Smith, *The Origins of the South African War* (London, 1996), 253–89; B. Nasson, *The South African War* (London, 1999), 15–45. There may have been twice as many Uitlanders as Boers. They were originally denied citizenship and voting rights until they were forty years old and had resided in the country for 14 years. This was later reduced to 7 years during negotiations. The British insisted on 5 years. The foreigners were taxed at higher rates than the Afrikaners.

manipulated by Jewish financiers[1] and their treatment by the republic was of no concern to the British government. But the Afrikaners had, after all, invaded British territory. Campbell-Bannerman and the majority who followed him, including, of course, the Triumvirate, voted for supplies, but sharply criticized the diplomacy that had preceded the ultimatum, and attacked the conduct of the war. Overconfident and poorly led, British armies had suffered embarrassing defeats in the opening campaigns. This was a less popular position after the relief of Mafeking in May 1900, when the tide began to turn. The vocal "pro-Boer" contingent was reduced to 30 on a vote on the defense estimates the following month. But then, a year later, in June 1901, came revelations from Emily Hobhouse about conditions in the camps that Boer families had been herded into after the guerilla phase of the war began.[2] Some 116,000 women and children were incarcerated, of whom over 26,000 died by the end of the war. On June 14, after meeting with Hobhouse, Campbell-Bannerman, issued his famous condemnation of the "methods of barbarism" in South Africa. This set off a firestorm in the country.

Grey was already distressed. In the general election of September 1900, the Tories had won a crushing victory, capturing 402 seats to the Liberals' 184.[3] Four days before Christmas, he wrote a 15-page letter to his political confidante J. A. Spender. The Party, he said, is

> discredited, dissipated and ruined because, except for Asquith, every one of our leaders let the 'factionalists with ardent eyes' run the whole party unreproved in a time of national crisis; with the result of disgusting a section of the

---

1 Alfred Beit was the only Jew among the German-born Randlords, though several, like Cecil Rhodes, were protégés of Jules Porges, originally a Viennese Jew.
2 After Pretoria was occupied in June 1900, about 14,000 Boer soldiers and several generals surrendered, but another 15,000 remained in the field, under the leadership of Steyn, de Wet, and de la Rey.
3 In fact, the results of the first khaki election were not so good for the Unionists as the previous contest in 1895, where the combined Conservatives and Liberal Unionists won 411 seats to 177 for the Liberals. Sentiments about the war had reversed an electoral swing away from the ruling party.

party and a mass of the electorate, and… moderate men on the Conservative side…, who might have been a valuable reinforcement of sane and tolerant opinion through these wild times. It is for all this that a few of us have tried to rescue the party; we have succeeded only in sacrificing ourselves; to the other side we are trimmers, to our own we are hateful; and there remains for us nothing, but to cling to the faint hope that the genius of Rosebery may succeed in redeeming a party which seems past redemption."[1]

But Rosebery contented himself with delphic utterances from the sidelines, and by the fall, Grey was in still greater despair, writing to his mentor, "We shall go ahead for what we are worth and the Liberal party will either get better or be smashed to pieces; in other words the party system will either be re-established for the working of our politics, or it will disappear."[2] Five months later he thought he saw the end in sight: "It is a great relief to see the 'status quo' broken up. The last seven years have been a nightmare of futility."[3]

He had not counted on Chamberlain wrecking the Conservatives as he had wrecked the Liberals seventeen years earlier—and uniting the Opposition behind one of the few principles all Liberals shared. Chamberlain's campaign for Tariff Reform, which divided the Conservative Party as dramatically as Peel's apostasy of 1846 and resulted in both the Colonial Secretary and the leading free-traders resigning from the Cabinet, handed the Liberals not only an issue that united them, but one with great support in the country. Balfour's Education Act galvanized Nonconformists in the north, and the introduction of Chinese workers into South Africa by Katharine Lyttelton's brother-in-law Alfred outraged public opinion.

---

1 E. Grey to J. A. Spender, 21 December 1900, BL
2 E. Grey to Rosebery, 2 Oct. 1901, NLS.
3 E. Grey to Rosebery, 22 February 1902, *Ibid.*

In January 1906 the Liberal government was swept back into power.[1] Though Campbell-Bannerman had refused to go to the Lords, the Triumvirs were all rewarded with high office.[2] But the rift in the Party never healed. After spring of 1907, and especially after summer, 1911, Grey would come under heavy fire from the Radical wing. "Always remember," Reid, now Lord Loreburn, the Foreign Secretary's most zealous critic, bitterly told the *Manchester Guardian* editor C. P. Scott, "this is a Liberal League Government."[3]

✐

It was my original intention to devote a final section of the introduction to the foreign policy of Sir Edward Grey, distilling several hundred draft pages on the subject. But on reflection, this seemed unwise.

Even a superficial discussion would inflict on the reader at least another fifty pages. There are precedents for introductions that dwarf what is introduced—the introduction to the most recent edition of Madame de Sablière's *pensées* and letters is 246 pages, while the *pensées* themselves take up two pages, her *maximes* ten pages, and her letters sixty-three pages—but it didn't seem desirable to emulate these.[4]

Grey's foreign policy and his conflicts with domestic critics have been discussed in innumerable books and articles. Readers interested in the immensely absorbing question of the origins of World War I will have read many of these. They and others will appreciate that great events have complex causes, going back centuries, and that the conscientious historian is a longwinded one.

---

1 It had taken office on December 5, after Balfour's resignation.
2 Haldane had hoped to be Lord Chief Justice, but this had been promised to Robert Reid, and he was given the War Office.
3 J. L. Hammond, *C. P Scott of the Manchester Guardian* (London, 1934), 152–7, cited by K. Robbins, "The Foreign Secretary, the Cabinet, Parliament and the parties," in F. Hinsley (ed.), *The Foreign Policy of Sir Edward Grey* (Cambridge, 1977), 14.
4 Vicomte Menjot d'Elbrenne, *Madame de Sablière* (Paris, 1923).

A brief summary of the diplomacy of 1905 to 1916 will be as unsatisfying to them as to the writer.[1]

---

1 Grey was in many respects merely the executor of the great shift in foreign policy inaugurated by his predecessor, Lord Lansdowne. Any account of Sir Edward's term in office would need to describe at least briefly the failed Anglo-German negotiations of 1898–1902, an often-overlooked turning point in European history, the Anglo-Japanese Alliance of 1903, and the negotiation of the Entente with France in 1903 and early 1904, and the anticipation that it would be extended to France's ally. And to appreciate the significance of the reversal of sentiments toward England's two former arch-enemies (though the nineteenth century saw periods in which the relationship with France warmed, when Anglophilic ministries were in power in Paris, including an "entente cordiale" in the 1830s, the alliance of 1854, and a comprehensive trade agreement of 1860), further discussion would be required of an antipathy going back to the eleventh century in the case of France and to the beginning of the nineteenth century in the case of Russia—if not to British conquests of the Mughal Empire in the 18th century and Russian victories over the Ottoman Empire beginning in the late 17th century, which put the two young empires on a collision course in Asia.

But if one is going to glance at this prelude to the Anglo-Russian Convention, one is surely obliged to acknowledge at least in passing the roots of the rivalry that caused the Great War, that between the sometime allies in the *reconquista* of the Christian kingdoms defeated and subjugated by the Turks during the 14th, 15th, and 16th centuries. The English came to India to trade. The Russians arrived at the shores of the Black Sea in order, ultimately, to retake Constantinople, for the Czar regarded himself as the heir to the Eastern Roman Empire following its annihilation in 1453.

And Russia's Viennese rivals were the heirs, by a circuitous route, of the Western Roman Empire. Their prerogative, if not their genealogy, went back to Louis the German and the East Frankish kingdom of which he was made ruler in 843. The Roman Empire, by one of those ironies that recur continuously, then passed into the hands of the great tribe that had been conquered by Louis's grandfather, and then on to other German tribes and families. Their ancestors had never been part of the original Roman Empire, thanks to the ambush of Varus's three legions by Arminius, or Hermann, in 9 A.D. From the 12th to the 15th century they had renewed Charlemagne's *Drang Nach Osten*, conquering the Slav tribes that had migrated into Eastern Europe between the 6th and 10th centuries, converting them to Christianity by force, as Charles had done, or annihilating and replacing them. When the descendants of these rugged eastern colonists belatedly united Germany, they erected an enormous statue in Ostwestfallen-Lippe, near the site of his victory, commemorating Hermann.

For German intellectuals the First World War was a war against "Latins" as well as "Slavs," and the former were far the more ancient rivals. The heirs of the unlucky West Frankish kingdom, savaged by the Vikings in the 9th and 10th centuries, gradually expanded their base in the Seine valley, and then, after retaking the provinces acquired by their overmighty Norman vassals, began seizing pieces of Lotharingia, the wealthy Middle Kingdom over which East and West contended during the course of a millennium. By the end of the 15th century, they had even begun crossing the Alps, something the German Holy Roman Emperors had felt obliged to do, following Charlemagne's precedent, since 894—permitting power to concentrate in the hands of princes back home. More often than not, efforts to contain the French aggrandizers, from 1214 down to 1815, saw the Anglo-Saxons allied with their Germanic, and after 1756, their Prussian cousins.

In 1914 there was no longer a Roman Emperor in Vienna. But there was a ruler in Potsdam who, like his cousin and rival in Tsarskoe Selo, called himself after Caesar. The Kaiser interested himself in the Near East, but it was not out of concern for the Christians under Ottoman rule. It had been frustrating that, when blood and iron had united Germany at last, the Western Powers had already seized most of the desirable bits of the world beyond Europe. But the British, long-time ally of the Porte, had been made queasy by Hamidian massacres. In Anatolia and Mesopotamia there was a splendid opportunity for German investments, and, perhaps, colonies. The route lay through the Balkans.

The letters to Katharine Lyttelton, moreover, shed a great deal of light on Edward Grey himself, but not much on his foreign policy—with the possible exception of his reflections on Russia in letters written during the summer of 1909. We can infer from his replies that Katharine would occasionally ask him what the Czar and Czarina or the Kaiser were like, but she did not ask probing questions about the Entente or about the five grave crises Edward dealt with: the two Moroccan crises of 1905–6 and 1911, the first in media res when he took office, the two Balkan crises of 1908–9 and 1912–13, and the third and final Balkan crisis of July 1914. Naturally, he did not volunteer information as to the deliberations going on at the Foreign Office about these and other questions. When he alludes to various crises, domestic as well as foreign—usually to complain about how they impinge on his time—these are explained in footnotes.

Grey's letters to Lyttelton may change the sometimes glib characterizations of him that historians still indulge in, but they are unlikely to affect their assessment of his policies. It is the individual, not the Foreign Secretary, that these letters illuminate, and I hope he will be less of an enigma to those who read them.

When, in 1914, Germany opted for the solution it had chosen in the first Balkan crisis rather than the second (which had been resolved by a conference of ambassadors meeting in London under the chairmanship of Edward Grey), there were those in Berlin who hoped that St. Petersburg would not back down this time, as it had in 1909.

Russia, indeed, could not permit the dismemberment of Serbia, as the Kaiser and the Wilhelmstrasse had acknowledged in 1912. But in 1914, unlike in the late 18th century wars, the Anglo-Saxons joined the decadent Latins and the barbaric Slavs. The treachery of Edward Grey infuriated German patriots. He was demonized, and perfidious Albion quickly assumed the role of *Erzfeind*.

KATHARINE LYTTELTON

Katharine Lyttelton (1860–1943) was the daughter of James ("Jem") Archibald Stuart-Wortley (1805–1881), youngest son of a prominent Tory politician of the same name. The father, created Baron Wharncliffe, was himself the grandson of George III's mentor and first Prime Minister,[1] the third Earl of Bute, and the great-grandson of Lady Mary Wortley Montagu, celebrated for introducing inoculation for smallpox to the West, but also a notable, and controversial, writer and diarist, the friend—and occasional enemy—of Pope, Swift, Horace Walpole, Joshua Reynolds, and other Augustan luminaries. Jem Stuart-Wortley was paralyzed after falling from a horse in 1858, and his promising career ended. He was Solicitor General under Palmerston at the time. Katharine spent her childhood helping care for her disabled and very depressed father.

Her mother, born Jane Lawley, was the daughter of Paul Bielby Thompson, the first Baron Wenlock, a wealthy Whig politician from Yorkshire. Lawley was photographed by Julia Margaret Cameron when a young woman; the image was called "Resignation" and sold widely.[2] She was not resigned to her situation after her husband's accident, however, becoming an active philanthropist in London's East End. She served on the boards

---

1 The title officially dates only from 1905 but is traditionally used for Walpole and his successors as First Lord of the Treasury.
2 F. Campbell-Preston, *Grandmother's Steps* (Stanbridge, Dorset, 2010), 24.

of the British Women's Emigration Society and the East London Nursing Association, and visited the homes of the poor.

Katharine, the youngest child, had four sisters and two brothers. Three of the sisters married into the aristocracy, perhaps the most illustrious husband being Byron's grandson, who ascended up the ranks after deaths in the family from Baron Wentworth to Viscount Ockham to the Earl of Lovelace. The two brothers had artistic and literary inclinations. The older became a painter and the younger, a Conservative M.P. for Sheffield, married first the niece of Trollope, then the daughter of Millais, and was a patron of Elgar and an accomplished pianist. Grey liked him.[1]

The most remarkable relative was no doubt Katharine's cousin, Victoria Stuart-Wortley Welby (1837–1912), the "founding mother" of semiotics. Her 1903 study *What Is Meaning?* influenced Charles Peirce, and they corresponded extensively. As mentioned, her own daughter Nina, an historian, memoirist, and sculptor, was the wife of Harry Cust.

In 1883 Katharine married into the celebrated Lyttelton family, cousins of the Gladstones. Her husband Neville (1845–1931), the third son, was reputedly the least clever of the lot, but that distinction probably belongs to Robert or Spencer. The twelve Lyttelton children were by no means uniformly over-achieving prodigies.[2]

---

1 E. Grey to K. Lyttelton, 24 October 1909.
2 Their eccentric father, George, who married Mary Glynne on the same day the future Prime Minister married her sister Catherine, is perhaps best known for a famous letter he wrote to his brother-in-law urging that he be made an earl, on the grounds that he was about to become Viscount Cobham and disliked both the title and the name he was to inherit. The most famous brother was the paragon Alfred (1857–1913), charming, handsome, intelligent, the best cricketer in England, and Colonial Secretary under his patron Balfour. A leading ornament of the Souls, he married the ebullient Laura Tennant, Margot's sister, who died the next year in childbirth. When he himself died prematurely after being struck by a cricket ball, Asquith declared in the House that "he, perhaps of all men of this generation, came nearest to the mould and ideal of manhood, which every English father would like to see his son aspire to..." (K. Rose, *Superior Person* (London, 1969), 374.) Grey, his rival for the amateur tennis championship of England, wrote "There was glory and radiance about Alfred to an uncommon degree..."(E. Grey to K. Lyttelton, 5 July 1913.)

Nevy, as he was called in the family, was a difficult child. His older sister found him "defiant and hard"[1] and his father worried about him at Eton: "I fear Nevy is in disgrace... Nevy must mend his [ways] or he will die a pauper." His tutor reported he was obstreperous, idle, neglectful, and disrespectful. From an early age he knew he wanted to be a soldier, and practiced by fighting with other children on the beach during seaside holidays.[2] Though he had struggled unsuccessfully with mathematics at Eton, he passed the army entrance exam with flying colors, and was commissioned to a rifle brigade. Handsome, ambitious, and popular (he'd been president of Pop at Eton), Lyttelton rose rapidly through the ranks, serving as military secretary, private secretary, or ADC to various imperial commanders, and to the Secretary of State for War. It did not hurt that he was Gladstone's nephew and a Liberal. Lyttelton proved a competent field commander in the Sudan and then in the Boer War, one of the few senior officers who emerged from the latter conflict with an enhanced reputation. But he was judged a failure as the Army's first Chief of the General Staff, from 1904 to 1908. ("Not intellectually up to the post," said his brother, "a scandal... the army laughs at him," said the Secretary of State for War, and "a disastrous first CGS," according to the secretary of the CID.)[3]

In 1883, Neville married Katharine Stuart-Wortley. As he recounts it in his memoir, "On the 17th of June I went home on leave after rather a short spell abroad, chiefly in connection with an affair which I had in mind before I left England. This was my engagement to Katharine Stuart-Wortley, a second cousin, the youngest daughter of the Right Hon. James Stuart-Wortley, a former Solicitor-General and Recorder of London. I left the Eton and Harrow match at a critical moment to settle the business, and

---

1 S. Fletcher, *Victorian Girls: Lord Lyttelton's Daughters* (London, 1997), 38
2 *Ibid.*, 54, 73, 18.
3 P. Fraser, *Lord Esher* (London, 1973), 152; J. Gooch, *The Plans of War: the general staff and British military strategy*, c.1900–1916 (1974), 100; cited by R. T. Stearn, "Sir Neville Lyttelton," *ODNB*.

it was well worth it. I had to go back to Gibraltar to get a house and arrange matters there, go home again to be married on the 1st October, 1883, and then back to Gibraltar on the 31st of the month."[1] The reader cannot be entirely sure the reference to the cricket match is ironic. Katharine is mentioned only in passing a few more times, and there are none of the appreciative platitudes one might expect.[2] What Lyttelton doesn't relate is that he was apparently engaged to another young woman, Kathleen Clive, at the beginning of the year, but she threw him over for his more interesting and intelligent younger brother Arthur.[3]

Katharine may have had second thoughts as well. Neville was fifteen years her senior, and not her intellectual equal. "He is the dullest dog I ever met," Jackie Fisher reported, and no one reading Lyttelton's memoir is likely to disagree.[4]

---

1 N. Lyttelton, *Eighty Years: Soldiering, Politics, Games* (London, n.d. [1927]), 147.

2 He mentions her returning to England from India without him on one occasion and his returning to India without her on another, the information that, on leaving South Africa, "she received a handsome present of jewellrey [sic], accompanied by a most appreciative address," and that she subsequently had a "warm discussion" with John Burns in the lobby of the House of Commons about South African matters. (*Ibid.*, 155, 157, 269, 280.)

3 Fletcher, 218. A student of Sidgwick at Cambridge, Arthur Lyttelton (1852–1903) scored a first in moral sciences, received an MA, a DD, served as tutor at Keble and Master of Selwyn College, and eventually became Bishop of Southampton. After her marriage, Clive (1856–1907) served as president of the National Union of Women Workers and on the executive board of the Central Society for Women's Suffrage.

4 Gooch, 48, cited by Stearn, ODNB. As in Eddy Tennant's unpublished autobiography, names are dropped, but the friends and acquaintances are not characterized, nor are conversations or incidents recounted. "My diary," Neville reports at one point, "records an extraordinarily pleasant time, many dinners and lunches, meeting my uncle Mr. Gladstone, John Morley, Arthur Balfour, Rosebery, Wolseley, Browning, Lowell, and many others. I only wish I had recorded all the good talk we heard." (Lyttelton, 155.) Yet the memoir begins with a prefatory note, without a flicker of irony: "The writer of these Reminiscences is gifted with a singularly retentive memory..." The book's opening sentence is characteristic: "I was born on the 28th October, 1845, at Hagley, the county place of the Lyttelton family in Worcestershire, the fifth child and third son in a family of twelve, eight of whom were sons, a tall lot ranging from 6 feet 3 ½ inches to 5 feet 10 ½ inches."(*Ibid.*, 9.) Intellectual vivacity was never a requisite for Grey in friendships, and though they didn't share an interest in fishing, the Foreign Secretary seems to have been fond of Neville.

As is clear from Edward's letters to her, Katharine detested official life. When she and Neville married, her husband was military secretary to the Governor of Gibraltar, and was then assigned the same position under the Governor of Bombay. Following the Boer War he was named Commander-in-Chief in South Africa and was appointed to the same post in Ireland after his unfortunate stint as Chief of Staff. So Katharine's public duties were extensive.

Unlike Edward's other confidantes Louise Creighton, Maud Selborne, and Elizabeth Robins, and despite, or because of, the example of her own mother, Katharine did not take part in women's organizations nor join the suffrage movement, something that, in any case, would not have been easy for the wife of a major-general. Nonetheless, her astringent views on the role of women can be inferred from occasional remarks by Edward.

They repeatedly complained to each other about impositions on their privacy. "A good plan would be to keep some bombs in your boudoir to throw at anybody who impinged," Edward advised in November 1906.[1] After lamenting that he had had only one fortnight's holiday in over six years, he added, "However women are always in office in their own houses, so you may not sympathize."[2]

"Your life has been harder than mine, but then you couldn't help it and I could," he observed in 1914, after telling her "I should like just for once, for a year or two in my life, to live in places and do things that I don't detest."[3] "I hope you are having pleasant days," he wrote later the same year, "—as far as it is possible for a woman to have pleasant days—and that in your next Incarnation you will be born a man and like salmon fishing."[4]

---

1 E. Grey to K. Lyttelton, 9 November 1906.
2 E. Grey to K. Lyttelton, 18 February 1912.
3 E. Grey to K. Lyttelton, 13 January 1914.
4 E. Grey to K. Lyttelton, 12 April 1914.

In her boudoir, she read French literature, and published a translation of a selection of Joubert's *Pensées*.[1] This is not the sort of book that Neville Lyttelton would have picked up. The general would have been surprised to be told that "the hatred between the two sexes is almost unquenchable," or that "a multitude of affections enlarges the heart."[2]

Whatever her relations with her husband, Katharine was devoted to her three daughters, and the letters reveal her anxieties about them. Edward was fond of the girls and interested in their activities, particularly Lucy (1884–1977), the eldest, whom he called "Auburn." She married Charles Masterman (1873–1927), descendant of the Quaker banking family the Gurneys, and a promising Liberal politician, but who, as Grey noted, seemed poised between the role of social critic and seer, on the one hand, and a Parliamentary career.[3] Masterman was ably assisted by his

---

1 *Joubert: A Selection from his Thoughts* (London, 1898). She was encouraged to do so by the novelist Mrs. Humphry Ward, who was working on a novel based on the romance between Joubert's friends François-René de Chateaubriand and Pauline de Beaumont. She offered to write the introduction. The son of a doctor, Joseph Joubert (1754–1824), was a moralist and *homme des lettres* who published nothing during his lifetime. He was the friend and disciple of Diderot before his attachment to Chateaubriand, served as inspector-general of universities under Napoleon, and presided over a conservative *salon* during the Restoration. He had a great gift for friendship. Chateaubriand said of him, "His great aim was tranquility, but no one was so troubled as he. He was an egoist who occupied himself exclusively with others."(*Ibid.*, xi].) He spent entire days in bed, clothed in pink silk pajamas.(xix.) ("The use of one's bed, when alone in it, is to gain wisdom," he wrote. "'A man should make for himself a temple of his bed,' says Pythagoras."(46.) He said of himself, "I am like Montaigne, unfit for sustained discourse." "I am like an Aeolian harp, that can sound a few beautiful notes but cannot play an air. No constant wind has ever breathed upon me."(204.) He nonetheless wrote constantly: "If there be a man tormented by the cursed ambition to put a whole book into a page, a whole page into a phrase, and that phrase into a word, I am that man."(206.) And he was convinced that "maxims are to the intelligence what laws are to conduct; they do not enlighten, but they guide, they direct, they save us insensibly. They are the thread in the labyrinth, the compass during the night."(68.)

2 *Ibid.*, 26, 27.

3 18 April 1908, pp. 561–7. Masterman, as the verdict always runs, did not fulfill his promise (double-first at Cambridge, president of the Union, fellow of Christ College, and leading light among the New Liberals). He contributed an essay to the anti-imperialist *Heart of Empire* (1901) and wrote several books based on his experience working in the slum of Camberwell, *From the Abyss* (1902), *In Peril of Change* (1905), and, his most famous work, *The Condition of England* (1909). Under Asquith, Masterman served as undersecretary at the Labor Board and Home Office, drafted the National Insurance bill and was appointed the first National Insurance Commissioner. He finally joined the Cabinet as Chancellor of the Duchy of Lancaster in 1914, but twice lost the by-elections the appointment required. During the war, he was the first director of Wellington House, but the

58

wife. Lucy was regarded as more decisive and trustworthy than the moody Charlie, and politicians relied on her as a conduit and sounding board. She was a diligent diarist, and wrote a biography of her husband after his death from alcohol poisoning. Lucy Masterman stood for Parliament herself, but lost elections at Salisbury in 1929 and 1931. Grey admired her *Lyrical Poems* (1912). She became something of a Liberal icon in her final decades, along with Violet Asquith, a living link with the party's glorious past.[1]

The second daughter, Hilda (1886–1972), called "the fair one" by Grey, married in 1909 the Foreign Secretary's friend Arthur Grenfell (1873–1958), who had been married previously to Lady Victoria Grey, the daughter of his cousin Albert. Edward corresponded with Katharine about the advisability of the match.[2] The ethereal and impractical Hilda, an excellent pianist and exhausting conversationalist, developed late in life a passion for Teillard de Chardin, whose essays she translated. Her husband's fortune waxed and waned dramatically, and she and her seven children (three from Arthur's previous marriage) moved frequently. She did not always cope well with life's vicissitudes.[3]

The youngest and most conventional daughter Hermione (1894–1985), "the Rascal" or "the nice new baby," married

---

propaganda he produced was affected by his scruples, and Lloyd George replaced him. Attempts to re-launch his career after the war failed.

1 Her oldest daughter Margaret Masterman (1910–1986) studied with Wittgenstein and, like her great-grand-aunt, became a linguistic philosopher, and a pioneering computer programmer.

2 E. Grey to K. Lyttelton, 8 November 1908, 4 December 1908. A financier and speculator from a Cornish family of bankers and copper mine-owners, Grenfell was over a million pounds in debt when war broke out. He declared bankruptcy and accepted a commission as lieutenant, winding up as a colonel in the Royal Flying Corps.(F. Patrick-Campbell, *The Rich Spoils of Time* (London, 2006), 21–2.) After discharging his debt, Grenfell was hit again when the National Socialists took over the companies and mines he had acquired in Central Europe. Most of his earlier investments had been in South Africa and Canada. Edward had not invested with him, but his cousin Albert suffered substantial losses. (EG to A. Grey, 23 June 1914, Durham.)

3 F. Campbell-Preston, *Grandmother's Steps* (London, 2010), 31–6.

Lionel Hitchens, a colonial administrator and former member of Milner's "Kindergarden."[1]

In 1912, Grey secured an appointment for Neville as Governor of the Royal Hospital at Chelsea—not, in fact, a hospital, but a retirement home for soldiers. This was not only a coveted sine-cure (a life-time position, it included a large house and staff), but meant that the Lytteltons would not have to move again, and that Katharine was close by. Here she entertained, among others, Henry James, George Meredith, Alfred Lyall, and Grey and his colleagues John Morley and Augustine Birrell.[2] When Katharine thanked him for securing the appointment, Edward replied, "The man who has your gratitude is but one degree less proud than the man who has your love. I am very relieved that you are now safely Chelsead: it is such a safe permanent thing and dignified too. I am sorry I can't ever become an old soldier to be looked after by you."[3]

With Grey's growing involvement with Pamela Tennant, they exchanged letters less frequently, but the tone is still warm and intimate, and they remained close until his death. Katharine sur-vived Edward by nearly ten years, in increasingly poor health. Her granddaughter recalled her as a rather distant and formidable woman who was much more interested in her grandsons than their sisters.[4]

1 He was killed during the Blitz. Hermione lived in Oxford after his death, but foisted her tiresome sister off on other relatives when Hilda would come up to research Teillard de Chardin. (*Ibid.*, 33–35.)
2 Campbell-Patterson, *Rich Spoils,* 26.
3 E. Grey to K. Lyttelton, 2 August 1912.
4 *Rich Spoils,* 26.

SMALL WORLD:
EDWARD AND KATHARINE'S CIRCLE

The links among the oligarchs who governed Britain before the First World War were promiscuous, and nowhere more so than among Edward and Katharine's friends and relations.

The patronizing Bishop of Winchester, Edward Talbot, whom Katharine was occasionally obliged to visit, was her first cousin, the son of her father's sister. He was the cousin also of one of her brothers-in-law, Sir Reginald Talbot, and, to compound the connection, had married one of Neville's sisters, and so was a brother-in-law in his own right. (Neville and Katharine themselves were second cousins.)

Another of Katharine's many brothers-in-law, the illustrious Alfred Lyttelton, Edward's tennis rival in the late 1890s, had married Laura Tennant in 1885. Eight years later, according to his diary, Pamela Tennant's cousin Wilfred Blunt slept with Laura's younger sister Margot.[1] In a post-coital chat, Blunt advised her to marry H. H. Asquith. This she did the following year. In 1888, Pamela had an affair with Harry Cust, a distant relative of Dorothy Grey, who was forced to marry Katharine's intellectual cousin, Nina. Pamela then married Margot's and Laura's brother Eddy, Edward's future best friend.

---

1 Margot Asquith's biographer discounts the story. (D. Bennett, *Margot* (New York, 1985), 216.)

Katharine's middle daughter married into the Grenfell family in 1909. The vivacious Ettie Grenfell, Lady Desborough, wife of Arthur Grenfell's cousin and the family patriarch "Willie," was the leading hostess of the Souls, along with Pamela's sister Mary Charteris, Lady Elcho. Ettie was reputed to be the lover of Violet Asquith's boyfriend, Archie Gordon. The Prime Minister, notoriously, had girlfriends of his own, and the favorite after 1912 was Venetia Stanley. She was the daughter of Edward Lyulph Stanley, 4th baron of Sheffield, but her best-known relative was her great grand-uncle, the Victorian luminary A. P. Stanley, liberal Dean of Westminster and star pupil and biographer of Thomas Arnold.

Humphry Ward, fellow of Brasenose, was intent on marrying the clever and attractive Louise von Glehn, though he had earlier flirted with Arnold's granddaughter and Matthew Arnold's niece Mary. But Louise found Humphry "a most unpleasing mixture of an evangelical parson and a fox hunting squire."[1] Ward's friend Mandell Creighton swooped in, and Humphry transferred his affections back to Mary. The two women nonetheless became close friends.

After her husband's death, Louise hoped to marry Edward.[2] But she was a dozen years his senior, and he insisted on addressing her as "Mrs. Creighton."

Edward inherited from his grandfather a house in Hertfordshire, Stocks. He sold it to the Humphry Wards in 1892. Mary Ward was now a famous novelist, thanks to *Robert Elsmere* (1888)— and particularly to the 10,000-word denunciation of it in *The Nineteenth Century* by Neville's uncle, William Gladstone.[3] The

---

1 J. Covert, *A Victorian Marriage* (London, 2000), 2.
2 "I do love you for having written this memoir," Edward told Louise. (E. Grey to L. Creighton, 16 March 1907, Bodleian.) The phrasing is usual for Grey; apart from the very rare mention of the word "love," the "do" raising the obvious question as to whether he was responding to something she had said or written. Louise's family, at least, was convinced she hoped he would ask her to marry him.(Email from James Covert, 13 January 2010; also, J. Covert (ed.), *Memoir of a Victorian Woman* (Bloomington, IN, 1994), 142, n. 22.)
3 Gladstone was nonetheless enthralled by the book. It was as riveting as Thucydides, he declared. (E. Jones, *Mrs. Humphry War* (New York, 1973), 169.

book was dedicated to Laura Lyttelton (whom, Mary Ward wrote, "I think I was simply in love with…from the first time I saw her).[1] Mary, whose sister Ethel was one of the Greys' closest friends, was herself a friend of Katharine Lyttelton, and the Lytteltons occasionally stayed at Stocks. Mary encouraged Kate, as she called her, to translate Joubert, and wrote a lengthy foreword. (Mary's uncle had written an essay introducing the French litterateur to English readers.) The Wards' son Arnold, Archie Gordon's best friend, hoped to marry Violet Asquith after Gordon's death, but his Unionist sympathies blighted that prospect.[2] Arnold's sister Janet, "the clever child" of the family[3] and less conventional, married Grey's friend and biographer George Macaulay Trevelyan. The blood of the two great non-doubting Thomases of the sunny Victorian spring, Arnold and Macaulay, thus mingled in their progeny.[4] (The friend also of Grey's nephew and heir Cecil Graves, long-time acting director of the BBC, Trevelyan lobbied him to hire fellow-Apostle—and Soviet spy—Guy Burgess.) The couple was linked to the Huxleys: Mary Ward's sister Julia had married Leonard, son of "Darwin's Bulldog," and Julian and Aldous were Janet Trevelyan's cousins.[5] It would be easy enough to multiply connections like these *ad nauseum*, if that point has not been reached already.

What's remarkable today, though not to the Edwardians, was how the friendships among political elites cut across party lines. Grey was friends with a son and a nephew of W. E. Gladstone,

---

1 J. Sutherland, *Mrs. Humphry Ward* (Oxford, 1990), 95.
2 *Ibid.*, 268, 284. Both Violet and her acerbic brother Raymond were apparently willing to overlook his addiction to gambling and a personality others found repellant.
3 D. Cannadine, *G. M. Trevelyan: A Life in History* (London, 1992), 9.
4 Trevelyan's grandfather married Macaulay's sister, so the genes came from the historian's father Zachary, the evangelical abolitionist.
5 These latter relationships were famously explored in Noel Annan's 1955 essay, "The Intellectual Aristocracy."

but he was closer to the oldest daughter and youngest son of Lord Salisbury.[1]

Any consideration of the small world of high politics leads inevitably to Salisbury's nephew, and Janet Trevelyan's second cousin, Arthur Balfour. Balfour proposed to Katharine's sister-in-law,[2] and then had a long, quasi-platonic relationship with Pamela's sister. He was the patron both of Pamela's brother and her lover, and of Katharine's brother-in-law.[3]

✑

By December 1899, Margot Asquith had become perturbed about her husband's prospects. After leaving office in 1895, he had been obliged to resume his legal practice. Though it netted at least 5,000 pounds annually, the Asquiths had four sons to educate, their Cavendish Square home required fourteen servants, and Margot had a taste for expensive clothes.[4] She had been granted a dowry by her father of 5,000 pounds a year, but that was not nearly sufficient. Margot turned to her friend Balfour, whom she regarded "as the person of most weight with papa," and begged him to ask the Bart to provide an additional 3,000 pounds per year. That would enable her husband to curtail his legal practice and devote more time to politics.[5] Balfour was First Lord of the Treasury and Leader of the House in Salisbury's third administration. Margot didn't imagine for a moment that he would hesitate to do what he could to help her husband sharpen and intensify his attacks on Uncle Robert's government from the Opposition's front bench.

---

1 Herbert Gladstone and Alfred Lyttelton; Maud Selborne and Lord Robert Cecil. Grey was on a first-name basis with all. He was closer still another nephew of the G.O.M., Neville.

2 Arthur was infatuated with May Lyttelton. Neville did not approve: "I don't think much of Spencer's friend, he's always hanging around the girls." (B. Aswith, *The Lytteltons* (London, 1975), 178. For the relationship of Balfour and Mary Wyndham Elcho, later the Countess of Wemyss, see J. Ridley and C. Percy, *The Letters of Arthur Balfour and Lady Elcho, 1883–1917* (London, 1992).

3 George Wyndham, Harry Cust, and Alfred Lyttelton

4 Bennett, *Margot*, 129; R. Jenkins, *Asquith* (New York, 1964), 89.

5 P. Jalland, *Women, Marriage and Politics, 1860–1914* (Oxford, 1986), 223.

Margot's assumption was correct. Balfour approached Sir Charles Tennant and asked the Liberal Maecenas to increase his subsidy to the Conservative Party's most formidable adversary.[1]

✑

In the *Times* obituary for Eddy Tennant, no doubt written by Pamela, there is a slightly petulant observation midway through. "Although the brother-in-law of Mr. Asquith, Lord Ribblesdale, George Wyndham and Alfred Lyttelton, he himself did not figure very largely as a politician."[2] Whatever they made of the invidious comparison, even at this date it was not likely to have struck readers as unusual that the deceased should have been connected by marriage to exemplary representatives of Liberalism, Conservatism, and Liberal Unionism. Among Grey's Parliamentary Under-Secretaries, along with the sons of Rosebery and Acland, were Edmond Fitzmaurice, Lord Lansdowne's younger brother, and Robert Cecil, Salisbury's son, who became Grey's staunchest sup-

---

1 The episode is a reminder that the world of Katharine Lyttelton and Edward Grey was largely a world of individuals with incomes well in excess of 500 pounds per year. From Edward's replies, one can infer that Katharine complained about her lot copiously and vehemently. But she was not obliged to shop for food, cook, clean dishes, wash clothes, or dust and polish, or to take care of her daughters when they were young. Nor, naturally, did she juggle domestic responsibilities with a full-time career. Servants were ubiquitous in this world, though only occasionally referred to in correspondence.

Louise Creighton, offered, after her husband's death, a "grace and favor" apartment at Hampton Court formerly occupied by Grey's cousin Lady Georgiana, had four servants for herself and her four girls.(Covert, 297). A large house like Fallodon would have required double that number, without the butler and footmen Dorothy and Pamela abhorred, and without gardeners, groundskeepers, and woodsmen. Edward pitied his poor sister Jane in Oxford, the wife of a clergyman in the Indian Ecclesiastical Establishment, who scrimped by with but one servant. The Greys themselves stayed at Cottage without a servant—a radical departure from convention. But a woman came from the village every day—Susan Drover and then, later, her sister Emily—to bring them food, cook their meals, and wash their dishes, clothes, and linen.

The first fully-automatic washing machine that resembled today's models only appeared in 1937, the first modern tumble dryer around the same time, and vacuum cleaners in the early 1920s. These became affordable for middle-class households only after the Second World War, along with refrigerators—when appliances finally replaced servants. But even in 1951, over 24% of working women in the U.K. were domestic servants, down from 45% half a century earlier.(J. Lewis, *Women in England, 1870–1950* (London, 1984), 156.)

2 *Times*, 22 November 1920. Ribblesdale was hardly more of a political figure than Tennant. George Wyndham is dragged in a second time, and two sentences are devoted to Edward Grey, to whom Lord Glenconner "was particularly attached."

porter after the war, lobbying for his mentor's appointment as Prime Minister.

But all this was changing, even while Grey was in office.

In 1909 Edward met Katharine Lyttelton's brother in Sheffield. "It put me pleasantly in mind of you," he told her. Charles Stuart-Wortley, he continued "has real ability I am sure and would have made quite a good Cabinet Minister of a good English type. A generation ago he would have been in Cabinets, but now there are new men and manners; less solid men and worse manners."[1]

Two years later Arthur Balfour was ousted as leader of the Conservatives in the House of Commons, after serving for two decades, and seven years later Asquith was forced to resign, along with Grey himself. Engineering the coups and replacing the two men as leaders were a Glasgow iron merchant, the son of a Scottish Presbyterian minister who had emigrated to Canada, and a Welsh solicitor, the son of a schoolteacher turned farmer, who, when his father died during his first year, was raised by his uncle, a shoemaker, in an unpronounceable village in Caernarvonshire.[2] Neither was an Etonian, Harrovian, or Wykehamist. Neither had been educated at Oxford or Cambridge. Neither spent weekends at Stanway, Panshanger, Taplow Court, or Clouds—or at Hatfield House or Bowood.

Then came the war, ruthlessly winnowing the ranks of the families that had governed Britain for generations. And the war, as Grey predicted, brought socialism. Within a generation, the taxes on the stately homes would exceed the means of their owners, and they would be thrown open to tourists. Within half a dozen years, being a peer had become a nearly insuperable bar to the Prime Ministership.[3] Ambitious aristocrats worked hard to pass legislation enabling members of the Upper House to renounce their

---

1 E. Grey to K. Lyttelton, 24 October 1909.
2 Llanystumdwy
3 Curzon's imperious personality also didn't help when he was considered and rejected in 1923.

peerages.[1] As early as 1920, Paul Cambon, the French Ambassador during Grey's entire tenure as Foreign Secretary, remarked to Winston Churchill that he had witnessed "an English revolution more profound and searching than the French Revolution itself. The governing classes have been almost entirely deprived of political power and to a very large extent of their property and estates; and this has been accomplished almost imperceptibly and without the loss of a single life."[2] Journalists today celebrate the fact, but it's worth recalling that this elite, some 164 families, was "envied as a model which French, Russian, and other nobilities sought to emulate,… presided over the birth of the first modern society,… ruled with commercial logic in aristocratic style,… curbed the power of the monarchy and inadvertently bequeathed liberal government and a language to a large portion of humanity."[3] And after ousting the Stuarts for good in 1688, the oligarchs also created the most powerful and wealthy kingdom, and the most extensive and best-run empire, in European history. The governing class was able to accomplish this, as Ellis Wasson notes, because it had "fluid flanks."[4] It was from the 16th century an open elite.[5] Grey's aristocratic predecessors as Foreign Secretary were as clever and capable as they were thanks to infusions of good middle-class blood.[6] The Channel had enabled the descendants of the Normans to acquire tastes and habits which would have astonished their forbears as much as it dismayed their Prussian counterparts.

✎

---

1 The 14th Earl of Home did this before becoming in 1963 the only aristocratic Prime Minister since 1901.

2 W. Churchill, *My Early Years* (London, 1930), 90.

3 E. Wasson, *Born to Rule: British Political Elites* (Stroud, Glous., 2000), 159.

4 *Ibid.*, 160.

5 L. and J. Stone, *An Open Elite?* (Oxford, 1984) attempted to challenge the consensus on this issue. For telling critiques, see E. and D. Spring, "The English Landed Elite, 1450–1879," *Albion*, v. 17, n. 2, 1985, 149–166 and H. Perkin, "An Open Elite," *J. of British Studies*, v. 24, 1985, 496–501, and Wasson's book.

6 of the Gascoynes and Pettys, respectively

In a Cabinet during Gladstone's final premiership, a quotation from Juvenal was disputed between the Prime Minister and Campbell-Bannerman. Everyone took an interest, and Lord Rosebery suggested a division on the question.[1] The next Liberal Cabinet included a popular essayist, a distinguished biographer, a leading historian and political scientist, a respected philosopher, and a prolific journalist, military historian, and biographer.[2] The world of letters and Liberal high politics overlapped. Grey was the friend of the historians H. A. L. Fisher and G. M. Trevelyan, the actress and playwright Elizabeth Robins, the novelists Mary and Jane Findlater, the nature writer W. H. Hudson, and the poets Henry Newbolt and Siegfried Sassoon. He dined with Meredith, James, and Yeats. Culture had not gone counter, despite the impression created by the focus of later scholarship on the Bloomsburies and other Edwardian harbingers of the *dégringolade*. This, too, was a consequence of the Great War, a watershed in so many ways.

1 H. H. Asquith, *The Genesis of the War* (London, 1923), 19.
2 Augustine Birrell, John Morley, James Bryce, Richard Haldane, and Winston Churchill.

THE LETTERS OF SIR EDWARD GREY
TO KATHARINE LYTTELTON

31 December 1896
Dear Mrs. Lyttelton,

I wonder whether you have been thinking very hard things of me for not having answered your letter before: at any rate I will give my only justification, apology, excuse, explanation, and reason (could Joubert himself suggest any more synonyms?) which is, that I did not get your letter till I came to London this morning. I haven't been here since the 18th and I have only been in London one night since I last saw you. But now the Commission in which I am caught,[1] has begun to sit and will sit dutifully next week. Will you be in London then? If so I should like to come to tea any afternoon next week.

We have had a large family party at Fallodon and a Christmas cake and 5 hunters and one driving horse and two tame squirrels. Dorothy has been hunting and doing her share of it, but I did my share of nothing, except going to church, and failed even to eat

---

1 A Royal Commission to investigate conditions in the British West Indies, particularly problems with the sugar trade. It was chaired by Sir Henry Norman and included Sidney Oliver and Sir David Barbour. Grey accepted the appointment by Chamberlain in part because he was advised the Caribbean climate would be salubrious for Dorothy. The Commissioners left London in January, 1897, returned in May, and published their report in August. The subsidized cultivation of sugar beets on the Continent had devastated West Indian exports. The Commission stopped short of recommending retaliatory tariffs, but proposed grants and loans to West Indian growers.

as much of the almond paste of the cake as the others. Haldane has lent me his flat and a line to 3 Whitehall Court will find me there on Monday.

5 August 1897

I am in London again but I am afraid I shant have a day to get down to Stocks.[1]

Tomorrow I am to struggle for the 2nd M.C.C. Tennis Cup, having lost the first;[2] the next day the West India Commission, which is the real cause of my being in London, will meet all day, and in the evening I go back to Fallodon.

Dorothy was very well when I left—really improved, but I hear there has been a setback again since:[3] there always is, as soon as the improvement is marked enough to raise one's spirits and "God fulfills himself in many ways, lest one good custom should corrupt the world"[4]: but these setbacks are getting more rare and more short. All the same this might not have happened if I had been there. Don't I speak just like a mother?

Please come and see us, if all goes well, in September: there will be no one else at Fallodon—"only ourselves and nothing but a mutton chop," but you shall have a writing table and a room to yourself, and your tyres blown up for you and when after much translating[5] you "have your eyebrows vexed and tired" you shall

---

1 A large house in Hertfordshire built in 1773 and inherited by Grey from his grandfather, and sold in 1892 to the Humphry Wards, friends of the Lytteltons. After Mary Ward's death in 1920, the house became an exclusive girls' school, the Playboy mansion of the U.K., a resort and spa, and once again a private residence.
2 Grey had defeated Alfred Lyttelton to win the Golden Racket at Lord's Club the year before and had also won another amateur championship at Queen's Club. He lost both titles in 1897.
3 Dorothy was diagnosed with Graves'Disease in the autumn of 1896, after experiencing weakness and fatigue while fishing in the Shetland Islands. Graves' is an autoimmune disease of the thyroid, hyperthyroidism, with symptoms including muscle weakness, increased heartbeat, palpitations, tremors, insomnia, and irritability.
4 From the penultimate stanza of "Morte d'Arthur" by Alfred Lord Tennyson, first published in 1835 and included, revised, as "The Passing of Arthur" in *Idylls of the King*.
5 Lyttelton was working on her translation of Joubert's maxims, for which Mary Ward had agreed to write the introduction.

go and "feast thereupon the wideness of the sea."[1] In middle age one falls into quotations—you will come to it.

6 August 1897

Dorothy is better again I hear. As I told you yesterday that she wasn't so well, please cancel the previous news.

I don't believe I said yesterday that I was really sorry not to be able to get to Stocks before I go north again. I am sorry, but we are counting upon you coming to Fallodon and that makes me mind less and say little.

You will no doubt observe that his letter has now said two distinct things: I wonder whether you will have any decided instinct as to which of the two is the chief reason for my writing. I am not sure that I know, though one came into my mind before the other.

Littlecote, Hungerford[2]
25 November 1897[3]

I am coming up to London on Friday, but I want to make a push to get all the work done on Friday so that I need not come up again on Saturday. I shant be able therefore to come to luncheon.

Dorothy has been to see her doctor in Edinburgh, who gives a very good account of her: he says the heart has recovered and she may go up to London in the early part of the year. She still has to avoid getting tired or excited for fear the heart should get out of tune again, and there is still the swelling in the neck, but I feel as if we had got onto firmer and freer ground.

---

1 From the sonnet "On the Sea" by John Keats.
2 An Elizabethan mansion in eastern Wiltshire, owned by the Popham family, now a hotel and resort.
3 At the top of the letter are drawings of a man's and woman's face, the man's in profile.

Fallodon
23 December 1897
Dear Katharine,[1]

You have given (us)(me)[2] a much better book than "Style": to begin with it is printed with so much care and "sold at the sign of the Dial." I'm afraid "Style" is not sold at the sign of anything. But Mrs. Browning's sonnets deserve all care in printing and reading for they are the expression of the deep feeling of one who had a living soul. I suppose other men besides Browning have had pure sweet incense burnt to them by women, but I do not know where else it has found expression, so that the world could know of it. I don't wonder that Browning was furious at the comment of casual depreciation of Aurora Leigh which appeared in Fitzgerald's letters.[3] A woman who had written and felt for him so must have been sacred to him.

I thought they would be a good Christmas lesson for Dorothy and have read them aloud to her: she doubts whether she has ever yet been so humble and is going to try to be more so: but don't let our having had this little play with them mislead you into thinking that we have not read them seriously.

Dorothy is really rather well and it is now more a case of taking care not to get bad again rather than trying to get well. We have taken Legge house[4] from Feb 14 to the end of May. It has been done greatly for the sake of others who live in Grosvenor Road, so it is hoped you will not mind our expecting you to come in often.

---

1 Hereafter the salutation is "Dear Katharine," then, beginning in June 1898, usually "My Dear Katharine" and the closing is "Yours very sincerely" or "Yours ever, Edward Grey." Henceforth, only when Grey uses a jocular salutation is it included.
2 "Us" is above "me." Both are in parentheses.
3 A long poem in blank verse by Elizabeth Barrett Browning published in 1856, *Aurora Leigh* tells the story, in nine books, of the relationship of the eponymous heroine, an aspiring writer, and her cousin Romney, an aspiring social reformer. FitzGerald's *Letters and Literary Remains* was published in three volumes in 1889. Robert Browning died at the end of that year.
4 A home near Swindon, Wiltshire, dating from the mid-19th century, now a conference center.

There is no change here, except that of the seasons, and we are having still bright days: but there is always a sense of storm and disturbance about Christmas: there are services and servants' dances and evergreens and irregular posts and turkeys and unusual things, however peaceful the weather is.

Did you read John Morley's speech at Bristol? I am sure he enjoyed saying that he would not put Salisbury's concessions under the microscope, and I know the chin with which he said it. It has been the one little human touch in all the platform speeches this autumn.

No date: "Homing day"

I looked in to say goodbye this morning, but found you had gone out even earlier than me.

We are starting for Fallodon in very fair health and good spirits. I am glad that our first and worst spell of London is over without any harm done, I really believe: and we are very glad that we came to spend it so near to you. You have been very nice to us.

Many many thanks.

20 June 1898

I have thought about writing to you often: at least once every day in which there has been a notice in the papers of Sudan preparations. But it is what one thinks of seldom that one does soonest for fear one should forget: what is thought about often there seems to be no such special reason for doing at the moment, and one lives in constant view of a prospect, which keeps just ahead.

I can't help being glad that all this has come about for both your sakes: it is so good to be stirred by something big, and nothing does this better than great work with some risk about it.[1] Don't you feel already how all the trivial things are losing their hold? All the horrible little worries and busy-nesses and planning, which creep upon one in numbers and cling and cluster upon the spirit and drain its energy and make it anaemic and weak—all these cannot stand the throbbing of a pulse which is stirred, and fall from one and shrink and perish on the ground, and you feel that you are standing erect and strong and clean. This alone is worth any amount of anxiety: it is the exchange of the unworthy for the worthy. I hope you won't meet me with the old story that this is all very well for men, but not for women, who stay at home or at Cairo—the "men must work and women must weep" argument. I believe women know very well what there is in them that answers that argument: it may be true in a sense, but at best it's only part of the truth and a poor part, and I think women know it. Does this sound very hard? It isn't meant to be, and I feel a very real sympathy, but it is rather a glowing sympathy, one that is both conscious for you and sanguine. There is a sort, which is like a limp figure climbing out of a weedy pool dripping, but there is no good in that and it is not healthy.

Now when it is all over I hope you will come to Fallodon, and Dorothy and I will prove that we have been thinking about you at the time by being extra glad afterwards and Neville shall make me feel a better man, as he has done before.

I have just come from a Richter concert, where they play as nowhere else, and they played the great choral Symphony.[2] Music like that puts me in a place where one seems to see the whole

---

1 Neville Lyttelton had been appointed to command the 2nd British brigade under Kitchener, Sirdar of the Egyptian Army in the Sudan campaign. The objective was to re-take the Upper Nile valley from Abdulah Al Taaisha, successor to the Madhi, the self-proclaimed messiah whose forces had overwhelmed Gordon at Khartoum. The decisive battle would take place at Omdurman at the beginning of September.

2 Beethoven's 9th. Hans Richter (1843–1916) was then the leading conductor in Britain, with his own orchestra, and would be appointed director of the Hallé Orchestra the following year. He introduced audiences in London and Manchester to Wagner, Brahms, Dvorak, Bruckner, and Tchaikovsky.

of life: the struggle and sorrow are not hidden, but one sees the whole with the splendid light upon it, which is so often hidden in times of depression: it is magnificent and real.

Now for news: please tell me when you go from the cottage, that I may either see you once there or in London. We are settled at our Cottage for some time. Dorothy is better than ever and we have ceased to count pulses, considering that the ground is at any rate firm under us, if not as strong yet as it will be. I spend about 2 nights a week in London, which means however 4 days.

29 July 1898

Dorothy has given me your postcard and alas! I don't see how I am to get to Stock Cottage on any day when you can be there. I come to London on Monday or Tuesday. There are West Indian and F.O. votes in the H of C for which I must attend all the sittings and prepare. Thursday and Friday I have business at York and on Saturday speak on Tweedside. On Wednesday you are away and that is my only possible day. But you must come here later on, which will be better.

I have been in Mull[1] and enjoyed it immensely and we are both going there in the middle of August. There seems to be no news from the Sudan and I suppose there will be none for some little time, during which Neville will no doubt have all the delight of action, without any of the danger of it. He may like the latter too, but the absence of it won't prevent his feeling the other.

We get neither letters nor telegrams here on Sunday and it occurs to me that there may be both from you lying in the post office: if not, you have no right to this letter and if you are a lady of honour will return it unread.

Dorothy is very well.

---

1 An island off the west coast of Scotland.

14 September 1898

You ought this afternoon to receive a telegram signed "Dorothy Grey": it's really from me but I couldn't explain in a telegram and I sit down now to tell you the state of affairs, so far as I comprehend them. I have just come back from Scotland: on the other platform I found Dorothy and a friend of hers (female) waiting for a train to Berwick: (it appears they have a committee to attend there). I had about two minutes talk with her during which she explained that you would come next week, but that the various relays of people who seem to be on their way here had overlapped and there might be difficulties, and I was to telegraph. It seems to be doubtful whether we have enough sheets (this of course is very private), but I have brought some white shroud-like things in our lodge in Green Mull, which I take to be sheets, and I fancy we could get others reach-me-down at a pinch.

Having entered the house and opened my letters, I find that a couple (of persons, not sheets) who were coming next week cannot come, so that settles it clearly that from the 19th to the 26th, there is plenty of room for you. I find various letters and a telegram from you about Dorothy's table, which give me the same reason to suppose that this may just be possible for you, and as far as I can make out if you can come on Monday the 19th and stay til the 26th, you will not now encounter anyone except perhaps Lady Rothschild alone for a night or two. Do come and we will have a really nice week: it all seems beautifully simple and smooth now at this end; all you need do is to pass a steam roller over all plans at your end which stand in the way. This is the true state of the case; we really do both most awfully want to see you, and now that Providence has come and cut the knots which tied up next week and set it free, I feel as if the sun had suddenly come out brilliantly or rather as if there had been a splendid downpour of rain, which is the thing most wanted.

I won't write to you about Omdurman, because it's easier to talk about these things at leisure. I'm delighted that it is over and that apparently no more fighting is needed: if the French are at Fashoda, we can talk to them about it, which we wouldn't do with the Mahdi.[1] And I am very glad that Neville has been in it: life is made much richer by experiences of this kind for good soldiers and I am sure he is much better than the ordinary "cockies" and "gummies" who are good soldiers. Can you say what it is about all Lytteltons which makes them better in their respective lines of life than the ordinary good? People might say it was just aristocratic blood, but it isn't either of the common types of that. The one type is the ordinary "noblesse oblige" and the other is the phlegmatic "you be damnedness" of the Duke of Devonshire. Neither of these types quite accounts for Lytteltons, who seem to have a peculiarly finely tempered spring in their family, which is all their own.

22 Grosvenor Road
12 February 1899

I am so sorry to hear you have really got something and that it is infectious, which means that the millions, of which you called yourself mother, may also get it—and the servants, who are an illness-catching race.

Now you are known to be ill, I will tell you my physical woes. Providence has been brutal to me. On Monday I had a great tooth

---

1 The battle of Omdurman took place on 2 September 1898, about 7 miles north of the city, capital of Al-Taashi's empire. The Khalif's forces numbered about 50,000 and faced 8,000 British regulars and 17,000 Egyptian and Sudanese troops under Kitchener. The British, with Maxim guns, artillery, and a flotilla of gunboats, killed around 10,000 of the attackers—armed with rifles and spears—with a loss of 47 dead and 382 wounded. "It was not a battle but an execution," said one eye-witness.

Kitchener then moved up the Nile to Fashoda, where a party of 12 French officers and 120 African troops under Major J.-B. Marchand had occupied a fort and hoisted the French flag. The expedition had crossed the center of Africa from Brazzaville in the Congo. Both sides waited for instructions from their capitals and the stand-off was peaceably resolved when Marchand took a British steamer down the Nile.

out[1] and got cold in the cavern left by it and haven't been quite out of pain in consequence, till this morning: and now Providence has changed from open hostility to a policy of pin-pricks, which has taken the form of a pimple on the tongue, which never lets me forget it, though it is rather better since luncheon. If we must be ill, why not have a correspondence about our ailments?—and show Provvy we know what he is doing and aren't afraid?

Fallodon
9 April 1899

I have got 4 days' letters on my table, all unanswered and many unopened, but I don't see one amongst them from you and I am so grateful to you for not having joined in the bombardment of enquiries about Dorothy that I shall write to you and nobody else today how she is.

She had a relapse of influenza 10 days ago—troublesome but not serious—only sending the temperature up slightly now and then and causing a little neuralgia in the face, and of course weakness, as it does with everybody. But early on Wednesday morning a most terrible bilious attack began: she could take no food for 36 hours and there was violent sickness for 12 hours and at last the heart began to give way and there was the greatest anxiety. On Thursday she began a diet of two tablespoonfuls of soda water every 45 minutes and that was only taken with difficulty. Today she has just eaten a good luncheon of chicken and rice pudding and the pulse is 72 instead of 44. Apparently all danger is over, as long as the influenza doesn't return and nothing new turns up: the lungs have never been touched, and the old ailment has been in cheque. I can't give details of medicine in this letter, but you may like to know that we have the doctor and the trained nurse staying in the house and that we telegraphed in the crisis

---

1 Through the 1930s, British physicians believed that extracting teeth was the sovereign remedy for a wide range of ailments.

for Grainger Stewart[1] from Edinburgh, who stayed while it was necessary. I write trivially, but that is because we are so cheerful today. I feel in a sort of silly reaction after been down very low. She can today read in bed, which marks a great step.

Fallodon
20 August 1899

In the last few months I have had enough good intentions of writing to you to pave the whole of—Aldershot.[2] And now that I am set down to write, there is no particular reason why I should be writing and I must just follow my pen. I have no ideas and no news, except about Dorothy's convalescence, which has been the main thing in our lives since she was so ill in April. She is now better than I dared hope to see her within the time, and is in some ways better than for a long time past. But we have looked over the edge of a precipice and are going to walk quietly and circumspectly for some months.

We are full of grave sympathy for you at the prospect of Aldershot. It seems to me as I pass it to be the dirtiest, ugliest, most repulsive place in the world, but it must be a sort of metropolis for the British army, and it is as natural for Mrs. Generals to go there as for Cabinet Minister's wives to be dragged off to London. (I fear most of them don't need much dragging.) Your gallant planning of a garden is quite piteous: geraniums and nasturtiums are the only flowers that seem at all suitable for the surroundings, but (being a Major-General's wife) you might have some large red poppies as well. You mean, I hear, to have hotbeds, so I shall think of you as surrounded by hotbeds, enclosed by stucco, with nothing but glare and dust and marching outside. The air must be full of the sound of men shouting words of command in hoarse

1 Sir Thomas Grainger Stewart was a distinguished Scottish physician, a former president of the Royal Society of Medicine and Physician-in-Ordinary to the Queen, specializing in diseases of the kidneys and neurological illness.
2 The country's largest military base, located in Hampshire, about 40 miles southeast of London.

voices. Surely enough has been said now to convince you that my feelings and sympathy are real, but don't let his letter get into the hands of the general staff (whatever that may be) or it will be thought unpatriotic, and I am not really that.

Does our army talk about Dreyfus much? And if so which side does it take? And if it is pro-Dreyfus, is this mostly from love of justice or dislike of the French? Feelings in the Dreyfus case might be headed two ways. 1. Dislike of the French leading to love of justice. 2. Love of justice leading to dislike of the French. Which is it?[1]

Now to return to yourself. Is the sentence for a definite number of years, or is it during Her Majesty's pleasure? I mean how long will you have to stay at Aldershot? All the time you are there we shall think of you as being under a cloud, but quite an honourable cloud. We shant miss you in Grosvenor Road, for Dorothy will not go to London next year before Easter. She has so often been unwell in London in February and March, that we shall give that up for the present. It will be easy for you to come to see us at Itchen Abbas, which is on the Aldershot line.

I could not get to Stock Cottage for a day, for the few days which I spent in London were crammed with politics, tennis and interviews: there wasn't a corner nor a chink nor a crevice of time left.

I am so pleased with what you wrote to Dorothy about my book:[2] it has given me a sort of lasting pleasure. It is a very nice thing to have one's work liked and in a nice way.

---

1 The second trial of Captain Alfred Dreyfus began in Rennes on July 1, 1899, following a long and bitter campaign to exonerate him after Emile Zola's *J'Accuse* had appeared in January 1898. When the military court again found the Jewish officer guilty of espionage, there was outrage in Britain. Dreyfus was promptly pardoned, but only cleared in 1906. The spy had been Major Ferdinand Esterhazy, and Dreyfus was convicted on the basis of forgeries by Major H.-J. Henry.
2 *Fly Fishing*, 1899

17 October 1899

By all means send in to me at the House on Wednesday, but do it either about 2:00 or 4:30. I may not be free at any other time as I do not know what is likely to happen in debate. The terrace is no good now, but if you come about 2 I will give you luncheon at Willis's room[1] or some such place, when the House adjourns for its luncheon.

I am going to Fallodon for Saturday and Sunday and I should have come to Aldershot and said farewell to Neville.

I am depressed about this war: I admit the necessity of it and that it must be carried through, but it has no business to be popular and the cry of revenge for Majuba dishonours us and destroys our reputation for good faith. I should like to break the heads of all the Music Halls first and then go out and teach the Boers gravely and sternly the things which they do not know.[2]

18 June 1900

Your letter to Dorothy came just before I left Itchen Abbas this morning and I drafted a telegram in answer to it, which she sanctioned and I sent off on my way to London.

I can't well come in Friday because I may have to go to London that day... But on Sunday I can be at Blackmoor by 1 and bicycle back at leisure in the evening. I should like to see Selborne[3] and talk trees, but there is a sentence in your letter with an ambiguous "he" in it (unworthy of the translatress of Joubert) which

---

1 The famous mixed-sex social club on King's Street in St. James, formerly Almack's.

2 The Boer War had begun on October 12, 1899, with a Boer commando raid into Cape Colony, after an ultimatum from Pretoria had been rejected by the British. The war created a serious rift in the Liberal Party, with a small but influential faction of Roseberyites, including Grey, Asquith, and Haldane, supporting it, though criticizing its conduct and the failed negotiations with the Boer republics at Bloemfontein in the spring. Majuba was the site of a major Boer victory in the first Boer War on February 27, 1881.

3 William Palmer, Grey's friend and former fagmaster at Winchester, 2nd Earl and a prominent Unionist politician. Salisbury's son-in-law, he would be named First Lord of the Admiralty later in the year. One of his homes was in Blackmoor, a village in eastern Hampshire.

leaves me in doubt whether he (Selborne, not Joubert) may be at Blackmoor on Sunday or not. If he is, "tant mieux" (I have lately been in Paris), if not, "n'importe," so long as you will be there.

I am staying in London tonight to go to Mrs. Gladstone's funeral in Westminster Abbey tomorrow; it is the last act of that great part of one's life.[1]

After it is over I return to Itchen Abbas: London is not a proper place at this time of year and I am glad you are not there, so that we can meet in the country.

Itchen Abbas
25 June 1900

It was not till I had mounted in the road that I realized all that your sister and daughter had done for my bicycle, when I wasn't looking. Not only had it been put in out of the rain, but the dirt which my sloth (I use the word in its opprobrious post-diluvian sense) had allowed to accumulate for several days, had been wiped away. And I never expressed my thanks before leaving! As I cannot be at Blackmoor today to do this on my knees, please do it for me.

As soon as I was thoroughly wet through on the way home I became one with the weather and would not have changed the day. It is only while one is dry that one is out of sympathy with rain, when one is wet through ("to the skin" as they say in the nursery) one minds it no more than the trees, having become part of the day oneself. And beyond East Tisted, if you go by the big road and take the second, not the first, turning to Alresford after East Tisted, you will go a mile through a magnificent wood full of bracken and all sorts of green things that delight in soft June rain.

---

1 Catherine Gladstone had died on June 14, at 88, two years after her husband. Neville's aunt had been something like a surrogate mother to the Lyttelton children after her sister's death in 1857. Perhaps Grey expressed condolences in a separate letter to Neville.

12 April 1903

I have here a letter from of November last preserved—not forever—but to be answered... I have been rather ground down at
times by political work and business and hateful letters, which get
more every year. Did you ever hear of "Gresham's Law." I believe
it is to the effect that bad money drives out the good. So it is with
correspondence—the annoying and wearisome part gets done at
the expense of the pleasant. That is why your letter of November
hasn't been answered til April. But time passes so much more
quickly and seems so much less important as one gets older; it is
a very upside down affair that it should be so, but so it is, and as
you are not so much younger than me as to belong to the next
generation, I suppose you find it so too;[1] which all means that
four months' delay in writing nowadays seems as week did when
I was younger.

You haven't got much news of us I should think. I don't see
how you can—we were more out of the world than ever.

Dorothy's pulse got quicker last year and in October after a
three day attempt to spend the Session in London, and she was
peremptorily told to give up visits, people and things and retire
to the country... She spent November at our Cottage, has been
in semi-retirement at Fallodon and is now salmon fishing with
me here... She is much better and in May we go to a place called
Grosvenor Square in some confidence that we shall be able to stay
the Session out.

I hate politics as much as ever and can't write about them. I
think the Govt. will flicker out in a year to two and a ministry
will be reformed under Chamberlain. I see no prospect of Liberals
coming in before 1910 and have no more thoughts of office than
for the last several years; but I have a Railway Board and other
business, which is definite work, at which one can sit with one's

---

1 Though he seems to have believed Katharine was younger than he, she was in fact two years older.

feet on the ground, instead of standing on one's head hurray-ing with one's heels, which is about all we can do in opposition, though one goes on mouthing about public affairs.

Fallodon is let again this year—that is another of the delights of politics: it confers on you the double privilege of being some hundreds a year out of pocket and of being unable to live at home.

What did you think of Chamberlain in South Africa? I thought it was a great performance physically and otherwise and that the immediate result might be good. Whether it could have any permanent effect I do not know.[1] How is Milner?[2] Tell us something about what is happening—we hear very little of it now and we are always interested to know even if we can't use our knowledge: and how are you and how is Neville and how is your "distinct" family as an Indian Rajah once put it. Dorothy charges me to say she is going to write you.

22 Grosvenor Road
30 May 1904

This seems to have hung fire, while we have been away. There can't, I should think, be any objection on our (N.E.R.) part to deal direct with such reputable not to say distinguished people as the First Land Lord and Land Lady.[3] I don't see why you shouldn't go direct to our Mr. Field, whom I don't know however.

I will ask at York on Thursday who of our many officials you had better deal with as most responsible.

We have just come back, and feel very glum and Cottage sick. (N.B., This doesn't mean "sick of the Cottage" any more than

1 The Colonial Secretary visited South Africa from December 1902 to March 1903 as the first of a projected series of trips abroad to unite the Empire. He was 66 at the time and his health had deteriorated after a cab accident in July 1902. Appointed in June, 1902, Neville Lyttelton was serving as Commander-in-Chief of the Army in South Africa.
2 Balliol-educated Alfred Milner (1854–1925), Governor of Cape Colony and High Commissioner of South Africa, and since 1902, Governor of Transvaal and Orange River Colonies, had returned to Britain briefly.
3 Neville Lyttelton had been appointed the first Chief of the General Staff in February 1904.

"home-sick" means "sick of your home." Have you ever considered teaching your children at your knee the various and opposite ways in which "sick" is used as a compound? e.g. "Home-sick" = "longing for home" but "sea-sick" does not = "longing for the sea" and "love-sick" is I take it used in the same way as "sea-sick") so that if I were to sign myself

    Yours sickly
    instead of
    Yours sincerely
    it would be ambiguous,

22 March 1905

I can't lunch today because I am going to meet Sir R. Soliman at luncheon. I think I can lunch tomorrow (Thursday), if you will have me at 1:30. "Dear" Dorothy is at Fallodon. I live in a whirl of trains and speeches and weekends in the North; sometimes I imagine I am Chairman of a Railway, sometimes that I am an M.P., sometimes that I am married, sometimes that I am not; I have all these by turns every week, but not one of them for long enough to make it seem real. This is why I haven't got to Manchester Square yet. I never in my life have been to Manchester Square; I shall go there tomorrow: it will be a great day.

Itchen Abbas
20 June 1905

Thank you very much for your letter. We have been much distressed by my mother's death: she died suddenly when we were counting upon her recovery and all anxiety seemed to be over. In these last years she had begun to be dependent on her children in a way that was very touching and which made her a centre and home, where they met. Now that is all gone, just when it seemed happily assured for some years. It is when the children have come to middle age and are scattered and entrenched in separate homes and occupations that the mother becomes the one centre without which they fall apart and get altogether out of touch: and when she dies there is a sense of desolation.

The death of one's mother brings mortality home to one so: I feel as if I had become a whole generation older than I was; as if I had passed the summit of life and was going down the hill and had lost touch with the young side.

Have you got a free evening next week, when you and Neville could come and dine alone with us? Say Tuesday, Wed., or Thursday. We don't want to see many people, but we should like you to come and we should like to hear the other side of the Morgan affair. I haven't read about it yet except newspaper extracts.

3 Whitehall Court
14 December 1905

I have been so hustled in the attempt to get into F.O. work and keep my head up[1] that I am not sure of any facts outside it but I think that when I came back to London on Monday I found a telephone message (sent a day or two before when I was at Fallodon) asking me to dine with Lady <u>Hamilton</u> alone to meet Sir Ian Hamilton who was coming to dine with her. From this I gathered that Lady Hamilton was anxious to see Sir Ian Hamilton and wanted me to be present as chaperone. On Tuesday <u>at dinner time</u> (being engaged to dine with Sir T. Sanderson on F.O. business) I found a letter from you asking me to dine with you that same evening to meet Sir I. Hamilton.[2] This letter has since dis-

---

1 Balfour submitted his resignation on December 5, and the King asked Campbell-Bannerman to form a government. After resisting until the evening of the 7th—honoring the "Relugas Compact," the pledge not to join any Liberal government unless Asquith would lead the party in the House— Grey accepted C.B.'s offer of the Foreign Secretaryship and received the seals of office on the 10th. He had to get up to speed in particular on the Moroccan Crisis. Though France had agreed to a conference in Algeciras, the possibility of a European war still loomed large.
2 Hamilton (1853–1947) was then a Lieutenant-General in charge of the Southern Command, two divisions and eight regiments based in Wiltshire. He was one of the few generals, along with

appeared, if indeed it was a real letter and not a dream one. This is all I remember of what has passed and will explain my silence hitherto and my absence from your table last Tuesday.

I am very sorry I could not come.

I hear of mighty things happening in the War Office. Councils seem to come and go, but Neville remains.

15 February 1906

I knew you would feel for and with me.[1] All that I shall feel I cannot know yet; every day I am grasping a little more of what it means and the difference it makes in my life. I feel some unexpected things—a sense of the unreality of time and of death and of continuing companionship with Dorothy. Too much of her has passed into me for me to feel altogether lonely; I could go home and live in the past altogether. I am doing my work, but I am living on the memories—they are too happy to be painful even now. Some day I shall ask you to come see me and shall want to hear you talk of her.

3 Queen Anne's Gate
9 March 1906

I must send this back to you. I think anyhow it would have made me cry that anyone who ever wrote so nice a letter should have died. I see what you say about talking of other things, but I'm no good for that yet. I have many hours a day of effort over my work, and when I am not doing that I can't make other efforts. Either I think alone; or if I see anyone, it must be someone to

Neville Lyttelton, who was a Liberal. The reference seems to imply that the Hamiltons were estranged at the time, but there is no evidence of this. Sanderson (1841–1923) had been serving as Permanent Under-Secretary at the Foreign Office since 1894. He would retire early the following year, shortly after the administrative reforms he had reluctantly agreed to went into effect.
1 Dorothy Grey had died early in the morning of February 4, three days after her accident.

whom I can talk of what I think and there are not many people I can talk of that to.

P.S. I am glad you sent me Mr. Fitzgerald's letter. I took no part in that business and wasn't so good or encouraging to Dorothy as I might have been; but she used to tell me about those hansom drives and talks, and I am very grateful for the letter now; it's a real good warm hearted letter. Oh! dear what a stone I feel!

Itchen Abbas
8 April 1906

My second Sunday here has been quieter; the first time was like going through it all again and some parts of the day are blank to me now looking back. But today I have listened to the birds and pruned my roses.

9 April 1906

Tuesday is no good for luncheon: it is one of my question days in the H. of C. and I shall lunch at the office—indeed I have no free time tomorrow at all. I should have liked to see you and I wrote yesterday.

Someone told me that they had seen in the paper that someone had adopted Neville and that he was to have an estate: I hope it is true and that you like your new father-in-law.

I am beginning to feel that I have had a great deal taken out of me and should like to sit down and rest: I was grateful for my work; this is the other side.

Fallodon
15 April 1906

It is very touching that you should have thought of me in this way and I will tell you about myself. There need be no fear of my being alone here: it is true that I am alone, but in that way I learn about what sorrow teaches and that is to the good. For instance I ask if Dorothy joined me again should I be more or less loving now? And the answer is "more loving." I had learnt all that happiness would teach me and now I have learnt more, for sorrow and happiness both teach love and both teach the same things, only each leaves so much untaught, which only the other can teach. And so if I am learning and growing, my spirit is becoming more fit to meet hers and to go, when the time comes, wherever hers has gone.

These thoughts come to me in solitude; we both had an unusual gift of solitude, the power to enjoy being alone, but she had used it more than I had done, and in the last ten years she had grown more than I had, partly by illness, partly by being many days alone, partly by strong friendships; while I in the same time had been always more hustled and bustled by public life and work and business, so that I was getting left behind. Now in a time like this, when I am constantly thinking and longing, love goes on growing and realizing itself and I would not have it disturbed by having anyone else with me just now. Much of each day is very sad; there are times when I quiver and my face feels drawn with the expression of misery; but I am used to that and before each day is over there come thoughts which turn to peace and at the worst I am never angry or impatient or in despair. Of course there is poignancy in being here; there are so many memories, so many external things and small things which make for tears; but there is also a sense of comfort in the familiarity of the home, which was my home in childhood; the very sound which the wind makes in these windows is so well known it is like having one's mother in the room.

As you wondered what it was like I have told you something of what it is; and if it were not so I could always go back to the Foreign Office.

I am glad you are having a happy time; you ought to, if you have got a nice cottage, because there is extraordinary joy and health in such weather at this time of year—warmth and the great singing time of birds don't last for long together nor are there many days of these, very often none in April, nor many in May, and early in June the songs begin to cease. So make the most of them and try to teach the daughters to enjoy them, so that next winter they may still be thinking of them and begin months before to wonder whether next April will bring such days again.

But perhaps the daughters are too young yet for such great things, or perhaps they must find love or be loved first, or are so made that they are moved by other great things more than by these; and remember always that May is still better than April at its best, because of the new leaves and blossoms. But then you may be in London! How that used to fill me with rage and despair! Now I bear it easily because I am filled with other thoughts and am ready to leave it all though I see it is beautiful still.

Fallodon
20 April 1906

If you are in London on the 27th will you come to tea or to dinner with me at 3 Queen Anne's Gate that day? I don't know about the Upton letters and their author,[1] you shall tell me.

I haven't read much; there are several hours a day of F. O. work and then letters; and I still fall to thinking.

In these fine days too I spend my spare time in the open air, walking much about the garden retracing old steps.

Fallodon
6 August 1906

When I saw such a fat envelope from you I was afraid it couldn't be all you and that there must be an enclosure; then I was pleased to find that it was all you, but the paper was rather thick and I

1 *The Upton Letters* (1905) by A. C. Benson (1862–1925), Master of Magdalene College, Cambridge, was a collection of brief literary essays in the form of letters. Son of the Archbishop of Canterbury, Benson was a prolific diarist and writer, as were two of his brothers.

found I was at the end, when I thought there was another sheet to come, and that gave me a little twinge of disappointment. This was in London.

I have been very low; the Session left me tired and out of sorts; and on the journey down there were not the proper sleeping cars, it being Saturday, and I had a slow and broken night journey with changes and waits.

My first day here I felt as if I were swaying over an abyss and ready to drop. As long as one's body and mind are vigorous, one has strength to learn what sorrow teaches and then one feels that one is being fitted for still more perfect love and to be used for God's purposes. But when one is tired, one feels as if one could not learn and could not be used and as if one's suffering was purposeless and one was not going to be worth a future.

If only there were not so long to wait! I could manage a few years bravely, but there may be so many and it seems impossible to keep up for 30 or perhaps more years. And yet I know it is not wise in these things to worry about what may be; if one can bear the present one may be able to bear each bit of the future as it becomes present. Do you know the lines

"He who afflicts me, knows what I can bear,

And when I fail and can endure no more

Will mercifully take me to himself."[1]

But she was ill and dying when she said it and had not got to go on doing work in the world.

Here I broke off to read your letter again and find in it that "the fair one"[2] said "I go on for the present in the hope that I shall meet someone who will take me out of it." The appositeness of the words to what I have been writing and the inappositeness of the allusion is quaint. It is a nice saying of "the fair one" all the

---

1 The lines are spoken by the character Ellen in Book 6 of Wordsworth's *The Excursion* (1814).
2 Hilda Lyttelton

same. They shall now be "the fair one" and "the auburn one"[1] in my letters, as you have chosen to begin describing them.

Young George Trevelyan's book I have got, but have not yet read.[2]

I am glad you have read "On the Heights" again.[3] I feel as you do that the Walpurga and peasant part was the most wonderful, but the Irma part is also wonderful when one was quite young, it would have been tremendous and thrown the rest into the shade. Now the Walpurga part seems the more uncommon, it is so wonderfully well done, and the quality and touch of it are so rare. The book hangs about one afterwards and haunts one's thoughts. I can't read much here; to find this place in summer has quickened so many memories that I can't attend to any book.

Fallodon
14 September 1906

I have just come back from London, where I had to go for business…

Haldane is coming for two nights to tell me about his new German friends; Mrs. Creighton is coming to go over material for what she is writing[4] and Constance Herbert, whom you know of, is coming also for a few days. My brother George arrives from Africa; that takes me till the 24th; after that I shall probably have to run up to London for a few days and then comes the end of the month.

---

1 Lucy Lyttelton
2 *The Poetry and Philosophy of George Meredith* (1906). Trevelyan was thirty years old.
3 *Auf de Höhe* (1865) is a novel about adultery by Berthold Auerbach. A king has an affair with a lady-in-waiting, the Countess Irma, while the peasant Walpurga, the nurse of the king's son, contemplates, but doesn't consummate, an extra-marital relationship. After Irma breaks off the affair and leaves the court, the chastened king vows to be less autocratic
4 Louise Creighton had begun work on a memoir of Dorothy Grey. It was her idea, not Grey's, as Trevelyan states, and Edward hesitated before giving his consent.(E. Grey to L. Creighton, 17 February 1906, Creighton Papers, Bodleian.)

Now wouldn't it be good for you to come to Fallodon for a change and rest from the 24th to Oct. 1st?...

So think it right to come because I expect it is a duty for you to rest sometimes (Duty with a big D.) I feel that you are being hard driven by a lot of things and are probably being over gallant, as is your way: try to be wise as well as gallant and come here.

I saw that Lord Lovelace[1] had died very suddenly; I wish I could just walk out of this door and find myself in the next world; it is so easy for some people to die and so hard for others, and I have such a hard struggle some days against the desire to sit down and wait and do nothing but remember till the end comes. But I have some thoughts to fight against that with, and after all it takes more energy to get out of things than to get into them.

I am afraid you are having a hard time; but the red (? auburn) haired one and the fair haired one are such big girls now that they would surely run the Priory for you for a bit and let you come here. Bless you.

18 September 1906

Yes—you are in the direct line between Fallodon and London, but that doesn't help for I pass you about 2 a.m. in a train which doesn't stop; if I take you on my way to London, I can only do it by breaking into two days, whereas now I go up and down by night and break into no day. I am in London again and am rather worrying because I cannot get time to go to Fallodon and go over the memoir with Mrs. Creighton—not even that.

I begin to think that I shall lose all my friends, if office lasts much longer for simple want of time to see them.

I do hope you are better or if you be not, that you are resting.

I read a nice account of your brother-in-law somewhere.[2]

---

1 Ralph King Milbanke, 2nd Earl (1839–1906), grandson of Byron and husband of Katharine's sister Mary.
2 Major-General Sir Reginald Talbot (1841–1929), then serving as Governor of Victoria.

Fallodon
29 September 1906

I must go to London tomorrow night and I do not see any more holidays before me except weekends. You must dine at 3 Queen Anne's Gate some time. After the 10th I shall be there.

Mrs. Creighton has practically done the memoir and I am happy that it is done as it is.[1] I love the material she has collected and she sees things as they are and says them so sanely and well. It is a great relief to me to have been able to get through the material before my holiday quite ended and to know that it has been faithfully and lovingly handled.

I wonder how you are. You have your children round your knee and I have my office and it isn't easy to keep in touch. We make friendships when we are young and free and then the cares and work of life separate us and shut us up in different compartments.

Do you think as we get older that life will relent and when we are quite old let us out occasionally to meet and sit on a bench in the sun, speaking at ease or doing nothing? Or shall we go being driven by life till we are too weak and ill to keep up friendship.

3 Queen Anne's Gate
20 October 1906

I am afraid Monday is no good; it's the day before the Session and there is a Cabinet at tea time, which will make a horrid hole in my afternoon and I shall have to make up for it by working all the evening afterwards, except for a short dinner hour, when I am dining with my brother.

I do long to see you again, but you must have your rest first and then we will arrange a Wednesday luncheon or a Friday

---

1 *Dorothy Grey* by Louise Creighton (1907). It was privately printed.

dinner—those will be my best times. I expect a bad Session—full of rows, but it may not be so.[1]

I am going to my Cottage today til Sunday.

I have thought of you very often and wished I could rest you.

9 November 1906

I could give you supper at 8 tonight or tea at 6 at 3 Queen Anne's Gate. If not will you come to luncheon some day next week?

I hope you are rested and you must find so many hours close time every day. A good plan would be to keep some bombs in your boudoir to throw at anybody who infringed the close time. You would very soon kill off the persistent infringers and lead a healthy free dignified and whole life for the rest of your days.

10 November 1906

What you told me about R. B. H.[2] has rather disturbed me. I do not pretend to know the ins and outs, but it seems to me that in this last row he must have been right in his position to work for peace and if he has secured it without in substance compromising the position of the Army Council I think he must have done the right thing. I haven't seen him since I saw you, so this reflection comes out of my own head. The great difficulty in these matters is to make allowance for the difficulties of other people; we know our own so much better than theirs.

---

1 The most contentious issue was the Liberal's Education Bill, which was being mangled in the House of Lords. It placed all tax-funded schools (which included Church of England and Catholic schools) under the control of elected local authorities.

2 Richard Burdon Haldane, Minister of War. Neville Lyttelton was then Chief of the General Staff and did not get on with Haldane, who had reorganized that body in September and eventually brought in Haig to head it. The previous month the report of a Royal Commission criticizing Lyttelton's administration in South Africa was released, and he had offered his resignation. Also in September, Haldane had visited Germany at the Kaiser's invitation, against Grey's wishes. The trip coincided with Sedan Day, and the Foreign Secretary worried about the effect on French sensibilities.

This is a real stuffy letter.

When I got home last night I found my spectacles had come, so I put on a pair and read the daughter's lines on the Abbey.[1] I like them very much indeed. It is a fine thing to have a daughter who is going about with such thoughts in her head and can express them like that. I shall always love her because of that letter to you from Dorothy after the visit at Novar. Do tell her I like this Abbey piece really much; it's stately, like the Abbey.

P.S. I return the printed sonnet—the first thing I have read in spectacles. Some day there will be a last thing read. I hope it will be good too.

3 Queen Anne's Gate
23 November 1906

I hear you have telephoned but I cannot get your mumble on the telephone. I am no good for this evening—I have just had someone to tea. I have got Sir G. Gibb[2] coming to dinner for whom I have been trying to find an evening for weeks and with whom I have a good deal to talk over and I must get at Winston Churchill somehow in the evening and work on an urgent piece of African business.[3] And I am in heavy arrears with the day's work, et voila vous êtes, as the Englishman said.

Luncheon at 1:30 tomorrow would be very nice. Will you come? Tonight there is nothing to be done but to wish me well through the evening.

1 "Westminster Abbey at Midnight" by Lucy Lyttelton, eventually published under her married name, Masterman. It's a meditation on the anonymous architect who designed the Abbey.
2 Sir George Gibb, General Manager of the North Eastern Railway.
3 Churchill was then Parliamentary Undersecretary in the Colonial Office.

3 Queen Anne's Gate
5 December 1906

I will gladly come on Thursday to dine. I shall like to see you with your children "round your knee."

I could go to Tate gallery Saturday morning from 11 to 12.

Fallodon
26 December 1906

What a nice little book and letter with it. I am glad to have them. My years are going to date now from Feb. 1; I long to have the first year completed—some of this last part of this year is very bad. I keep comparing it to last Feb. 1. I shall at any rate be able to say—this day is less terrible than it was a year ago. But I long to hurry the years and get them over and sometimes I totter and feel as if I should go under. No doubt one gets used to all the thoughts of grief and an outer crust forms, but on the other hand one's stock of strength and courage is being drawn upon more or less every day and sometimes it seems more nearly run down than ever yet.

I wish you were through this time of London office and into a good solid army command outside. Somehow I feel that is the right thing for you both. I haven't yet read R. B. H.'s papers.

The winter is rather depressing to me—I feel it would be better if the birds would sing, that gives me more conviction of the existence of joy than anything.

God bless you and help you.

3 Queen Anne's Gate
13 March 1907

Ichabod! I am ordered to dine at Marlborough House[1] on the 19th. Farewell to the Bach Mass. Truly in office one can say like St. Paul "I die daily."

I have asked the Francis Buxtons to lunch on Friday so I look to you and Mary Buxton to chaperone me. I have asked the Austrian and Russian Ambassadors,[2] both easy people. Madame Benckendorff is in Russia.

Fallodon
1 April 1907

You told me that you had some unpaid bills and like others in such plight you have as far as I am concerned gone away and left no address, so I send this to the last address that I knew of. You are more Katharine Houseless than ever, but I do hope you are enjoying Italy. Are you basking in the Italian sun? I am basking here. There is a standing order that til the weather changes no fires are to be lit till evening and that a pocket lunch is to be put out for me in the morning; with that I disappear to the moors or sea when the morning's work is done, or sometimes I get no further than the garden and eat it there because the garden is so nice. Nevertheless (or shall I say "cependant" which you used to say with an accent and a French manner?) I shall welcome rain and go out in that too when it comes, if it ever does again.

I am reading nothing; the time which can be spared from work is given to out of doors; for the first day here I was flat—want of time from being overtired with London work—and had only the mind of a drudge.

---

1 The Westminster home of King Edward and Queen Alexandra. It had been his London residence while he was Prince of Wales, and he still preferred it to Buckingham Palace.
2 Count Albert Mensdorff-Pouilly-Dietrichstein (1861–1945) and Count Alexander Benckendorff (1849–1917). The two were related through the de Croy family.

The first sign of ceasing to be tired is that one hates one's work; that means that one has recovered the power to enjoy freedom: it's only the fresh horse that smashes the harness and kicks the trap to pieces; the tired one will stand between the shafts for ever. But there isn't really that sort of freshness about me; I just want to be left alone and to be out of things.

I went to the Bach Passion Music at St. Paul's; it is a great thing. Do you know the history of the words? I don't, but they are so simple in the great chorales that they make me cry; simple words and great music that isn't afraid of repeating itself.[1]

I had an interesting contrast in church here on Sunday—they struck up the Athanasian creed,[2] which always offends me; it starts me analyzing its smug dialectic, its cocksureness and its damnating intentions, til the unchristianness of it seems to start up and hit me in the face; so to avoid it I opened a Bible and went on with the lesson which was in Revelations and I came upon this: "and I will give him the morning star." It's a verse all by itself. Isn't it nice and doesn't it make the Athanasian creed faint? I do believe if I had been a clergyman I could have been a very good one, but Hugh Cecil[3] would have turned me out of the Church.

This isn't at all the letter that I thought I was going to write.

I am quieter but in some ways sadder than I was last Easter; there is less pain but more longing.

---

1 In the St. John's Passion, in addition to the Gospel, Bach used texts from several 16th and 17th century writers for the chorales, including Martin Luther's *"Vater unser im Himmelreich."* The chorales of the St. Matthew Passion draw on nine hymns from the same period.

2 The creed, not in fact written by Athansias, is a long and didactic exposition of the doctrine of the Trinity, and declares that salvation depends on a belief in the Incarnation of Christ, who will judge everyone and consign individuals to heaven or hell according to their works. It dates from around 500 and is accepted by all the major Western Christian denominations.

3 The youngest and most conservative of Salisbury's sons, Cecil (1869–1956) was a zealous defender of the Church of England and its privileges.

Itchen Abbas
14 April 1907

I am sorry about this illness. It's cruel—just in your one chance of a good holiday; but you write a very good letter—I liked it as much as any. You must let the Auburn one go about alone; if you and she were both my daughters and only one of you might be allowed to go about alone, she is the one I should think it safest to let go.

My holiday was broken up by Cromer's resignation.[1] I had been for a beautiful long walk at Fallodon, taking out my lunch and got back about 4:30. Now, thought I, there will be nice time to go round my ducks before tea—I hadn't had time for that before I started out because of my pouch work—; and then I saw a telegram, opened it and found a lot of cypher. So I got out my cypher book and before I had got far found that I was face to face with Cromer's resignation. I went back to London that night and shant see Fallodon till August.

The going of Cromer is very pathetic. I have just tried to do it all in the way he wanted and it has been done so and he is to have the man he wants to carry on his work.[2] My first little job was to be called his private secretary for a month in 1884 when he was in London for the Egyptian Conference. Lord Northbrook got that for me. Since then Cromer has made his great reputation and built up Egypt and now he is worn out and his work is over, and Lord Northbrook is dead; and I have lived a whole life time since 1884 and am alive. I find grey hairs coming forth in new places on my head and am glad. I long to be old.

---

1 Evelyn Baring, Lord Cromer, (1841–1917) resigned ostensibly on grounds of health. He was unhappy with the prospective liberalization of British rule in Egypt under the new government following the Denshawai incident of June 1906. Liberals felt the authorities had overreacted to the killing of a British officer after a misunderstanding while some officers were shooting pigeons.
2 Eldon Gorst (1861–1911), the Egyptian financial adviser. He pursued a policy of conciliation with Egyptian and Ottoman elites and served until shortly before his death.

It's curious that you should think it strange that I can do the same things that Dorothy and I used to do together. If I couldn't do that I should kill myself, for what else could I do? It's impossible to make a new life and do things which I didn't like before; I must do the old or nothing. And the things we liked were so pure that though I can't get the wonderful happiness any more, I feel them to be…those common everlasting outdoors things which are all part of God.

I will get Church's book. I even remember seeing it or writing about you in it. Do you say I did that in John's room—it's incredible!

When you want to spend a night in London, remember that I can put up you and Neville and the auburn one, if you didn't bring a maid; or a maid instead of the auburn one.

Mrs. Creighton tells me that the Bach chorales are translations of old German hymns going back to Luther's time.

I have had a letter from Mrs. Paul. She is a real brave heart. Poor Herbert Paul[1] has been badly ill—quite broken down and if you are well when he comes out, you must stroke him and be very good to her; if you are ill too you can't help and must just nurse yourself.

3 Queen Anne's Gate
22 April 1907

I am a little proud that you are coming, but I hope you will be comfortable. Here are your instructions.

1. Say, when you arrive, what time you would like breakfast

2. Luncheon is ordered at 1:30—that suits me, and Neville is coming—he and I are on the same committee in the morning.

---

1 Herbert W. Paul (1853–1935), journalist, man of letters, and M.P. (1892–5, 1906–9). He wrote biographies of Gladstone, Arnold, and Froude, and a five-volume *History of Modern England*. Paul experienced a "nervous collapse" in 1907. His wife was Elinor Ritchie.

3. I shall be down by nine o'clock in the morning and after that you can all use my bathroom without fear of collisions, if you prefer a proper bath to sloppy little baths in your own rooms.

Itchen Abbas
19 May 1907

I looked at my letters this morning to see if there was a nice one to read at breakfast and I found there was and it was yours. I couldn't help just asking you about the book[1] in that crowd, just to be sure that you felt right about it and you told me enough to satisfy me entirely. I want the feeling about the book to be something which unites friends and makes sympathy and understanding between them. If they feel the same about the book it will give them confidence in each other. That is one thing; the other is that some people, if nice, understanding minds, should be helped to see how strong and real pleasure in common pure things may be—in books and out of doors, if only you will be real yourself.

That, I gather, is what your Auburn one has felt. One has to draw the line, if one is free, and to settle how much pleasure it is fair to take and how much time must be given to work or duty—to politics in our case; that was our problem and we always doubted whether it would not have been better to live a country life entirely with books and birds and garden and night and day and all the rest, because so few people seemed to enjoy all these things as we did and it seemed as if they would be less wasted if we gave ourselves up to them. But for you and most people the problem is different; it is not how much will you take but how much can you get and will you be let to have? How few people, who have the desire to enjoy, have the freedom and money? And how few people, who have the money, have the desire? This world is jealous and chokes them. If the book makes the Auburn one

---

1 *Dorothy Grey*

102

feel that, come what may she will not let herself be choked, not even if she marries a duke; that will be a good start for her.

I know Lady Salisbury is a nice minded woman and I am quite easy about her seeing the book, but I don't want it read by people who won't understand or are narrow and have no reverence in them, and who would just use it for gossip.

I could pass the rest of the summer here; it is a real temptation to resign and to stay. I went to the great beechwood grove 10 miles away, to which we went together when the leaves were new; I would have died there so happily; there is something which seems perverse in one's heart going on beating against one's will. But I hold to the thought that when life is over, whether it be a few months, or whether it be many years hence, I shall see that the length of time was nothing more than a moment and that what love has gained by separation and sorrow is eternal. So I keep on, keeping the same pleasures, the same thoughts and the same places as far as I can, so that I may go out of this life unchanged, better and stronger I hope, but with the same likings and sympathies and fit for all that they may lead to.

Bless you

P.S. I should like to hear the Bach and Handel, but I am so pinched for Cottage times that I can't give one up. It may be that there will have to be two Windsor Castle weekends in June and if there are I hope you will be at Windsor and I will come to tea.

5 June 1907

Rooms will be ready for you and the fair-haired one tomorrow (Thursday) any time after 3 o'clock. I have to dine out in uniform and go to a Court, but I will order dinner for you and my brother George, who may be dining at home.

J. M.[1] has the great night of the year in the House with the Indian Budget and a very critical debate, so I cannot approach him.

In case we do not meet tomorrow (for I am having a desperate week), please order breakfast at the hour which suits you best and "I will see you in the morning." (There is an allusion in those quotation marks which I can explain if it won't shock you.)

Itchen Abbas
7 June 1907

As I lunched under a hedge looking at buttercup meadows and listening to larks, it seemed very unkind that I couldn't help your Auburn with her book. If you would tell me exactly what the book is and give me a list of the birds that want mottoes, I would write to Hudson[2] and ask him if he couldn't send some references. I can't help myself because all my books are at Fallodon and I haven't time to go on the search, but I should think there must be some book in which this sort of thing has been done before and Hudson might know.

P.S. I have been lying down in this little room with its large glass doors wide open onto the grass and the wind moving gently in the leaves in the dark outside. This cottage is so small that the trees grow about it as if it wasn't here; it is not like being in a house. And such restful things come floating into one's mind—things like "casting all your care upon him for he careth for you"[3] and "thou wilt keep him in perfect peace whose mind is stayed in thee."[4]

You may say in a London breakfast mood that those things don't tell you much, but here one feels that there is something great at the back of them. The spirit of understanding moves in

---

1 John Morley
2 W. H. Hudson (1841–1922), the famous naturalist and ornithologist. He stayed at Cottage several times, and writes about it in *Hampshire Days* (1903).
3 1 Peter 5:7
4 Isaiah 26:3

these trees and meadows and there comes that "blessed mood in which the burthen and the mystery, in which the heavy and the weary weight of all this unintelligible world seems lightened."[1] And it brings a very grateful feeling of patience and faith. I do wish everybody could have a cottage of this sort and were so made they could enjoy it.

I get comfort when I have these moods alone here, in feeling that I am continuing what Dorothy and I loved together and in the assurance which they give that if I died and joined her, I should be fit to continue my part—more fit perhaps than ever before and that is the most comforting thought of all.

I don't altogether like telling these private thoughts, but there is pleasure too in saying them to a friend and one never can tell what may help a friend, even when the friend's life and problems are different from one's own.

Brooks's Club
14 June 1907

Next time at the Court Ball we must have a rendez-vous. I never saw either you or the Eddie Tennants, but I never got into the big room at all. You need not have bothered that I got no talk with Pamela Tennant. I particularly wanted her to get some talk with John Morley, who was new to her, which I am not: so having put you by John's good ear at dinner I wanted him to sit by her a little after dinner and you arranged that. So I repeat don't bother at all; and if you <u>have</u> bothered, then stop, and be extra glad now that you did the right thing and remember the man who said when he was dying, "I have had a great deal of trouble in my life and most of it didn't happen;" and don't bother again on my account till you have asked me whether there is need.

---

1 from Wordsworth's "Tintern Abbey"

I bothered a little afterward because I wanted you all to have nice talks with each other and kept thinking what much better talks you might all be having if you could have been all in pairs in 3 separate rooms. I saw in John's eye at the end that if we could have left him alone for a tête-à-tête with you, you would have had a real good talk. But I always think this sort of thing, and believe in one person at a time for conversation. Nevertheless John told me on the bench next day that he had liked his evening.

I am glad you can come on the 20th.

P.S. I am glad you have asked my George to Windsor.

Itchen Abbas
21 June 1907

I shall keep the first half of October for you at Fallodon—by you I mean all of you that like to come, and if you let me know about the middle of August, that will be time enough, so you need not settle yet. I was very glad that you came last night and Barton liked you and you liked him, which pleased me. Dorothy specially wanted to help him and the best way I can do it is to put him in the way of nice friends.

I have been thinking about Simon[1] since you told me of him, and I still think that everything must depend upon what he feels about the future; if he has no feelings and no hopes it is impossible to help except just by giving him pleasure in the present, and woman are better for giving sympathy and comfort to men than men can be to each other. Women have that privilege and gift, though they have a bad time in many ways.

Today I broke loose after a long conversation with the Muslin-il-Muilk—a Persian—during which I spoke some of the most astounding French that ever was uttered, so strange and bad was it; even his oriental face could not quite conceal his astonishment,

---

1 Possibly John Simon (1873–1954), then an M.P. and protégé of Asquith and Grey. He joined the Cabinet in 1910, and would later serve as Foreign Secretary and Home Secretary.

his French being very good. When he went I fled from the F.O. and went to the gardens of the R.H.S. at Wisley with Mildred Buxton and the Eddie Tennants and we took a basket lunch and ate it under trees and spent the afternoon in the gardens talking gardening talk and taking notes, and they went back to London by train and the Tennant motor took me on and dropped me here on its way to Wilford and here I am.

16 July 1907

Mrs. Fizgerald came to luncheon yesterday and brought me Dorothy's last letter to her. I kept it for a day to real alone and in moved me strangely. I got back into the past and the future seemed to be coming quite close; the sense of time shriveled up and I seemed almost out of the present. Sometimes it seems as if by a little more act of will I would get away into a spiritual life altogether, but it isn't so and I have to come back and wait.

I hope you will come for the first half of October. George has been asked to some of the best stalking in Scotland for the very best 10 days or so of it. It's the one enjoyment he cares for in this country so he will be away part of the time, for which I am sorry, but you must just regard Fallodon as a house lent you with me in it, and not a place where you are paying a visit and being entertained. You have no right to be dull wherever you are so long as you are you.

Did you know that the engagement of the Creighton son has been broken? That sort of catastrophe is very painful.[1]

6 August 1907

There are sparks of the divine fire in this poem and I like it. The sentiment and thought remind me of G. Herbert, whom I

_____

1 Probably Cuthbert (1876–1973), who married six years later and became headmaster at King's School, Worcester

call Holy Mr. Herbert and whom I love, though it isn't in his peculiar quaint style, which it would never do to imitate now. Do you remember too the Wanderer's account of himself in the Excursion where he says "By Thy grace the particle divine remained unquenched"?[1] I like the communing of thought between pure minds.

I am interested to see the list of ducks; I expect the numbers of quacking mallards and the muscovies will look rather top heavy, but it is evidently a larger water than mine.

My sister lives at Oulton Lodge: she has a friend, a Mrs. Bagnall whom I have never seen and whose husband is I think in India, living with her. Mrs. Bagnall is dying slowly and Alice is seeing her through.[2] Dorothy was always kind to Alice and she has an affection both for Dorothy and for me.

Mrs. Fitzgerald has written me a nice letter about the memoir, with very true feeling in it.

P.S. My servants have gone to Fallodon and I am finishing the Session in Haldane's house no. 28[3] with the bright green door.

26 August 1907

George has come to London to see Charlie's doctor and has had rather a disappointing account of him. George is rather sad and depressed in consequence and meanwhile Charlie has gone to Fallodon alone. It is thought he wants looking after and ought not to be alone, so George is going back to Fallodon to look after him. I am sorry that he can't go to Mannington[4] and he is sorrier, but he is right to go after Charlie and would not be comfortable if he did not, so I hope you will understand and if all goes well

---

1 From the beginning of the Fourth Book of Wordsworth's long poem, "Despondency Corrected."
2 Elizabeth Bagnall and Alice Graves lived together for many years after they separated from their husbands. Helen Bagnall, Elizabeth's youngest daughter, married Cecil Graves.(C. Graves, unpublished memoir.)
3 Queen Anne's Gate, midway between Grey and the Tennants. Haldane had moved from Whitehall Court the previous year.
4 A moated manor house, dating from the Middle Ages, in Norfolk.

we will all meet at Fallodon in October and say it didn't matter after all.

I am very glad to have seen Mannington; it is pleasant to think of you all in such a nice place: to spend a month or two in such a nice place must be something to the good in your lives and probably it is only now and then if ever that the place has such nice people to live in its rooms and walk about its garden and go in and out over its moat.

Fallodon
8 September 1907

There is alas no piano at Fallodon and has been none for many years. I never regretted its absence more. Your rooms will be ready on October 1. There are a few partridges and the harvest may be in full swing by then (it isn't yet) so I hope Neville will bring a gun if he cares to shoot. Someone will have to get partridges when wanted for the house. A cloud threatens. I am to be summoned to Balmoral[1] for a few days some time, but it only threatens my plans not yours, for the rooms and servants will be here all the time. I shall have a motor while you are here and it can fetch you from Alnwick. You won't find this place as beautiful as Mannington, so see that the daughters' expectations are not pitched too high, but I shall show you some fine country if it is good weather, and there is the sea.

I was very sad for the first days, but am now better: it was right that I arranged to have the first week alone to take it all in; and I was unstrung at first by the weariness of the Session.

Fallodon
10 September 1907

---

1 The royal castle and estate in Aberdeenshire where Queen Victoria and her successors usually spent part of the fall.

The Balmoral blow has fall; it leaves me free happily in your time here, but it has hit the week when I was to have the E. Tennants, Ella Pease, and Barton and I am just writing letters to put them all off.

Fallodon
14 September 1907

I am going to London on Sunday night for a few days and shall try to arrange to keep the 1st to the 7th clear, so as to be here when Neville is here. Barring accidents I can do it all right and you shall find me at Fallodon on the 1st. Barton will also be at Fallodon til the 8th and the Francis Buxtons come on the 12th, so you will have some other company.

P.S. One of my printed telegrams yesterday had as follows: "Spanish govt. contemplate compensating themselves (see rat trapper)." Can you guess what it meant? It was the printer's version of "se rattraper."[1]

17 September 1907

I go back to Fallodon tomorrow night. You need not be anxious about meeting too many people at Fallodon. Here is the list of strangers... And I shall <u>make</u> you be quiet and rest—all of you, and if you won't do it, I shall put you in the drawing room and the men in the smoking room and lock the doors every morning till luncheon—keeping the daughters out to play in the garden or do their knitting in the summer house. Will that be quiet enough?

Till when do you want to stay?...

The F.O smells horrid—the private secretaries' room is being cleaned out and it's next to mine and I think they must be cleaning it with iodiform or some very strong anti-septic. There is such a tiresome day ahead of me and I am so bored. I go this evening

---

1 to recoup oneself

to dine and sleep at John's house at Wimbleton: that will be all right, if we are in conversing moods.

P.S. Extract from conversation at dinner at Fallodon.

E.G. "They say Morley got 10,000 pounds for writing Gladstone's Life."

Charles Grey: "How much did he get for his Cromwell?"

E.G. "Oh! I don't know, that was a much smaller book of a different kind."

C.G. "Oh! Yes. I remember it was like 'the last phase' of the other man."

Aren't the last three words nice?

9 October 1907

I wish I could help you more about Hilda's journey. I am sure the best place to wait in will be the Station Hotel at Newcastle: it has an entrance on to the platform and a drawing room in the first (not ground) floor, which is always quiet and where I have no doubt they would bring her tea. Her luggage could be wheeled by a porter into the hotel to wait there and a hotel porter would go with her and it to the train at the proper time.

If you liked to write a line to the manager, Station Hotel, Newcastle-on-Tyne, to say that your daughter was traveling alone and would like to have tea or something in the drawing room while she waited for the train, it would secure every attention. The hotel belongs to and is managed by the railway company.

I suppose it wouldn't do to send daughters by rail in a labeled crate—like one does with fragile and valuable things when the are large.

I hope you are comfortable at Fallodon: I am sorry to have had to run away, but glad that I am coming back.

15 October 1907

I suspect this and the Mass book of being yours or Auburn's. On the other hand I do not find Vol. I of Fitzgerald's "Remains"[1] and it may have been packed by your zealous maid in mistake for the last hair of the camel's back.

I am so glad that you came and stayed here. It has given me confidence as well as pleasure; the feeling of being grateful to friends for inward things is new in my life. I shall have to try for the rest of my life to find out what gift I have for friendship and to use what I have. It is as if Dorothy had left me some good friends as a legacy; they must be few in number, because one can't give much to many: and they will be those who can feel that she has in a way left me as a legacy to them. That will be the bond, which helps us. I am very much in favour of the daughters and I do wish them well with all my heart.

I am afraid you had a horrid journey—I kept feeling as if I might have helped it more by going to the station, but I don't see how I could and there was no room in the motor.

Itchen Abbas
27 October 1907

I shall have some free luncheon times this week. Will you come to 3 QAG or should I find you in Eaton Square?

P.S. It has been a very beautiful day and this place is very dear. I keep thinking of all I have had and with that comes the question "how is it possible to go on living with all that taken away?"; and the answer is "It is just because I have had so much that I can go on," and then there is the life after this to be lived for; and then I cling to the beauty of the world and my feeling for it as a sign that life goes on.

---

1 *The Letters and Literary Remains of Edward FitzGerald* (W. A. Wright, ed.), 1903–4.

I saw Mrs. Fitzgerald on Friday afternoon and came away very pleased with her pleasure at having seen Nigel. I shall see Rufus Isaacs[1] and consult with him as to whether some of us can't bring pressure to bear on Henry Norman to make him keep his word.[2]

Friday evening I kept to spend with George. I am sad that he is gone—there is real affection between us.

3 Queen Anne's Gate
7 November 1907

I did enjoy the music this evening more than I can tell you. I was hungry for it and I do like Hilda's playing and your singing. I wish I knew enough about music to be able to say things, which would make you feel how much pleasure you were giving me. As it is I can only go on saying "Like, Like, Like, Like awfully much" as if I was a child.

You don't a bit change or have the manner of someone else when you sing, as many people do: I could hear you in your singing and feel it was you that I was listening to.

"Balde rühest du auch"[3] made me cry very much—I liked and felt it so; that was why I daren't risk it at the end, it would have started me off again; but I shall want to hear it often.

---

1 Isaacs (1860–1935), later the first Marquess of Reading, had represented Reading in the House since 1904. A successful barrister, he specialized in trade union legislation. Isaacs would go on to serve as solicitor-general and then attorney-general under Asquith, and then Ambassador to the U.S.
2 Sir Henry Norman (1858–1939) was a widely-travelled and well-connected journalist who entered Parliament in 1900. A Liberal Imperialist like Isaacs, he had chaired the West Indies Commission Grey sat on and was at one point viewed as a future Foreign Secretary. The matter to which Grey refers is obscure.
3 Schubert's 1823 setting of Goethe's poem *"Ein Gleiches,"* from *"Wandrers Nachtleid."* "Above all summits/It is calm./In all the tree-tops/You feel/Scarcely a breath;/The birds in the forest are silent./Just wait,/ Soon you will rest as well."

3 Queen Anne's Gate
15 November 1907

I feel that I have had a very narrow escape. It would have been terrible if I had given my spare ticket away and then found on coming to dinner that you were not going to the concert for want of a ticket. You really must be careful; if you go on sacrificing and effacing yourself in this way, you will one day disappear altogether or turn into a faint shadow, which can only just be seen.

Itchen Abbas
22 November 1907

I will speak to Herbert Gladstone about (jails/gaols) for Barton.[1] I don't know what Borstall is—it sounds like some sort of Swedish massage, but I can ask about that.[2]

I have got Bernard Holland[3] to lunch with Barton and me at 3 Q.A.G. tomorrow, because that may help the C. O.[4] thing.

Barton was very good at the Wallace collection[5] to which he took me: first of all he showed me things to be liked and some heart-felt dislikes came out: "come and look at this particularly detestable person," etc. It is very satisfactory to make him laugh. I did it the other day at breakfast by something I said about elephantiasis.

---

1 Captain Frank Barton (1865–1974) was one of the Greys' closest friends. They met in the West Indies. Barton had served as Governor of New Guinea, but lost his position after a conflict with a subordinate who had Colonial Office connections. Grey was trying at this time to secure him a new post. Herbert Gladstone (1854–1930), the Prime Minister's youngest son, was Home Secretary.

2 Borstals were detention centers for juveniles. The first one opened in the village of Borstal, Kent in 1902 and the Liberal government established them nation-wide in 1908.

3 Holland, Cambridge Apostle, biographer and historian, had served as private secretary to Alfred Lyttelton at the Colonial Office and continued in that position under his Liberal successor, Lord Elgin.

4 Colonial Office

5 Specimens, mostly birds and insects from the Malay archipelago, donated to the Natural History Museum by the naturalist and co-discoverer of the theory of evolution, Alfred Russell Wallace (1823–1913).

I am glad you told me about Methuen and Duncan; it is good to hear of strong clean souls being moved by Beethoven: in the next state we may be able to be moved and to move each other as music moves us, without all the limitations of brass and strings and ears and material waves of sound; just as Beethoven I am sure felt music when he was stone deaf.

I wanted to ask Neville about the symphony at the C.I.D. Committee, but when it was over I had to get Ottley[1] talked to about an F.O. matter and then French[2] came to tell me about his visit to Russia and then Neville was having a talk to someone else and the whole room was very unmusical and I went away.

This really is the last Cottage day till March: the last day was to have been 3 weeks ago, but I felt I must say goodbye to it once more. I had a big ache today; it comes with the feeling that it is so long since I have seen Dorothy and that I cannot bear being without her any more, but in time that will also bring the feeling that I am getting nearer to the end of this life and separation.

29 November 1907

I am ashamed that I told you I was tired last night and had so much work. It was true, but I think I only told you to convince you that I was not running away early because I was not enjoying my evening. I did like it and it so composed me that I had the best sleep after it for some days past. There is magic in the Goethe song.

I hope Hilda is better; some future day it will be nice to hear the Waldstein[3] and you shall tell me at what point it was that Joe Vance said "Of course if that's so"—etc.

---

1 Sir Charles Ottley (1858–1932) was director of naval intelligence and had served as the chief naval advisor in the British delegation to The Hague Peace Conference earlier in the year. He had recently succeeded Sir George Clarke as secretary of the C.I.D.
2 Sir John French (1852–1925), then commander at Aldershot, had been appointed to the C.I.D. in December 1905. Some influential individuals wished him to replace Lyttelton as Chief of the General Staff, but he took the post of Inspector-General of the Army at the end 1907.
3 Piano Sonata #21 in C Major by Beethoven.

Barton returned from Caesar and Cleopatra[1]—interested in the play, but saying that he was very glad I had not been there and that "it was the quintessence of Bernard Shaw with his tongue in both cheeks."

9 December 1907

Do come to Hatfield[2] if you can since I promised to go. I have rather relapsed into a mood of not wanting to see any people except a very few and you are one of those.

I shall never get over having been deprived of the "Eager Heart."[3]

12 December 1907

Dear Katharine Faithless,

I enjoyed my evening at Hatfield very much in spite of your having failed.

I like Lady Salisbury and had a nice fellow creature talk with her, and I like the naturalness of Cecils and the sense of space that there was in the house, when no party was there, and the tranquillizing effect of the oak paneling and the quiet that comes from the feeling of many centuries sleeping or laid to rest in the house.

I am very glad that I went and I found it very easy and refreshing.

P.S. I call you Faithless, but we are really quits, for I failed about the Eager Heart and am not at all sure that you don't think badly of me therefore.

---

1 The five-act play with two prologues by George Bernard Shaw was written in 1898 and first staged in 1901.
2 The home of James Gascoyne-Cecil, 4th Marquess of Salisbury, the Prime Minister's son.
3 Alice Mary Buckton, *Eager Heart: A Christmas Mystery Play* (1904) ("Inscribed to all who see and worship the One in the Many"). Buckton was a spiritualist, associated with Glastonbury.

Fallodon
20 December 1907

I came here today and have had my little treasures out and looked at them and have read our Cottage Book and they all seem to say "be patient and the end will come," and I have been able to cry a little and feel restored.

I do wish all of you happiness.

North British Station Hotel, Edinburgh
27 December 1907

I am on my way to Fallodon after a very kind and refreshing stay with the E. Tennants, which has been very good for me. I liked seeing the children enjoy their Christmas, and as there was no party there was plenty of time for all nice quiet things just as if it wasn't Christmas.

I burnt your letter telling of poor Masterman,[1] so that the secret should be safe with me. You think he spent a sleepless night of misery afterwards and that reminded me by contrast of the night after I had asked Dorothy to marry me, when I lay awake all night because I couldn't sleep for happiness. That is the sort of contrast which shames me out of impatience on repining by the thought of how much I have had in comparison with so many others. But this must have been rather a shock in your household and it cannot have been without pain. Some day I hope love will find his way in.

---

1 Charles Masterman had presumably asked Lucy Lyttelton to marry him and had been refused. The couple became engaged on February 23, 1908. Masterman (1873–1927), after graduating from Cambridge, where he'd been President of the Union, lived in the East End and wrote about his experiences in *From the Abyss* (1902). He edited a collection of essays *In the Heart of Empire* (1901) and then published an essay collection of his own, *In Peril of Change* (1905) and a biography of F. D. Maurice (1907). In 1906, he was elected M.P. for West Ham North. He was closely associated with Winston Churchill and Lloyd George, and helped draft the latter's "People's Budget" and National Insurance Act. Best known today for *The Condition of England* (1909) and his work as the first director of Wellington House, the War Propaganda Bureau, during World War I, Masterman's promising political career was cut short by the collapse of the Liberal Party and alcoholism.

Many thanks for Eager Heart. I am taking it home to read, because I had another book at Glen, which I was trying to finish, but am glad to have Eager Heart and if there is difficulty you shall come and expound it to me in London.

Farewell and may all go very well with you for the New Year.

Fallodon
15 January 1908

I have been thinking much about your Auburn problem. It is a woman's question and I feel I don't know what to say about it, except that I am sure it ought not to be unless there is a real great love on both sides, which is worth all risks and all sacrifice.

I should like to see you. Could you come to tea at 3 Queen Anne's Gate about 5:30 on Monday or Thursday.

3 Queen Anne's Gate
4 February 1908

I never said that I was going to Fallodon—only that I should spend Sunday alone. I went to the hotel which Dorothy found for me in the New Forest[1] and was out in the Forest for many hours on a beautiful day and came back by starlight. That is the sort of thing I am really made for—not politics. Sometimes as I walked I felt full of the things that Dorothy liked best in me and thoughts come to me, which I know she would have liked me to say to her. These last two years have taken a lot out of me and I am now just perpetually tired, except physically—I can walk and all that. So it is no good goading me to take more politics upon me than I have. You will be enthusiastic and high spirited to the end and I see that you and Winston have been talking a lot of nonsense together. I know that he knows nothing about the F.O. work and thinks that because a Parliamentary under-secretary can travel and pick and

1 The Forest Park Inn.

118

choose and gallop about the field and toss his head and sniff what breeze he pleases, therefore a Foreign Secretary can do the same. And I am sorry to see that you know no more about the F.O. work than he does.

What I might do would be to do my railway work again, and live mostly in the country and be nice to a few friends when I saw them and wrote to them, if they would remember that I was on the ebb tide. Would you like to come to lunch or tea on Saturday? I would make you very welcome and tell you something of what Dorothy really did expect of me in office.

3 Queen Anne's Gate
4 February 1908

You mustn't take my depression to heart: I ought to consume my own smoke and I should hate to hurt you. Yes do come to tea 5:30 on Friday.

There's no objection whatever to Barton seeing Winston. I'll speak to Winston too.

I have kept plugging away at Elgin-Hopwood and B. Holland, but Winston may certainly be enlisted, too.

3 Queen Anne's Gate
12 February 1908

I was longing last night to ask you how many daughters were now engaged, but it didn't seem discreet to ask it, even when the servants were not in the room. I foresee that within two years you will be left with just your "nice new baby" and Neville and no more. But I hope it will come about smoothly.

I do like the quality in your voice and the songs you sing. It really isn't safe for Hilda when a simple innocent like me is highly wrought by the Waldstein Sonata to say she is playing it badly. What is that to one who has never heard it played at all except as she plays it? The danger is that out of gratitude and loyalty to

Hilda, who has played, I might rush at whatever said the playing was bad and shake it, till it unsaid it: and what confusion and fuss that would make in your Eaton Square drawing room!

Dorothy's "two little Findlaters"[1] are coming to tea on Friday, so I can't go to the Temple[2] with you that evening, but some other Friday I could do it and should like it very much.

3 Queen Anne's Gate
21 February 1908

I will be, unless told not, at the Temple Church at 6:30 on Friday Feb. 28.

As to dinner I can do nothing next week till Macedonia and the Congo are over. The F.O. work is heavy and with these two debates on top of it, I must sit tight.[3]

…Would you come to lunch on Wednesday the 11th or lunch on Friday the 13th? P.S. Let me know if the 20th is settled and I will try to bring J. M.

3 Queen Anne's Gate
26 February 1908

Please call me here on Friday.

My heart goes out to your Lucy in the longing that she may be very happy.

---

1 The novelists Mary and Jane Findlater, best known as co-authors of *The Green Graves of Balgowrie* (1896), *Ladder to the Stars* (1906) and, later in 1908, *Crossriggs*.
2 Temple Church off Fleet Street, adjacent to two of the Inns of Court, built in the late 12th century for the Knights Templar
3 On February 25, Grey spoke at length in the House on Macedonia, in response to a hostile question by Masterman. The issue concerned the scope of the reforms to be imposed on the Turkish government by the Powers. The Congo question involved the transfer of the colony, the personal property of King Leopold II, to the Belgian government and the ending of abuses in the Free State. As always, the difficulty for the Foreign Secretary was reconciling humanitarian impulses with perceived British interests. German diplomacy was happy to exploit resentment toward the British in Brussels and Constantinople.

"You were as cold as ice and almost repellent to men in your manners, never seeming to care for one of them save as things to dance with—but they admired you and I think were piqued for they came back and hovered about but got less than nothing for their pains."
Dorothy as a young woman.

Edward with his oldest sister Alice and middle sister Jane, about 1880.

"I never saw a perfect marriage before." (Miss Soulsby to her mother, after visiting Fallodon, 1899.) Dorothy and Edward, about 1885.

"It took people's breath away when they entered a room side-by-side."
Edward and Dorothy, not long after their marriage.

"Ultra-virginal." Dorothy about 1887, after two years of marriage

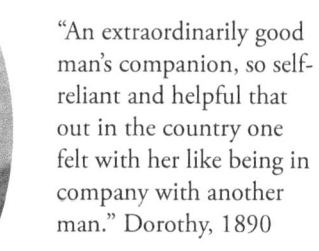

"An extraordinarily good man's companion, so self-reliant and helpful that out in the country one felt with her like being in company with another man." Dorothy, 1890

"Not unto us, O Lord,
Not unto us the rapture of the day."
Pamela about the time of her
ill-fated relationship with
Harry Cust.

"I am afraid she is rather
losing her look of distinction."
Pamela, about two years
before her marriage to
Edward.

"I have been leading a life that does violence to all my natural feelings and I'm broken in spirit and temper: but perhaps I shall recover after a few weeks out of office." The Foreign Secretary.

"The spring sun shone full on the rich plumage of the three mandarin drakes as they stood motionless as though on guard, on the statesman's head and one on either side of him. They were without fear or uneasiness, and one of the drakes actually closed his eyes and dozed for a brief space." Viscount Grey and ducks, 1932.

"Are there many people who like any one place as much as I like Cottage, Fallodon, and Rosehall?" Fallodon before 1917.

"Dear Cottage, with its happiness and peace
And quiet breathing leisure, sweetly spent
Far from all ugliness and tiresome show
A place for watching nature's still increase,
A refuge from all hurt till life shall end,
A nest where love and wisdom still may grow."

"You have your children round your knee." Katharine with her daughters, Hilda, Hermione, and Lucy, about 1895.

Hilda, Hermione, and Lucy, about 1897.

"When I got home last night I found my spectacles had come, so I put on a pair and read the daughter's lines on the Abbey. I like them very much indeed. It is a fine thing to have a daughter who is going about with such thoughts in her head and can express them like that… Do tell her I like this Abbey piece really much; it's stately, like the Abbey."
Lucy, "Auburn," about 1900.

"It really isn't safe for Hilda when a simple innocent like me is highly wrought by the *Waldstein Sonata* to say she is playing it badly. What is that to one who has never heard it played at all except as she plays it? The danger is that out of gratitude and loyalty to Hilda…I might rush at whatever said the playing was bad and shake it, till it unsaid it: and what confusion and fuss that would make in your Eaton Square drawing room!"
"The Fair One," about 1900.

"I hoped that Hermione had been Damed. Dame Hermione of the British Empire! How grand that would sound! But titles don't matter: she is splendid as plain Hermione."
"The Rascal," about 1915

"It does me good to see Neville in these troublesome times. He is so unworried."
The Paterfamilis, about 1897.

"I am glad you are feeling young and well and I am sure you are looking it. (This isn't quite my usual style I think, but no matter.)"
Katharine, late 1890s.

Post Office, Rosehall, N.B.
18 April 1908

This isn't a good place for writing in. I go out after breakfast
and when I come in in the afternoon a huge pouch of papers has
arrived from the F.O. and they last me more or less till bedtime. I
have been much taken up with recollections; the place is so familiar and it is so strange to be here alone; but I prefer the pain of
these things to any other pleasure now: it is a means of keeping in
touch. There is too little water and no fish in the river, but I don't
bother about that. I had a good walk yesterday over the moor
and saw the lovely hills; isn't that line "the sleep that is among the
lonely hills" most restful?[1]

Of course your Charlie Masterman is right to take office.[2]
There are two common ways of failing in politics—one is to be
an idealist, not in touch with the practical side, always advocating the impossible, never getting anything done—like an over
keen soldier firing all his ammunition at something out of range.
Another way is to lose all ideas, to be an opportunist—a place-
hunter out of office and a drudge in office. Your C. M. runs no
risk of the second failure, but he might of the first, and office will
help him to avoid [this]. What is wanted in politics is an idealist
who can estimate rightly the limits of what is possible in his own
generation. Or to put the thing from another point of view: C.
M. has got a gift of speech and writing with which he can educate
the public: a few years of office will give him an education and
insight and correct judgment, which he can get in no other way:
it won't impair his gift but it will add wisdom. So I am sure he was
right to take it. And he doesn't risk failure as if he was at the head
of the office. If there is a failure, it is all put down to the head. All

---

1 From "Song of the Feast of Brougham Castle" by William Wordsworth. The stanza runs: "Love
had he found in huts where poor men lie;/His daily teachers had been woods and rills, /The silence
that is in the starry sky,/The sleep that is among the lonely hills."
2 Masterman had been offered the position of Parliamentary Under-Secretary of the Local Government Board, serving under John Burns.

this is on the assumption that C. M. wants to continue in the H. of C. and not be a Ruskin or Carlyle outside it—a great writer who preaches and tells mankind what they should feel—that is another and a different career; the H. of C. is mainly a place for settling what should be done.

I have come across two things in a book which I will tell you as they are in my mind—"to love anything sincerely is an act of grace, but to love the best sincerely is a state of grace" and this: "St. Peter denied our Lord, but it was reserved for M. Renan to patronize Him."[1]

I leave here on Saturday and go on Sunday afternoon the 26th to stay with the Pauls at Cherry Orchard for two nights: Mrs. Paul is quite convalescent and made steady progress every day since she came home.

P.S. It is very natural that you should feel "attendrissements"[2] at having finished a chapter of life as you have just done; for me life is now a thing to be got through, but you haven't come to that yet and perhaps never may.

Rosehall, N.B.[3]
21 April 1908

The enclosed is evidently a reminiscence of last year.

It was very nice of you to say that my presence was fortifying: I really feel that it is much more I who need fortifying, but it does fortify to have that sort of thing said to one.

This is not a good place for writing letters. I go out in the morning and at 3:30 comes my F.O. work and when that is done I don't feel inclined to write more.

---

1 Ernest Renan (1823–1892), philologist, philosopher, and historian, best known in Britain for his controversial *Life of Jesus,* in which Christ is treated as an historical figure.
2 moved
3 a small village in Sutherland at the confluence of the rivers Cassley and Oykel

I shall look forward to your coming in May and will keep the last half free for you—that is to say I will keep the rooms free—I wish I could keep myself free.

3 Queen Anne's Gate
29 April 1908

You said 15th to end of May originally and in consequence I told McGonigle[1] I could put him up before the 15th; but he will go on the 11th (a Monday) and I can take you, Auburn and a maid on the 11th till whatever date you like. Please let me know for certain and then I can keep the rest of the world away. I shall very much like you to come.

There is a lot I should like to say but I have fallen into arrears and have begun my day by going to the wrong station at 9 o'clock to see Clemenceau off—thereby endangering the Entente and annoying myself.

3 Queen Anne's Gate
1 May 1908

This is all right and I am quite pleased I was originally keeping till the end of May for you and it is still free: so you can play with all that margin after the 20th. I shall be amused if Auburn is married from this house.

3 Queen Anne's Gate
8 May 1908

I am looking forward very much to your coming, but once here you must act as mistress of the house and ask who you like to come here and give orders about luncheon and dinner as you please, for I have a desperate three weeks ahead of me and I

---

1 W. A. McGonigle, vicar of Ellingham, near Fallodon. A friend of the Greys, he identified Dorothy after the accident and conducted her funeral.

believe I haven't one evening except weekends free from official dinners and functions to which I must go out every night. Even the weekends are clipped so that I can never get to my Cottage till Saturday evening. The house is therefore at your disposal altogether, but I am feeling very grim.[1]

24 May 1908

I am very glad that you stayed at No. 3; it was a pleasure to me though we were both so busy. I hope Auburn is well again. I had such a funny evening on Thursday at the Dudleys[2] where I dined with the King and Queen. After dinner something called Maud Allan[3] came and danced. Pretty movements, but very childish; I suppose it was meant to represent the artless innocence of a child and if that is what makes it popular, the world is a very innocent place. But I am told that at the music hall she is very diaphanous and dances with John the Baptist's head.

What amused me was that John Morley and I were looking at it together; such a thing for him to be asked to see: I laughed to see him there. Office does bring one into funny situations.

I have got a liver attack—it came on suddenly yesterday evening and there are four state banquets ahead of me: but they will be over before your wedding is. I wish you well though: you are very gallant and touching.

---

1 Campbell Bannerman resigned on April 3 and Asquith kissed hands at Biarritz five days later. Churchill became Home Secretary and Lloyd George Chancellor of the Exchequer, and both were determined to cut military spending. Preparations were being made for a visit of King Edward to the Czar and there was some pressure on Grey to accompany him. He faced mounting criticism about the Entente with Russia, particularly over Macedonia, still the most pressing foreign policy question.
2 William Humble Ward, second earl of Dudley, (1867–1932) and his wife Rachel. He had served as lord lieutenant of Ireland and would be appointed governor-general of Australia later in the year, at the King's urging.
3 Canadian pianist-turned-dancer Maud Allan (1873–1956) was at the height of her fame in 1908, her "Vision of Salome" being performed over 200 times. She herself designed her risqué costume and choreographed the dance.

P.S. My room is chock full of lilac and lilies of the valley and so sweet that I can't bear to pollute it with tobacco. Your Domenici[1] that was brought me from Italy stands between hawthorne flowers and lilies of the valley—rather a chaste setting for him.

3 June 1908

I am to be harried in the House about sugar this afternoon and worried about Russia tomorrow. I have probably got to see a sister about her affairs before I can get away and I must have interviews with various people before they start for Russia. I fear it is no good my trying to make a time to see you. I go to the Cottage Friday as soon as I can get off—it ought to have been Thursday but they have killed that.[2]

Well, I thought of you and your Auburn yesterday with prayers and good wishes.[3]

P.S. I shall be in town Wednesday and Thursday next week—is that any good?

3 Queen Anne's Gate
24 June 1908

I just return this.

I read Herbert's[4] article and like it and wrote to him about it and he is coming to lunch here next week.

I haven't time at this moment to write, but I will make a better letter soon.

I am amused that soldiers always seem to surprise you a little as if you were still just encountering them for the first time. Be blessed.

---

1 A painting by the Neapolitan landscape and genre painter Bernardo de' Dominici (1683–1759).
2 King Edward was to meet the Czar at Reval on June 9. Questions were again raised in Cabinet about Hardinge rather than Grey accompanying the king, and in Parliament about the visit itself.
3 Lucy Lyttelton and Charlie Masterman were married on June 2.
4 Herbert Paul

3 July 1908

Your Auburn and her husband dined with me the other night. She looks very well and happy and launched. They have at present only one latch key for their house, but no doubt they will get more in time. John Burns' illness has given him (C. M.) a good start in office, but I haven't been able to hear his speeches. Nor have I heard or read properly J. M.'s speech, but I gather it was good and he seemed pleased at the Cabinet next day, which is the only time when I have seen him for weeks. Curzon's speech was I gather as unwise and mischievous as it could be: he is a fine speaker but has no power of reticence and the defects of his qualities run to such excess as to destroy the good of them.[1]

I feel I can't tell you any of the things you would like to know because I do not know them myself. Would you like to hear that last week I went to the Horticultural Garden at Wisley with Mildred Buxton and Pamela Tennant? We went to see flowers and incidentally found a great spotted woodpecker's nest and saw both the old birds and heard the clamour of the young. There has been no such surprise since Saul went out to look for his father's asses and found a kingdom.[2]

I don't much believe in your A.D.C. being fond of birds and expect you were a little premature in showing him bird bits in the Memoir.[3] You always have to discount 85% of interest which any man appears to take in any subject in which he finds a woman sympathetic; at any rate if she is [three words crossed out] one on whom he wishes to make a good impression and I suppose every A.D.C. wishes to make a good impression on the wife of his commanding officer. It isn't very nice of me to have written this, but it is too much to scratch out and I really wrote it because I was amused and not displeased. I fear I am grumbling too much just

---

1 Curzon had again attacked the Anglo-Russian Convention, which he believed conceded too much to St. Petersburg.
2 1 Samuel 9:3–10:14
3 *Dorothy Grey*

now: I infer it because I got a sort of reproof from dear Birrell in his good humoured breezy way the other day. But one does work better if one can blow off a little steam; otherwise one might burst.

You ask me what I read. I am reading *Crossriggs* by the Findlaters and that's all. It is good—there is one woman well done in it and very alive. The man she is in love with and who is in love with her is shadowy and you have to take him on trust without feeling him. He has the misfortune to be married already; but he and the girl are both very proper. Once he nearly kisses her behind a hedge, but she stops him by saying "You will never forgive yourself if you do and I shall never forgive myself either," and you feel it's true of them. On the other hand, she does get kissed against her will by a very young man with whom she is not in love, but who is so much in love with her, that when he can't get her, he lets himself be caught by a girl who marries him because she has begun a baby by someone else. He finds out the full horror of his wife afterwards and drowns himself with the photograph of the kissed and loved girl in his hand. It's a shame of me to write in this bald way about the book: one can make any book seem ridiculous by treating it unfairly. But do read it; the hard grind of poverty, and the general hardship of life and yet all the while the possibilities of life and happiness which a little change might bring within reach—you are made to feel how real all this is.

Itchen Abbas
12 July 1908

You write very nice causing letters. Isn't there some French word like "causer" meaning to talk easily? It's this that I am after in inventing the epithet "causing." What a funny garden it must be in a tiny fence with a road round it. Is it like this?[1] And who

---

1 Grey drew on the bottom of the first page a map of the circular garden, with a thick road running round it and a little figure labeled "K.L." in the middle.

drives round and round the road that goes round the fence that goes round the garden?

So you read the Times hungrily from cover to cover? You are so much more suited to be a Cabinet Minister than I am. I am now as I was when I read for some Oxford exam in the vicarage at Embleton and got restless when I saw the gardener wheeling the wheelbarrow outside and wanted to change my work for his, having all my young affections out of doors. Some day when there is a storm and you are all hugging your homes and reading your Timeses, I shall take to the road and be no more seen and wander till I cease upon the midnight somewhere in the open air.[1]

Today I have had a long bicycle ride. A letter came from Barton telling me of his illness and I remembered that once, I should think about 1903 or 1904, I was trailing Dorothy and we came to a place called on the map Barton copse and we fell to talking of Barton and trying to plan how he might be got something in which he could marry his girl. So today I thought again of Barton copse and because I had had a letter from him I bicycled to it again. I had only seen it once before, that one time when Dorothy and I came to it. I am getting into a habit here of just re-living or trying to. This has been a good week end—I came on Thursday evening and I am much refreshed. It is a wonderful out of the world place and very beautiful.

As you tell me that J. B. Robinson has been made a baronet I suppose it is so—I do remember vaguely having heard two years ago that it was promised to him, and I expect Asquith inherited the promise.[2]

If I were Prime Minister I should not make any positively disgusting honours, but then my govt. would not last for more than

---

1 The passage references Wordsworth's "I Wandered Lonely as a Cloud" and Keats' "Ode to a Nightingale."

2 Joseph Benjamin Robinson (1840–1929) was a less than scrupulous South African mine owner. When he was awarded an earldom by Lloyd George in 1922 for additional contributions to the Liberal party coffers, this precipitated the "honours scandal" that contributed to the withdrawal of Conservative support from the P.M.

six months; and as for you, you would wreck your govt. by excess of virtue in even less time.

I remember Lindley at Winchester; he was older than me and I think his initials were J. E.; his younger brother (who I think was higher up in the school than he) was my contemporary and we sat next to each other in Riding's division. He was called "Tubby," but I didn't know J. E. enough to know if he had a nickname. However J. E. is a general and poor clever Tubby is I fear only a county court judge or something small.

Of course if your A.D.C. liked my book he must be a little bit of all right. (I am trying to use phrases that I imagine suitable to A.D.C.s) and there is no more to be said.

Certainly I shall be in London for the week of the 20th. Let me know the days you will be in London; we are being hustled to finish the Session, but I will give you the best free time I have. Would you like to come to no 3 Q.A.G.? I shall have room for you and Neville or a chaperone.

P.S. Barton's letter to me is dated July 8 and he has had a horrid relapse and great internal discomfort—he is now better again and has booked a passage to Zanzibar on Aug. 15, but if I wasn't so tied I think I should run over to Copenhagen to see him. He should however be soon back in England, but he must be horridly pulled down. I do hope he will have a very good next life with plenty of health and money and a beautiful marriage.

3 Queen Anne's Gate
15 July 1908

Alas! the 29th is too late—on that day the last of the servants go to get Fallodon ready for me—caretakers come in here and I go to stay with Haldane opposite. But if you are in London I will come to see you.

I am glad my letter made you laugh—it is very satisfactory to make people laugh.

Everyone tells me that Charlie Masterman made a fine speech on old age pensions last week. I had played truant to my cottage and so didn't hear it.

I lunched with the Pauls on Monday—I am afraid he gets on but slowly, but he has begun to write for the Times Literary Supplement again. He wrote the article in it on J.M.'s book the other day.

3 Queen Anne's Gate
24 July 1908

I expect I can be in today by 6 til 7:30 and you might come to see me then, if you have any margin of time left in this day.

Tonight I have to propose the King's health at an official dinner to the Olympic Games:[1] I think perhaps you might suggest an appropriate phrase or two—my mind is a blank and yours is always fresh.

Fallodon
2 August 1908

Barton came back and I saw him just before I left on Friday. He has married a Danish girl, about 19, he tells me. He didn't know her before he went to Copenhagen two months ago. He gave me a very straight simple account of it; I am sure she is nice, but I only saw him at the F.O. and had no time to see her.

Do you know the grass hill near the drive from which one sees Bamburgh and the sunset and the Cheviots? I lay out there for a long time after supper this evening: it is something to be out above the trees and under the sky.

---

1 The 1908 Games were held at the newly built White City Stadium outside London, after Italy withdrew as host following the eruption of Mt. Vesuvius. They lasted from April 27 to October 31.

Fallodon
14 August 1908

These are very good letters from Dorothy and I should like to talk about them. There is that about her letters which gives a feeling that she is living still and that is comforting. It seems incredible to me as I walk about this place and sit here that I should be living without her; sometimes the feeling is borne in upon me like a conviction that either she must come back to me soon or I must go to her. The thought that carries me on is that in the long run it will turn out that time is not real and does not matter, and that even if I live 40 years more it will at the end seem nothing, though I may have gained something by which it will endure.

I had totally forgotten my letters to you—if you had read one out to me I should have asked whose it was. I did like my friends even in those days, but when I was here with Dorothy the coming of friends might always seem like the interruption of a honeymoon. So you must just forgive that. Anyhow I like their coming now, though I like too to have some days alone, when the companionship of memory can be very close.

Today I bicycled to the Widdringtons and lunched and stayed the afternoon.[1]

I think I gave pleasure there. Mrs. Widdrington goes on talking as if only the bad in the world were real. "It should be dreadful if there were another life besides this" and so forth. It's a piteous thing to see anyone who has missed all happiness in life. She goes on doing good things, living a most patient life with her blind husband, and saying perverse things. As if she had a sort of feeling that she must undo the good that she does, for fear it should

---

1 Shalcross Fitzherbert "Fitz" (1826–1917) and Cecilia Widdrington (1840–1936) were Dorothy's parents. Newton Hall, the family home, was just sixteen miles from Fallodon. But Dorothy didn't get along with her parents and never saw them, and this is Grey's only reference to them in any surviving letter. Despite the estrangement from her daughter, Cecilia Widdrington was fond of her son-in-law; she was the only person who called him "Ed."

be proved that there was something good in a world which she insists is all bad.

I have told my gardener to make a list of stuff that could be sent you.

Turkey is being very interesting: I am more interested in that than in anything that has happened while I have been in office. The change in Turkey is pregnant with consequences.[1] Does this expression shock you?

Fallodon
8 September 1908

I have just come back from London; I spent two nights and a Sunday with J. M. at Wimbledon. He had a very light tweed suit; I told him it was the most holiday-looking suit I ever saw: it was a very nice soft suit, much better than my stiff dark thing and he looked very light-hearted in it. He said it was made by Pool. It was very good to be with a mind which has voyaged so far and long through seas of thought and I enjoyed it; fearing, however, that [all] the while that I could not be an adequate companion. We talked about the many clouds in the political sky, and he was sometimes thoughtful, sometimes grim, but often breaking into those gleams of humour, when his expression is so delightful: his wreathed expression I call it, if you know what I mean by that. I feel quite proud whenever I tell him anything that makes him light up and laugh. We talked of books and got taking down volumes to show each other passages, so that by the evening the great

---

1 The old Ottoman Constitution was restored on July 24, 1908, when the 3rd Army marched into Constantinople from Macedonia and met no resistance. The Sultan was not deposed until the following April, but was forced to appoint members of the Committee of Union and Progress to positions of power. The Constitution was liberal, but the C.U.P. was not. Its leaders were nationalists who wanted a stronger Turkey, and had no more intention of granting rights to Armenians, Greeks, and Jews in Anatolia than of liberalizing the Empire's rule over Christians in the Balkans. Grey was hardly the only Liberal to be overly sanguine about the events of July. Christian and Jewish minorities in Turkey had also welcomed the revolution.

library was littered with some loose volumes lying about, which is always a good sign.

Jusserand[1] and his wife dined in Saturday and Jusserand was very lively and amusing. He speaks very perfect English with a very foreign accent and imperfect pronunciation.

Haldane came to dine, fresh from what he called plain living and high thinking with the Marmers at some charming place in Styria.[2]

I saw the wife of the wretched Ayling[3] —a nice straight-looking woman and three of their children, little happy light soft-dressed girls, all unconscious of the clouded father. It was pathetic.

There is family here—my eldest sister and her two boys for a week. My brother Charlie also makes it his home and has his own motor car and is his own chauffeur which saves me from hiring. He is very sound and competent and I respect him: he is now I think cured. He urged me to fish the Coquet with him, and one day I made an effort and arranged my work so as to get time to go. We caught nothing as there has been no flood since last winter! but I had my waders on again for the first time in 3 ½ years, and stood with the water lapping round me and I shared the brother's keenness. We are both keen about fishing in the same way and are neither of us jealous of each other, so that we would like fishing together very well, if it wasn't for my office.

The Salisburys have been at Howick Rectory and I went to two picnics with them; she is excellent company, but I am afraid she doesn't get left alone much. There was a large gregarious Cecil tea at Dunstanburgh; the Salisburys and children; Robert Cecil, and I think a child of his, Hugh Cecil, Lady Selborne and a son,

---

1 Jean Jules Jusserand (1855–1932), historian and diplomat, served as French Ambassador to the U.S. from 1902 to 1925.
2 An Austria province, now in the southeast of the country, bordering Slovenia.
3 John Ayling (b. 1859 or 1860), Morley's stepson, was convicted in November 1907 of forging the signature of Morley and others on several promissory notes, totaling 13,350 pounds.

the Howicks and perhaps some more that I have forgotten.[1] It came on to drizzle rain with a cold wind; Hugh Cecil had no coat but got Lady Selborne's black mackintosh and put it on and it being too wet to sit down, he stood apart, hopelessly exposed and looking like a much-enduring Simon Stylites. The rest of us men threw stones at a bottle tossing in the waves and failed to hit it and the women collected stones for us to throw, and Lady Salisbury's humour never failed and we all enjoyed ourselves except I think poor Hugh.

I took down my fishing book[2] the other day and failed to recognize most of what I had written as being mine; just as with the letters to you. By the way don't think I was at all surprised at finding I had written those letters: you were always much liked and rather chivalrously felt about and I do remember being stirred when Neville began to be let in for great risky things and we knew how high your spirit and courage would be in spite of anxieties.

Fallodon
1 October 1908

Mrs. Creighton and my sister both want to know if I can take them in for a night or two in the week of the 12th or the next one. Please let me know your dates, as nothing should interfere with your visit and other people shall be kept off for the days you want my rooms: otherwise I should not see you till goodness knows when and the others I have seen lately at Fallodon.

---

1 James Gascoyne-Cecil (1861–1947), 4th Marquess of Salisbury. His wife was the former Lady Cecily Gore. Robert Cecil (1864–1958) would go on to serve as Grey's Parliamentary Under-Secretary and eventually win the Nobel Peace Prize for his work on behalf of the League of Nations. Grey's Winchester friend William Palmer, Lord Selborne, had married Lady Beatrix (Maud) Cecil (1858–1956) in 1883. She would become one of Grey's confidantes. Hugh Cecil (1869–1956) was the youngest and most conservative of Salisbury's children. The Howicks were the family of Charles Grey, the son of the 4th Earl.
2 *Fly Fishing*, 1899

I have had a really nice stay at Balmoral and like it: I fished, drank excellent wine, played bridge, did my work in comfort and was generally petted by the King and everybody.

6 October 1908

You and Neville can come on the 12th, but will you dine out that night as I have a business dinner at 3 Q.A.G. that evening with Benckendorff and Isvolsky the Russian Foreign Minister?[1]

3 Queen Anne's Gate
27 October 1908

Dear Katharine Courageous
(This epithet because of your independence of chaperones)
Probably you won't have time to look in to say goodbye but in case you have, this is to say that you could share my supper tonight or tomorrow up to 9:45 p.m. when I go back to H. of C. All tomorrow otherwise is filled up, but on Thursday morning I am free.

Don't trouble to answer unless you can come: I only write on the off chance.

I was up till after 2 a.m. last night at the House and found incidentally in the day that I had hurt the feelings lately of two different friends—not the most intimate friends happily—but I think if one stayed long enough in office one would lose most of one's friends. "I have lost a friend and gained an acquaintance" as the cantankerous Whistler said.

---

1 Alexander Petrovich Izvolsky (1856–1919) had been named Foreign Minister in April 1906. Like his friend Benckendorff (who called him "Mack"), he was a constitutionalist and had worked hard to bring about the Anglo-Russian agreement of August 1907.

On September 15, 1908, at a meeting with his Austrian counterpart Alois Aehrenthal, Izvolsky had agreed to support Austrian annexation of Bosnia-Herzegovina in exchange for Austrian support for the opening of the Straits to Russian warships. On the morning of Grey's letter, October 6, Vienna announced the annexation of Bosnia-Herzegovina, twenty-four hours after Bulgaria, in collusion with the Ballhausplatz, had unilaterally declared its independence. Izvolsky had understood that both would occur only after a conference of the signatories of the Treaty of Berlin.

Itchen Abbas
8 November 1908

I don't know how to write about these love matters. Love is a secret between the two people for whom it comes and too sacred and wonderful and mysterious for third persons to touch. It is like the making of a soul. You must just take a broad view and feel that with a good man, and there be real liking on the woman's part to begin with, things cannot go far wrong—whether or not it is to be the very best possible for her no one can tell; the possibilities of each marriage are different; some that have the greatest possibilities have also the greatest risk of failure and catastrophe. I should never dare to make a marriage between two people of whom I thought well, nor should I dare to interfere with one; any more than I would dare to decide about a new soul whether it had better be born or not. You must let God settle these things.

I am touched by what you say about A. G.[1]: it seems full of simplicity and strength and humility; approaching the woman he loves with reverence and honesty; and his having struggled against the new love because of the old and having the honesty to say so reveals a true heart.[2]

I still feel that for a young girl with all love and life before her I would like her first love to meet a first love. On the other hand I do know now that till one has loved and suffered a separation one knows only part of what love can be. I have so much more in me to give, so much more knowledge of all that there can be in love than I had at first; so much more than I had even three years ago. I could to another woman now give more kindness, more patience, more understanding; more unselfish sympathy than ever before;

---

1 Arthur Grenfell (1873–1958)
2 Grenfell had been married to Lady Victoria Grey, daughter of Albert, the 4th earl. She died in 1906, leaving him with three small children. He had just proposed to Hilda Lyttelton, whom he married the following year. A free-wheeling banker and speculator whose fortunes waxed and waned, he was over a million pounds in debt in August 1914 and declared bankruptcy. Grey family members had invested considerable amounts with him.

only I couldn't give the love to anyone but Dorothy. There is more to give than ever before, but to no one but her could I give it all; I give some things to friends and take all gratefully that they can give to me, but only in such a way that if Dorothy came again I could give all to her with undivided love.

But A. G. is younger and marriage is different with everybody. I feel he must have more to give than ever he had yet; and if having loved once he can give all that he has gained by sorrow and the love as well to someone else, I can only say that these things are mysteries and that with God all things are possible and that it is not for us to say what shall be possible for God's creatures and what not.

I am having my last Sunday before Cottage is shut up for the winter. The lawn is covered with what Dorothy called the "lovely cream coloured carpet" of fallen lime leaves—a thick carpet of them so that no grass can be seen. There is bright sun and autumn haze but a wintery wind, and my bedroom windows were glazed inside with ice this morning. There was a full moon last night and I walked out from Winchester under it. That was very refreshing after a hard week in London shut up in rooms.

The leaves turned very suddenly this year—all in one week, the week in which the German Emperor published his interview[1]— it was as if that had turned the leaves. I am very tired of the Emperor—he is like a great battleship with steam up and screws

---

1 in the pro-German *Daily Telegraph* on 28 October 1908. It was arranged by the Kaiser's friend Edwin James Montagu Stuart-Wortley, Katharine's second cousin, with whom Wilhelm had spent over three weeks hunting in Hampshire. The Kaiser resented that his feelings of goodwill toward Britain were not appreciated. In the interview Wilhelm observed that while most Germans were hostile to England, he was an exception. Indeed, he had rejected approaches of France and Russia to assist the Boer republics and had gone so far as to send Queen Victoria a battle plan for the war, which "by a curious coincidence, was very much on the same lines as that which was actually adopted by Lord Roberts." The fleet, he claimed, was not being built against England but merely to safeguard German commerce. The Kaiser expressed himself with his usual tact: "You English are mad, mad, mad as March hares. What has come over you that you are so completely given over to suspicions unworthy of a great nation?" (A still more inflammatory interview with an American journalist was suppressed the following month.) The article provoked derision in Britain, but widespread outrage in Germany. Bülow had approved a draft of the interview, though he denied it in the Reichstag, and the affair led to his dismissal.

going, but no rudder, and you cannot tell what he will run into or what catastrophe he will cause.[1]

Anyhow, the country with the biggest army in the world has been made a fool of in public by its own Emperor and that is an uncomfortable thing, for the country fooled and laughed at will seek some object on which to vent its ill temper and its strength. I am glad we are an island.

I don't know who the interviewer of the Emperor was—some dummy I suppose whom he ordered to draw it up, but it was the Emperor who settled it should be published. So you may dismiss the handsome cousin-once-removed from the question.[2]

All you say of Mrs. Jack Tennant is good and true—you know that as I should only have been able to go for a week to the Beauly and the little lodge in it which before office came we had taken for all April 1906, Dorothy decided after office came that she would ask Mrs. Jack Tennant to stay at the lodge alone with her to fish when I could not be there. I told the Jack Tennants afterward.[3]

I am writing to Henderson about garden things, but I expect he thinks they are not ready yet.

P.S. I do sympathize with your fear of losing Hilda if it wasn't for the thought that parents ought to want their daughters to love and marry. I should have liked now to have a daughter—very much attached to me, her father, whom I should not let marry at all. But one can't own children after they grow up. You will soon

---

1 Earlier in the year, in February, the Kaiser had written to Lord Tweedmouth, First Lord of the Admiralty, in a similar vein. This was a serious breach of diplomacy: foreign heads of state did not communicate directly with the ministers of another sovereign. Tweedmouth, with Grey's approval, replied with a brief letter, but enclosed the naval budget, which had not yet been presented to Parliament. This created a furor when the *Times* disclosed the exchange.
2 Montagu Stuart-Wortley
3 Harold John Tennant, M.P. (1865–1935) was the Prime Minister's brother-in-law and private secretary. He joined the Cabinet in 1909 as Parliamentary Secretary to the Board of Trade, and held other posts. Mrs. Tennant, May Abraham (1869–1946), was one of the first women factory inspectors and wrote on factory legislation. She was asked to sit on a royal commission investigating the divorce laws, scandalizing King Edward. The rose garden of the Tennants' home in Kent was immortalized in Frances Hodgson Burnett's *The Secret Garden*.

have the third (who I am sure ought to come out next year in spite of what you say about her age) as a companion.

3 Queen Anne's Gate
4 December 1908

I am sure it is good true love on both sides so that is all right. I won't write yet as you say that perhaps it is better not, and there is nothing to say except that one is glad and wishes happiness. I wondered when you said you had showed my last letter to Hilda, whether she shrank at all from knowing that her affairs were thought about. I don't say "talked about," because that I should never do. But I think quite reverently and kindly, so it needn't be minded.

As the wedding cannot be just yet you must have the wrench of being left for some time: you will want some consoling after it is over.

My servants will probably go to Fallodon on the 18th to prepare a place for me, but if you let me know in good time I could put you and Hilda or Neville up on the 14th, 15th, or 16th. I say "in good time" because this house is getting popular. I have had the E. Tennants and the Munro Fergusons[1] in different weeks since you were here and have enjoyed their being here though I see little of any guests except at breakfast. It has been rather a sad week this time for I have had Herbert Paul staying, partly as a change to try, if it would do good, and partly to give him a refuge from the noise of workmen who are pulling down the house in Tite Street next to his. He has made some progress, but it is only at intervals that the heavy cloud which broods over him seems to lift. Mrs. Paul isn't very well. Humphrey and Beatrix seem to be

---

1 Ronald Munro Ferguson (1860–1934), from 1920 Viscount Novar, was a colleague and friend of Grey, Haldane, and Asquith. The staunchest imperialist of the Limps, he was the closest to Rosebery, and served as his private secretary in 1886 and 1892–4. Campbell Bannerman excluded him from his Cabinet, and Asquith eventually appointed him Governor-General of Australia. His wife was Lady Helena Hamilton-Temple-Blackwood (1863–1941).

excellent through it all that I quite love them. But oh! the troubles in the world! I hear Ronald Ferguson is suddenly summoned to America because his brother is very ill.

I alone feel a sense of security because the worst that could happen has happened to me and cannot happen again. I can live as I am and each year draws me nearer to a desired end; and if illness or misfortune is before me it cannot be so bad as for others; for all trouble is comparative and it must be less than I have been through. I am very—I am inclined to say damnably—well. Now and then I get very tired towards the end of a week, but an easier day and two hours extra sleep sets me up again.

I have been amused and interested by a book called "My little boy" by Carl Ewald (translated), though I have never had a little boy.[1] I think I shall send it to you, though you have never had a little boy either.

Did you read a fine dignified Christian letter by that good man the Bishop of Southwark in favour of a settlement about education a fortnight ago in the Times? And did you see that at the Church Council yesterday when he got up to speak they hissed him because of it? A knot of little parsons and clerical laymen. "Budding Beelzebubs" was the name I called them, to the amusement of the man to whom I said it.

It is time that all moderate fair-minded people took big sticks and broke the heads of the extreme people.

I didn't mean to write a long letter when I began. I thought I had no time and writing in my head and didn't want to write; but it is easy to talk to you when once one begins and I have been drawn on by the pleasure of it.

Goodbye now for the present.

---

1 *Mein Kleiner Junge* (1899). Ewald (1856–1908) was a Danish novelist.

28 Queen Anne's Gate
25 January 1909

You might like to see this. I am going to write to Freeman
Thomas to ask him to let me have any news he gets of the Norman
boy.[1]

When you return Mrs. Fitzgerald's letter please tell me if you
can what the word in the address which looks like "Mbout" really
is.

I shall be here till Wednesday night then at Fallodon till
Monday; then back here.

Both brothers have been with me at Fallodon—they are now
south but go back there with me this week. We get on very well—
the talk is a good deal about fishing and motor cars with occasional comments upon life or people and a good deal of chaff of
each other and I win their money at bridge in the evening.

For a few hours each day I withdraw into the library and do
my work and think about other days.

I am now being braced by Haldane for the Session and Cabinet
councils.

P.S. I think often with sadness of your being soon to be bereft
of Hilda; but I know your chivalry will find compensation in her
happiness.

3 Queen Anne's Gate
15 February 1909

I have just opened the wedding invitation with your pleading
"do write soon, K.L." upon it. It's like the cry of a drowning thing
and you've got to let the waters go over your head. I know you

---

1 Freeman Freeman-Thomas, 1st Marquess of Willington (1866–1941). Eventually Governor-General of Canada and Viceroy of India, he wasat this time an MP serving as one of Asquith's
private secretaries. The Norman boy may be Henry Nigel Norman, son of the journalist and M.P.
Sir Henry Morgan and Ménie Muriel Dowie, novelist and travel writer. The parents were divorced.
Norman, then 11, went on to have a distinguished career with the R.A.F.

141

are going to be very brave about it. You have got chivalry, which I suppose means braveness and kindness; at any rate you have those two things in a special degree and they will carry you through everything. I do see what it must mean to you to be severed from Hilda, just as she has grown up and you know the wonderousness of her and I quite understand that you want to marry her your-self, but that can't be for many reasons—age amongst others. You seem very young to me, but she must join her life to someone younger; and because of the mysterious way the world is made it must be a man. I'm afraid this isn't consoling: shall I fall back on the stuffy things such as finding consolation in her happiness and so forth? I think she is going to be happy and I want to send a wedding present. I have been looking in a weary dilettante way into the windows of jewellers' shops, but the things seem all alike and she isn't alike. I did in an upstairs place—had proved to have a shop window—the sort of shop that pretends to be a first floor drawing room having a small at home—find a small green jade box with a plain gold rim, which I loved. Its price was 19 pounds -10 s-0 d and I wanted to buy it for her, but George said it looked as if it was really worth 10 s/- and I didn't think it looked as if it cost more than 15/- and George put me off it. And now Charlie Masterman, whom I have just seen in uniform, says that Hilda won't have anything but books, so I shall send books. But what books? I wish you would send me a telegram to say.

There's a lot to tell you about myself, but it's too long to write—it's all internal things, what I felt at Fallodon as my third anniversary went over me, so you won't see any of it in the news-papers—however it isn't relevant to your present affairs. We have also stern things to deal with politically.[1] I am quite clear as to my line and am being firm and conciliatory both together in the way that one can only do when one is very clear and resolute.

P.S. When the wedding is over, read "Araminta" by Snaith.[2]

3 Queen Anne's Gate
12 March 1909

By all means come on the 28th or 30th—you and kid and maid.

You won't need a chaperone on Sat. to Monday as I am always out of town.

What is "fitful chaperonage"? I'd want an illustration—e.g. would Mrs. Creighton coming to luncheon once a week come up to the definition? The brothers are both gone to Africa—otherwise I might have had one staying here. Would he have been a chaperone?

I expect you will have to suggest your own chaperone to dinner on those days, and when J. M. should be asked.

P.S. I felt very bare after both the brothers went.

---

1 The first Bosnian Crisis, which had begun on October 5, 1908, with Bulgaria's unilateral declaration of independence, followed twenty-four hours later by Austria's annexation of Bosnia and Herzegovina, had reached a critical phase. Grey, troubled by the effect of the twin blows on the new regime in Constantinople, in which he still had high hopes, as well as the breach of international law, had called for a conference of the signatories of the Treaty of Berlin of 1878, as stipulated by that agreement before any alteration in its terms could be made. Austria resisted, backed by Germany. But on 11 January 1909, Turkey agreed to accept compensation from Austria, and Russia appeared ready to bankroll compensation from Bulgaria. Serbia, however, demanded compensation as well, which Vienna refused to consider. (The Serbs wanted access to the coast, so their exports would not be subject to Austrian tariffs and regulations.) When Belgrade proved obdurate, the Austro-Hungarian army was mobilized and a punitive invasion seemed imminent. Germany, after appearing to join in working for a negotiated settlement early in February, abruptly disinterested itself. The following month, Berlin brandished "the mailed fist," delivering a stiff ultimatum to Russia, Serbia's patron, and St. Petersburg backed down.

The most controversial domestic issue was the Budget, introduced in the King's Speech on the day of Grey's letter. In order to fund old age pensions and increased naval spending, the "People's Budget" called for a tax on land and increases in the income tax and other taxes and duties.

2 An arch, Trollopian novel published in 1908 by John Collis Snaith (1876–1936). The eponymous heroine, a simple parson's daughter from Devonshire, is adopted by her elderly aunt, the irascible Countess of Crewkerne, "the sharpest-tongued old woman in London. And the least scrupulous."

26 March 1909

Console yourself by thinking that the debate will be nothing like as fine as the Bach Mass last night.

Fallodon
9 April 1909

Your letter about Cottage book[1] came to Q.A.G. positively just as my cab was at the door and my luggage being put in. I had time however to find and send off the book. I am very glad that you like it in the way you do. It is evident that your maid thought Cottage book was the last hair on the camel's back.

I came here with a heavy cold which however has been beaten by two days of sun and open air and is now nearly gone: but it has taken away my sense of smell: it is sad to press one's nose against Daphne mezereum and smell no more than if it was a begonia. Nevertheless these last two days have been very splendid. I went over the moor to Ross Camp today and lunched and read and slept a little in the heather. I have been reading some of Dorothy's letters to me and mine to her, and feeling how real all that time of happiness was. It makes me very impatient to be gone, but I see the wonderful beauty of the world as it still is and I think of the happiness I have had and do say from my heart "Oh! that men would therefore praise the Lord for His goodness,"[2] for I have had that which is worth being born for, or waiting for; and others may have it all too—the beauty of the world at any rate is for all who have eyes to see and hearts to feel. I shall die grateful for what I have had, whether I die soon or late and whatever happens to me between now and then.

---

1 *The Cottage Book*, a collection of diary entries by Dorothy and Edward between 1894 and 1905, was privately printed in 1909.
2 Psalm 107:8

Itchen Abbas
25 April 1909

Ethel Arnold[1] came to tea with me in London yesterday. She has had a very successful lecturing tour in American and is engaged for another tour of four months next winter. The work has been a great strain, but she has stood it and I thought her mentally and morally in very good case. Her talk was very good— it was that of a first-rate brain and with power in it. I am sorry to say she has one lung a little touched, but she is going to open air it at her Welsh place. I don't know anything about her friends that would have given Dorothy more pleasure than this news of Ethel Arnold and I am very glad therefore.

I have been much upset—it is as if I had a fever, but not one which could be told by the thermometer—or the pulse. I went to Rosehall and had 2 ½ days fishing and one fine Sunday amongst the hills and curlews. On the last day's fishing (Monday) I got nine salmon and had to decide while getting them to give up my holiday and go back to London because the F.O. telegrams were unsatisfactory. I did it, but it was very hard and I tried to get back to Rosehall. On Friday I had ordered my sleeping berth, when there came an uncomfortable telegram from Constantinople and I had to counter-order it and I didn't go and didn't even get to Cottage til midday on Sunday today.[2] It doesn't do in office to let yourself look forward to anything or begin to enjoy it and I have had real disappointment fever. I don't get the rapture out of fishing or anything that I used to. It even made me sad that five spring salmon in one day is better than I ever did and therefore

---

1 Ethel Arnold (1865–1930) was the granddaughter of Thomas, niece of Matthew, and younger sister of the novelist Mrs. Humphry Ward. A reviewer and reporter for the *Manchester Guardian* in the 1890s, she was best known as a lecturer on women's suffrage, and twice toured the U.S.

2 The sultan, Abdul Hamid, who had recognized in July 1908 the new constitution proclaimed by the Young Turks (The Committee of Union and Progress), renounced the decision on April 13. Revolutionary troops again marched on the capital from Salonika. The counter-revolution was marked by massacres of some 30,000 Armenians in Anatolia, killings that continued after the sultan was overthrown. The British Ambassador to Constantinople was Nicholas O'Conor.

better than anything that Dorothy shared with me. But I did like my river and the Scottish country and enjoyed the fishing and am very tired of office and state. There has been never a day of complete holiday now for nearly 3 ½ years and I am not the sort that likes work—all my affections are out of doors.

It is never safe for such as me in office to take off the lid and now I have done it and boiled over and there is a regular mess inside me and it isn't easy to get the lid on again. And yet I don't want to have so much life in me. I am 47 today and wish it was 77.

I read Miss Cholmondeley's "Red Pottage" at Rosehall for the first time.[1] It is a clever book and its cleverness all on the right side—showing up the shams and showing the reals.

I hope Hermione has done measling and that you have good news of Hilda—Auburn I look upon as settled down.

My chile teal has nested and its eggs are to be carefully hatched under a hen and the gardener writes "I have got a nice quiet light hen to sit on them." Aren't these epithets delightful? Are there many people who like any one place as much as I like Cottage, Fallodon, and Rosehall? And oughtn't I to be grateful for the power to like even when there is no present opportunity? And haven't I had more opportunities than most people?

P.S. I ought therefore not to grumble, but the lid is off.

3 Queen Anne's Gate
26 April 1909

We seem to have written to each other in the same day. I dread Punchestown[2] more than I can say for you and for everybody who has feelings and brains—and the balls—terrible! And you tired before they begin! I can't bear to think of it. The 4th is my

---

1 Mary Cholmondeley (1859–1925), the daughter of a Shropshire clergyman, published a number of novels between 1887 and 1921. *Red Pottage* (1899), the most successful, is a story of two girl-friends whose lives diverge. The book satirizes religious hypocrisy and social conventions.
2 A race course and resort in County Kildare, Ireland.

only free evening. I will keep that for Manchester Square on the chance of your being free too. I want to hear Uber allen Gipfeln.[1]

Will you have lunch here on the 5th, 6th, or 7th

16 May 1909

My bicycle has given out and I am waiting to go back ignominiously in a train.

Do you know that I am particularly clumsy at machinery? I have spent 40 minutes trying to mend the puncture in my tyre and the net result is that I have torn the inner tube and have failed to get the outer cover on again. However, there is a train; the same train that Dorothy and I used to go back on from here when we had trailed here and this is the same room in the inn where we used to have tea.

Four bicyclists, young healthy men, came in for tea at the same time. I felt a wretched cripple knowing that they were going to bicycle on and I couldn't because of my inefficiency in repairing punctures; but I was very well disposed toward them for they drank no whisky, just large cups of tea, and ate healthy dollops of bread and butter and jam and cake and their conversation amused me much.

"Pass me one of those mags" was the first thing, "mags" being short for magazine, but at tea the talk developed as thus.

No. 1 "When were clocks first invented? The slow ticking of that clock (a very old clock in the room) makes one think."

No. 2. "I suppose the sun dial was before clocks, but Alfred the Great was the first one to foster the clock."

No. 3 "And a very good foster father he would make—put them in an incubator perhaps." (N.B. this joke failed entirely—not a smile followed)

---

1 *Über allen Gipfeln ist ruh* (Above all the Summits it is Quiet), the second of Goethe's "Wanderer's Nightsongs," set by Schubert.

No. 1. "I have seen a place where they show you all the development of the chicken in the egg from the first stage just as it is in nature."

No. 4. "In Liverpool there is a place where you can see the same thing of a human being."

No. 1. "You mean see how one is born?"

No. 4. "No, the whole thing from the beginning."

This they thought impossible and No. 4 couldn't explain it, but said, "Well, Wilson of our place has been to Liverpool and he's seen it" and in all further difficulties he fell back upon Wilson, ending by saying "Wilson's been there and he reckons it would do any fellow a lot of good to see it—make him understand the consequences of what he might be likely to do."

And the subject ended by No. 1 saying "If you think what a prostitute was before she became one and what she developed into it does make you think."

Then the conversation was changed by No. 3 saying "How pure those narcissuses are!" (There was a glass of poet's narcissuses on the table.) "Yes," said No. 4. "Narcissus and sweet peas are my favorite flowers" and then they talked about various gardens and show places which they had seen and then discussed games and so forth.

This conversation pleased me very much, because it was so healthy minded—there was no prudery, but [sic] never a smile nor an unclean word; just natural healthy minds in healthy bodies—kept healthy probably by the habit of bicycling on Sundays.

They were apparently clerks or shop assistants from Portsmouth—quite common—but where out of England could you have heard 4 common young men talk of such subjects without reproach like that? In America perhaps, but there is more sound material in this country than one knows. I am now finishing this letter at Cottage. I couldn't write with the commercial pens at the Inn and had to borrow the waiter's pencil out of his waistcoat pocket, the stumpiest and dirtiest pencil[1] that ever was seen. This is the outline of it which I traced at the inn. I remembered carefully not to suck it however palely it wrote; it was so dirty.

Altogether this has been an unusual day; it is very unusual for me to have no pencil; the puncturing adventures were unusual. The last Romsey train was 40 minutes late—very unfeeling of a little Sunday train which only has a run of about 30 miles altogether—so that I nearly missed the last connection on the main line. I began to wonder whether I should ever see Cottage again: I might be going to die suddenly or be killed—things seemed to fight so against my return and I was amused to think how they would puzzle over my body with nothing on it to identify me but a strange letter unfinished and unsigned to someone named Katharine.

Are there any orchards near Foxwarren? If so, did you drive about seeing them today? It is apple blossom Sunday and a very fine apple blossom year—a thing not to be missed if you can help it: it doesn't last long and is extraordinarily beautiful.

I am reading an ugly book called "Fraternity" by Galsworthy, but it has power and some searching truth in it. Pages 108 to 110 have a very good analysis of the strength and weakness of political socialists.[2] I wonder if you will be amused or tired by this long letter—the result of enforced idleness at an inn. Now I must do F.O. papers

P.S. I hope you will be amused by some of the phrases of the men. "The first one to foster the clock" is very precious.

---

1 Grey drew after this word an outline of the pencil.
2 *Fraternity* was one of three novels published in 1909 by John Galsworthy (1867–1933). Like *Araminta*, it is a story of artists and their models, and class tensions.

Itchan Abbas
28 May 1909

I came here last night and am looking forward to six days
here—five only now, for one day is over. I want not only rest but
solitude and to have it in a place which is sacred to Dorothy. The
world goes on and gets to seem more and more of a separation
from her.

I like my friends nevertheless and felt quite proud when you
told me that you had laughed over my last letter to you. I was
amused too by your forecast of Hermione scattering dismay by
the free and innocent use of the word "prostitute." But is it really
not safe to let young girls know that there is evil in the world? The
knowledge would never corrupt a girl who was naturally good. Of
course actresses do happen in the best regulated families, but that
is not from knowledge but from inclination or perhaps even from
the want of knowledge. Surely to be told what a prostitute was
and that it was an undesirable thing would not make a girl desire
to be one. However it is perhaps best for you to settle, and I am
not really wishing to alter your opinion.

3 Queen Anne's Gate
28 June 1909

I have for a long time had the intention to write you and am
now much amused by the way you took my remarks upon what
to tell a daughter. I have never had to consider the bringing up of
young people with any direct responsibility and my observations
must be taken as obiter dicta. At what age you ought to cease to
beat about the bush with the gigantic but youthful Hermione
I will not say: but I should think that bush beating prolonged
too far into years of discretion might stimulate aspirations and
artificial curiosity, which would be worse than natural knowledge
cleanly come by. Nevertheless whatever you think or do in such

150

matters I will handsomely admit that it is just possible you may be right.

Barton's Scandinavian wife languished in the climate of Zanzibar and went home for a few weeks. Being sad and lonely in her absence he began to write and I had two letters from him— the first sad because she was away, the second glad because she was returning. It is a very good sign when a man ceases to write after marriage, writes when his wife is away, and then stops when she returns. It means that when she is with him he feels the need of friends less. Both letters were delightful, one telling me two delicious stories and the other suggesting a clock for my wedding present to him "not a large bland-faced thing with loud insistent tick, but a nice gentle lady clock that never goes wrong." Who but Barton could have written that now that Edward Fitzgerald is dead?[1]

I reproached him for not letting me know where his wife could be found, for she was in England for a little. I was sure that you and one or two more of his lady friends would have tried to see her.

I went as usual to lunch and spend the day in the R.H.S. Garden at Wisley on the King's birthday. The usual party of E. Tennants, Mildred Buxton and me. We had tea at Foxwarren and found Hilda looking very nice and quiet. Only Flora Grenfell there, who was apparently painting Hilda while Hilda played to her. I did like seeing her—she looks so beautiful and gentle and so nicely serious and restful. I do hope they let her rest.

I really haven't had time to read anything. "A Room with a View" was the last book: it is very good and so I hear is "The Longest Journey" by the same man—Forster.[2]

At this point I was interrupted and the thread is broken.

---

1 Edward FitzGerald (1809–1883), translator of *The Rubaiyat of Omar Khayyam*.
2 *A Room with a View* was published in fall of 1908, *The Longest Journey* the previous spring.

I am amused at your asking my opinion on the Budget, Duma, Czar and Turks and then ending by saying you don't expect a long letter, only a note.

As to the Czar. The I.L.P.[1] say there were some 800 executions in Russian last year—that is true, but they don't say that there were about 1500 murders and some thousands of terrorist outrages.

The Czar is a kind moral family man, who as an English squire would be much respected in his parish. His direct control over the huge machine of Russian bureaucracy is necessarily slight. He will be remembered as the Czar under whom Russia received a Duma and a Constitution. But we have in this country a number of people who don't want to know the truth as to do good, but to express their own emotions. Dram drinkers, I call them, for they must be in a state of emotion and when you attempt to dilute their emotions with the truth they are as angry as the drunkard whose whisky you dilute with water.

For us to insult the Czar, when all the rest of Europe receives him, is to play straight into the hands of the reactionaries in Russia. The Russian revolutionaries who wish to embroil their country with any foreign country in order to overthrow the Russian govt. come here and find it easy to play upon the emotions of our dram drinkers—in fact supply them with the stimulant they crave for.

Russia is slowly and with pain and throes working toward better things: she has progressed more in three years than seemed possible considering how slowly human affairs must move in such a vast country; our attitude toward her internal affairs should be one of benevolent neutrality and hope.

I send you two pictures, which my private secretary has just sent in my box—you need not return them. I am always consoled for my nose by remembering that Hazlitt thought the smallness

---

1 The socialist Independent Labour Party, founded at Bradford in 1893.

of Coleridge's nose was an indication of weakness, and spoilt his appearance. "The nose," said Hazlitt, "is the rudder of the face.

The lady pictured at the back of mine is pretty, but I don't know her

When are you likely to be in England?

Itchen Abbas

25 July 1909

This is to tell you that I know you were alive a few days ago, for I met your Talbot sister[1] and she told me you had been heard of. I had another evening of her glorious music, at the John Talbots' this time. It is not only her playing, but the way in which she selects what to play: her own feeling leads her to one thing after another which carries one on whither one is delighted to go. This was a Wednesday evening in the middle of one of my thickest and most odious weeks and it was a most refreshing oasis to me: an evening spent on the Delectable Mountains, just when the Pilgrim was at his weariest.[2]

Today I am at Cottage as usual: there hasn't been one hot day this summer and not much sun; and you can't have the full glory of Cottage without hot sun and still weather to let the shade be felt and to set off the moist [illegible] and fresh green of the water meadows. But Cottage can adapt itself to every mood and no complaint has been heard in it, though today has a garden-wrecking

---

1 Margret, Lady Talbot (1841–1929)

2 Site of a rest haven in John Bunyan's *Pilgrim's Progress*. Bülow had recently resigned as Chancellor and his successor Bethmann Hollweg was thought to be more conciliatory toward Britain. But Russia was still a source of trouble. The British Ambassador, Nicolson, pressed for a full alliance to reassure St. Petersburg of the value of Western support after its capitulation before the Kaiser's "mailed fist." But tensions between the two Powers in Persia were exacerbated when the Shah, deposed on July 16 by forces loyal to the constitution and parliament, fled to Russia to prepare a counter-revolution. The sniping from the Liberal and Labour back benches intensified.

Meanwhile a sub-committee of the Committee of Imperial Defense was inquiring into charges leveled against Jackie Fisher, First Sea Lord, by Lord Charles Beresford, Commander-in-Chief of the Channel Fleet. In addition, the controversy over the number of Dreadnaughts to be built was reignited in July when it was learned Italy and Austria had commenced building versions of the new battleship. Grey had twice threatened to resign over the issue.

wind and a leaden grey sky. Nevertheless it is soft and the country is very green.

I have had a mood this week of feeling the past very near to me and when that comes I always feel as if I might die very soon, but I don't think it means anything.

I suppose you understand the position as regards Russia. The Revolutionaries are neutered and broken in Russia and are trying to make trouble here. In Russia itself there is a severe struggle between the Reactionaries on one side and Stolypin (a really good man) and the Duma on the other. The Reactionaries wish to abolish the Duma; the Duma is intent on working out reforms by Constitutional means. The question for us is whether we will help Stoypin and the Duma by being civil to the Czar as long as he stands by them, or whether we will play straight into the hands of the Revolutionaries by insulting the Czar as Keir Hardie[1] and co. want us to do. But for us to do this in public would obviously be fatal. It is made a reproach against the Czar that some time ago he received a deputation of the Union of the Russian People which organized "pogroms"; he did this when he was told that this "Union" was the bulwark against Terrorist outrages. Now he knows its true character and has recently refused to receive a deputation and its leading paper has been heavily fined. And so forth: but I can't say a word of this. Imagine what our feeling would be if a German Foreign Minister in the Reichstag discussed what deputations of his own people our King should or should not receive and blamed or praised him accordingly.[2]

---

1 Co-founder of the I.L.P. and the Labour Party, and its first M.P., along with John Burns and Havelock Wilson, Hardie (1856–1915) had resigned as Labour leader at the end of 1907, but continued to attack the Entente in the House with undiminished energy.

2 Two things weighing on Anglo-Russian relations over the summer were St. Petersburg's anxieties about the resumption of talks between Britain and Germany over collaboration on a railroad line from Bagdad to the Gulf coast. But Berlin's price, as always, was a "political agreement"—neutrality in a European war—and the talks fizzled out. In Persia, Russia had supported the Shah and Britain the *majlis*, the fledgling parliament, and Grey had issued a stern warning when Russia was poised to send troops into Azerbaijan in the spring. "Persia tried my patience more than any other subject," he later confessed. (*Twenty-Five Years*, v. 1, 164.) Eventually Russia was persuaded not to intervene on behalf of the Shah, and when nationalist troops entered Teheran in July, the Cossack brigade in

How awfully dull this is! It has bored me to write it: but I thought you would expect something about public affairs and so I began and went on like this. Perhaps it will help you to understand how odiously disinteresting political work is. Now if I tell you that one of two bread-eating Cottage robins, which comes into this room, has fallen into a most deplorable moult and lost its tail, but that its manners are just as perky as ever and that it amuses me to see how very unconscious it is of its personal appearance, that is something pleasant and interesting, which it pleases me to write and ought not bore you to read, if you are any friend of mine. (This is a dreadfully long sentence nevertheless.)

On Saturday I am going to see Paul at Cherry Orchard—I hear he is better, but Birrell who has seen him tells me there is still lethargy. On Monday the 2nd I go to see the Czar and at the end of that week I hope to get three days at Fallodon else I shall not see my garden till October nor my young ducks at all, till they are dull and grown up. I could cry with vexation when I think of this: it is criminal. You needn't think it necessary to answer this because it begins with a jibe.

24 August 1909

I am glad you liked my speech at Leeds and still more that you liked what I said about Lord Salisbury. It amuses me that you should say that what I said was exactly like me to say. I never know what I seem like to other people. I don't know what the Cecils thought of it: there were several of them there and it was rather like me not to mind saying what I thought of their father in their presence, though I had never met him. Perhaps it was also

---

the capital remained in its barracks.

The third Duma was in the middle of its five-year term. (Its predecessors had each been dissolved after sitting fewer than six months.) But it was elected on a different system and was a more conservative body, and British critics of Russia were not placated. (These same critics, in less than a decade and a half, would be pressing the government to establish cordial relations with an infinitely more brutal and corrupt regime in Russia.)

like them not to say what they thought or to like it as a matter of course. Or they may have been annoyed at the speech being too personal. I think I might have been that in their place. "What on earth has this fellow got to do with appraising my father etc., etc." To which I should have replied "…your father's character is public property and I am one of the public; and if you don't come here as part of the public you should stay at Hatfield."

When did I last write to you? I went to Fallodon for three days and stayed there with two sisters and two brothers-in-law, just a weekend. That is my only glimpse of it this summer. Cottage season ends in the middle of August.

I have been on one visit to the Sydney Buxtons;[1] tonight I go to the Glen to have three days grouse shooting, which will complete my Easter holiday, of which I missed part.

It amuses me that you live always either in a hut or in hospital.

What strange ideas you have about the posts to Zanzibar! Do you really think you can get a reply within a month? I should think a letter took a month to get there. But your habit of telephoning makes you expect things to be very quick. I see that it is women who really love the telephone. When the Tennants are staying with me, he never uses the telephone but she often does.

Nevertheless, I find that Barton only writes to friends when his wife is away from him—this ought to be a very good sign.

You ask about the Czarina. She isn't fat and still looks rather (not very) beautiful. In repose her face looks sad, as I suppose mothers' faces may be after they have found bombs in their baby's cradle.[2] The Czar is a gentleman; his pleasure is I imagine in domestic life; and he works hard and does his best at affairs of state.

---

1 Grey's old fishing friend, Buxton (1853–1934), from a well-known family of Quaker brewers in Norfolk, relatives of the Gurneys and Frys, was serving as Postmaster General. He would be appointed President of the Board of Trade the following year and Governor-General of South Africa in 1914.

2 Grey was speaking metaphorically. No such incident actually occurred, though there were terrorist attacks on government officials across Russia, as he notes in a previous letter.

The fleet was a very fine sight today for those who understood it and by night when illuminated it was a fine sight for everybody, including me. You see I like games so much better than guns; and I like sailing ships that are in touch with the elements.

Winston Churchill wants to buy a flying machine.

P.S. I am getting rather hungry to see you again, but I should have more appetite even for that, if the Session were over and I were less stale.

Brooks's, St. James
4 September 1909

You will find tea at 3 Q.A.G. about 5 o'clock on Monday and I shall either be there or come as soon as I can get away from the F.O.

A most delicious letter from Barton has just come which remind me to read you. I have also been told a story which has amused me for a week, whenever I have thought of it, but it is an improper one unfortunately.

I am going to Hatfield on Sunday; it is a pity you are not going to be there.

Fallodon
12 September 1909

You are not sending me back Barton's letter. I remember now that there is a sentence in it about Clarke[1] being too energetic which I omitted in sending. You mustn't repeat that to anyone: it is those sort of things repeated that put grit into the machine of an office and destroy people and work.

Now I have another letter from Barton in which he says that phloxes and zinnias will do at Zanzibar.

---

1 Possibly Sir George Clarke (1848–1933), former first secretary of the C.I.D., but more likely Grey's misspelling of G. R. Clerke, Senior Clerk in the Foreign Office.

I have had beautiful days here and am refreshed, but also loath to go back to London, which I do tonight.

P.S. I have not got your Broadstairs[1] address and should not like it if I had it: the name suggests crowds of people going up and down steps at the end of a long pier to embark and disembark from tourist steamers; and there is a kiosk on the pier in which a band plays sometimes, and on some of the steamers there is a poor fiddler.

I liked both your Mastermans very much the evening I dined there: his talk was sound and good and Auburn's face watching you read out the verses about her was very delightful.

Fallodon
1 October 1909

I am delighted with this story about George. It gives me deep pleasure, but I shall also make it a subject of chaff when he comes home. I don't know how to write to him now: he has sent no instructions. I am coming to Fallodon every week and am liking my days here alone: it isn't playing the game for I withdraw into myself and past days and don't think of politics; though I do my papers in a perfunctory way. There is a sort of machine in me which works when a F. O. paper is put before it, but it stops when the paper is put away, and it isn't me.

Do you see an article about Wolff[2] in the last Litt. Suppl. of the Times! He wrote of a favourite pointer as "my happiness, my very existence." I am reading Gibbon and Thackeray's "Adventures of Philip,"[3] which I have never read: if a new novel of Thackeray were published I should be keen to read it and so why not read

---

1 Resort town on the Isle of Thanet, off the east coast of Kent
2 Probably Henry Drummond Wolff (1830–1908). A Foreign Office clerk before becoming an M.P., he was a member of the "Fourth Party," with Balfour, John Gorst, and Randolph Churchill. Wolff returned to diplomacy in the 1880s, serving as high commissioner in Egypt, minister plenipotentiary to Persia, and Ambassador to Spain.
3 First published in *Cornhill*, 1861–2. The author's last and least respected novel, drawing on characters from previous works, about a fortune won, lost, and regained.

this. The beginning is sombre, but Thackeray's meditative wistful style suits me and rests me. I see that young George Trevelyan has written another volume about Garibaldi: it sounds good.[1] Young G. T. has literary fire in his belly.

I am thinking of asking J. M. to come here for a weekend when I am alone; but it is rather a bold thing of me to do. If he accepted I am sure he would have a phase of regretting before he came, and I should be afraid I should not be in a good mood when he was here and wish I hadn't asked him. It would probably do very well, but it might not, and is a terrible long way for him to come.

Fallodon
24 October 1909

At Sheffield where I had to speak last week I met your brother[2] and Talbot brother-in-law;[3] it put me pleasantly in mind of you, though I didn't speak of you. They both had to speak and did it quite well; the brother has real ability I am sure, and would have made quite a good Cabinet Minister of a good English type. A generation ago he would have been in Cabinets, but now there are new men and manners; less solid men and worse manners.

Today I went to church unintentionally, by which I mean that I put aside the church-going clothes when I got up, and put on others, intending not to go. Then after breakfast I changed my mind, though not my clothes, and went and enjoyed it. It seemed to be Harvest Thanksgiving when I got there: the Church was decorated with chrysanthemums and oats, and an occasional beetroot

---

1 *Garibaldi and the Thousand* (1909), the second of three volumes G. M. Trevelyan (1876–1962) wrote about the revolutionary leader. The "last Whig historian" had resigned his Trinity College fellowship six years earlier to write the kind of literary history that was out of favor in Cambridge.
2 Charles Beilby Stuart-Wortley (1851–1926), Unionist M.P. for Sheffield and twice Parliamentary Under-Secretary in the Home Office. An urbane man of with literary interests, he married successively the niece of Trollope and daughter of Millais.
3 Major-General Sir Reginald Talbot (1841–1929). After retiring from the army, he served as Conservative M.P. for Stafford and Governor of Victoria.

or carrot; and we had four harvest hymns all near together in the hymn book. Do you remember the touching simplicity of harvest hymns? They make me wriggle and purr with enjoyment.

"And keep us in His Grace
And guide us when perplexed
And save us from all ills
In this world and the next"[1]

The simplicity gave me such a *douce attendrissement*[2] that I felt as if I could kiss the whole choir for singing it.

But they missed out one verse of "We plough the fields and scatter" and I nearly made a fuss and interrupted the service then. We had too the 118th Psalm and a fine chant for it; do you know that Psalm? It is splendid and buoyant and says things two and three and four times over because it is so glad.

I go on with Adventures of Philip: it is very early Victorian and Oh! the difference between Thackeray's women and Meredith's! You cannot think of any of Meredith's women in a crinoline nor of any of Thackeray's out of one. If it wasn't for the fact that they had children I should be sure they slept in their crinolines. Nevertheless there is in Thackeray what belongs to all time and all ages of both sexes.

I also continue with Gibbon—he has a haughtiness which amuses me, as when he speaks of the "pious obstinacy" of the early Christians, when persecuted. But he has a respect for Athanasius,[3] which I hadn't before, but I have now.

I leave these books here—Gibbon and Thackeray—when I go to London, and find Gibbon in the library with my mark in it and Thackeray open where I left off on the reading stand by my bed when I come back. That is homey.

---

1 "Now We Thank Our God" ("Nun danket alle Gott"), written in the mid-17th century by Martin Rinkart (1586–1649), set to music by Johannes Crüger (1598–1662).
2 Sweet emotion
3 St. Athanasius of Alexandria (c. 296–373), defender of Trinitarianism against Arianism.

The leaves are turning and I go to look at the trees, which Dorothy and I knew and which we used to watch and visit every autumn at the height of their colour. It's 8 years since I have seen them colour, for Fallodon was let for our last four autumns and each office year but this I have been back in London before the colour came. I like to see them still, but there is the settled wish that I may be seeing them for the last time and be gone before the season comes again. It is strange how as long as one's body keeps well one can enjoy life and yet want to die. I should have said it was impossible, but it isn't. Death now seems like going home. If I was dying and found my friends sorry, I feel as if I should say, "never mind—you will die too," as if it was a thing to be desired, and this brings me up short with a sense of the difference of my point of view from theirs and from what mine was. In 1904 in these days I was making speeches and doing railway work and Dorothy was at Cottage and writing me such dear letters about it: I read them as the days come round again.

I have given John Morley his invitation, which he is considering: I don't think he will come, but I put it nicely and I think it has given pleasure.

Fallodon
21 November 1909

Barton asks me to send this on to Lady Lyttelton and Lady Tennant if I think it is good enough. I think it is not only good enough to send on but to be returned to me, so please ask Pamela Tennant to return it.

I am going to fight this seat again, though I am ill-prepared for election speeches.[1]

---

1 The long-anticipated rejection of a motion for a second reading of the Budget by the House of Lords came on November 30th, 350 to 75. On December 3rd, the House passed a motion that the Lords' action was "a breach of the Constitution and a usurpation of the rights of the Commons," and was prorogued.

For the next fortnight however I shall be mainly in London. I am in a hurry tonight, having to start off, but I will write you a better letter sometime. I am proud that my last made you laugh.

Fallodon
12 December 1909

I love your letters. I am in the thick of election speeches now and I fear there will be no more letters from me to make you go about smiling till the ordeal is over.

My base is Fallodon, but I shall be in London for the day on the 23rd and would breakfast or lunch with you. I shall have no house available but will give you luncheon at any place you choose from the Ritz to an aerated bread shop. Let me know your will.

J. M. didn't come to Fallodon: but was quite nice about it: I wish I had heard your sermon—can I join the Mother's Union and come next time?

I am reading "the Search Party": a frivolous book but very Irish and amusing.[1]

My brothers are very well. George expects to reach Nairobi about the end of the year. Barton writes now and then—always amusing—there are touches of Lamb in his letters.

It will be fun when you are a grandmother—no more talk of chaperones then I hope. And yet I don't seem to hear people saying "old Katharine" for a long time to come.

Tyrrell my private secretary[2] is here to help me with speeches and work: his presence helps oddly to make this election work

1 A novel published earlier in the year by George A. Birmingham (James Owen Hannay) (1865–1950), Church of Ireland clergyman and prolific novelist and playwright.
2 William Tyrrell (1866–1974), was private secretary to Thomas Sanderson, Permanent Under-Secretary at the Foreign Office, and secretary to the Committee of Imperial Defense before becoming Grey's private secretary in 1907. He went on to himself serve as P.U.S. and then as Ambassador to France. Grey was closer to Tyrrell than any other subordinate at the F.O., and wrote warmly of him in *Twenty-five Years.* A paragraph devoted to him concludes, "I had occasion, in office, to know the great value of Tyrrell's public service; but the thing that I prize is our friendship, that began in the Foreign Office, and has continued uninterrupted and intimate after official ties ceased." Tyrrell was extraordinarily secretive, had an aversion to writing, and left few papers.

seem different to other elections and therefore not to be contrasted so much with them. But I feel dreadfully dead with Dorothy not here and I daren't stop to think: for which happily there is no time.

I want a new second Chambre with about 50 of the best Peers kept there for life and some 200 other members elected, each for large areas by proportional representation and not elected at the same time as the House of Commons.[1]

Fallodon
20 December 1909

I only knew Archie Gordon by sight, but it is pathetic to think of that beautiful, strong clean-looking body being crushed and killed as it was.[2] For the rest both Margot and Violet Asquith have been particularly nice to me this year and I grieve for what Violet A. has to suffer. But it is only through love that people learn what is most worth learning in life; and love uses happiness and sorrow to teach them, and the best one can wish for others is that they should have the opportunities of learning and the strength to learn. This is only saying in my own cumbrous was what you have said about it more incisively.

3 Queen Anne's Gate
19 February 1910

I have had a strenuous time, but things are not going badly and I have positively been interested and still am. Alas! I get bored with all political situations sooner or later. You wouldn't, but then

---

1 In wishing to reconstitute the House without limiting its powers, Grey found himself in a minority in the Cabinet. Most members wanted to prohibit the Lords from vetoing finance bills and permit only two vetoes of any other bill. This Grey referred to as the "C.-B" plan, having been proposed by Asquith's predecessor, and it became the basis for the 1911 Parliament Act. Grey felt strongly about the issue, and threatened to resign over it in March 1910.
2 Archibald Gordon (1884–1909), third son of the Earl of Aberdeen, member of "the Corrupt Coterie," the children of "the Souls," rumored lover of Lady Desborough and intimate of Violet Asquith. He was killed in an automobile accident in December.

you are really much younger than me and more tolerant of town life. I wrote these lines down for you when you were here and never gave them.

Thank you for your letter and I have also had a delightful Collins from the nice new baby[1]: please thank her as I have little time to write.

3 Queen Anne's Gate
17 March 1910

I delighted in your letter and now as to April 30. Brother George will be back [and] I must keep the small room next to mine for him: but the other two bedrooms will be at your disposal.

I had a sudden pain and sickness yesterday, which caused me to go home suddenly from the F.O. and get a doctor, but I am all right today and going back to work. I asked Mary Buxton to send you a line when I was bad in case the thing got into the newspapers so that you would not need to be alarmed. Gravel[2] is thought to be the trouble.

I have never heard of the Green Curve[3] so I can't have recommended it to you. If it is good I will get it. I am much amused by your warning that Hermione is not to be confirmed by Swift and by your calling her a rascal—she shall be known henceforth as the nice new baby or rascal.

PO Rosehall, Sutherland
19 April 1910

I came here on Saturday afternoon and the river being in flood today I write to you. I haven't heard yet whether the govt. were

---

1 Hermione Lyttelton. A "Collins" seems to be a letter, but the reference is obscure.
2 kidney stones
3 *The Green Curve and Other Stories* (1909) by Captain Ernest Dunlop Swinton, who wrote fiction under the *nom de plume* O'le Luk-Oie. Later credited with developing the tank, Swinton became a Major General and the second Chichele Professor of Military History at Oxford.

defeated last night and am in no hurry to know.[1] If they were beaten we all resign, if not we go on, but either way I stay here for two days more, unless F.O. things, which are my special charge, go wrong.

I suppose it seems rather scandalous that I should have come here while there is a political crisis, but I feel very pleased at having bolted. I feel the same sort of reckless exaltation that I suppose one might feel if one had run off with another man's wife or perpetrated some triumphant scandal of that kind.

Nevertheless I am not really being naughty for it was settled before I went that no concessions were to be made on the Budget and that though we must precipitate a crisis of some sort, if the Lords won't have what we sent them, we would not commit ourselves as to what we would advise the King to do. If Redmond votes for the Budget now he must do it without knowing what he said he must know first. So there was no more to be said or done when I left London.[2]

I do enjoy being here: I never tire of watching the river even when it isn't fishable, and of hearing the spring greetings of curlews, and seeing the bare birches on the hill sides turn purple after every shower, when the sun comes out and their twigs are still wet. I even begin to think, which one never can do in the political atmosphere. It seems to me more and more that much speaking and much writing are fatal to thought and that politicians and journalists cease to think and become simply expert in the use of words without thought. They have I think no deep feelings but lots of emotions founded upon phrases. Have you read Europe's

---

1 The vote was on Asquith's guillotine motion setting a timetable for consideration of Lloyd George's Finance Bill, the "People's Budget." The bill passed by a comfortable majority, 345 to 252. The previous week, on 14 April, the P.M. had introduced the Parliament Bill. If the Lords rejected it, Asquith declared, the Cabinet would resign or Parliament would be dissolved. The Lords, however, would be considering the bill only after spring recess, which began April 29.

2 After the January general election, the Liberals' majority depended on 40 Labour Party members and 82 Irish Nationalists. John Redmond (1856–1918), leader of the Irish Parliamentary Party since 1900, had requested details about the government's intentions if the bill was rejected by the Lords.

Optical Illusion?[1] There is some thought in that. Oh! what a deep dislike I have of London and public life and how it grows upon me when I am in the country and alone!

I haven't had any more attacks of pain, but I don't feel secure in health. That glory is gone I suppose for the rest of my life. I now diet and a chill might make me ill.

3 Queen Anne's Gate
5 May 1910

First please convey to Auburn my blessing and tell her that I rejoice in this new happiness of hers. Also give my congratulations to the "criminal."[2]

I am sorry to be leaving you but my Cottage hunger is great and I must go there when I can.

I shall be in to dinner on Wednesday and to luncheon on Thursday—going to Cottage again before dinner on Thursday evening.

I am asking J. M. to dine on Wednesday to talk politics after dinner with me, but it will be nice if you can dine—we will all have good talk at dinner and I fresh from Cottage shall chaff J. M. about his copper beech at Flowermead.[3]

Southwestern Hotel, Southampton
10 June 1910

Thank you for the latch key and the Collins. I am pleased and satisfied that my house should have been of use to you. London is London—a place where people cannot meet to much purpose— even I can neither make it restful nor be restful there myself—at

---

1 by Norman Angell (1909), republished the following year as *The Great Illusion*. The illusion was Angell's: he made the case that war would be unprofitable, owing to the economic interdependence of the European states and to the unwillingness of subject populations to work for their conquerors, and this realization would have a chastening effect on Europe's leaders.
2 Lucy Masterman was pregnant with her first child, Margaret, born 12 October 1910.
3 Morley's home in Wimbledon, Surrey.

any rate while I am in office—but I liked seeing you and talking when we could.

I have just had my day with Roosevelt—it was yesterday—we had some hours of walking and listening to birds and still more hours of excellent talk about bird books, poetry and some politics. It was congenial on every subject and he imparted to me a sort of healthy vigor and courage: he has a wonderful gift of doing that. I fairly loved him.

I have now brought him here to join his family on the boat train and am writing this while he is talking to a cousin in the hotel. We spent last night at the Forest Park Hotel in the New Forest.[1]

Itchen Abbas
2 July 1910

It is time that you heard that Barton has come back. He and his wife came to luncheon with me yesterday. The wife is very sweet and touching, and as for Barton, his laugh and his humour are more delightful and infectious than ever.

Before he had been 10 minutes in the room I felt as if I hadn't really enjoyed humour since he went away...

George has toured to the north of Scotland in my motor car. He came back to London on Thursday evening and went off the next day to stay with Albert at Howick. Albert is not only volatile himself, but keeps other people on the move. When he was in England a year or two ago I considered him to be about 22 years old. I now think of him as 18. But his exuberance is very delightful. George likes him immensely.[2]

I am getting no time to read anything, but we are to adjourn Parliament at the end of July and I shall then go to Fallodon and

---

1 Grey and the former president spent about twenty hours together. They walked first in the upper Itchen Valley and then the New Forest, arriving at dusk at the hotel in Brockenhurst. It was a little late in the year for birds, but the two men saw about forty species and heard twenty.
2 Lord Grey, in his sixth year as Governor-General of Canada, was 58.

read some more Gibbon. I am well and feeling rather content but at this moment sleepy and shall take a nap before my 5:30 dinner.

P.S. 90 Ebury Steet So. is Barton's present address. They have a nice new baby with them but I haven't seen it.

Fallodon
11 July 1910

You are worse off than me really with all your functions and no quiet time, and as I grumbled to you, are entitled to grumble to me. I should run away from the sort of time you have and let off a bomb in the middle of one of my own smart parties and then kill myself, but you do like people better than I do and so, though your time is bad for you, it would be worse for me.

I have come here for a three night and four day weekend with George so that he may sleep under this roof before he goes to Canada on the 15th. We fish and have a sea walk each day and I dote upon young ducks. Tonight we go back to London.

Now as to this Derby day story—I went through four stages over it.

1. Sheer compunction/commiseration and penitence that I who have some 10 sacred weekends should have spoilt the most sacred day of a man named Watson.

2. Slight annoyance with the private secretaries, who made the appointment and never told me it was Derby Day and who know that Derby Day would come and go without my knowing unless I was told.

3. Reflections upon the character of Watson. If I have gumption enough to let the King know that I want all weekends free with the result that King Edward in his kindness never appointed me for audiences on Saturdays and Sundays, what sort of worm must Watson be who hasn't gumption to tell my private sec. that he would like to be free on Derby Day.

4. The truth. In consequence of mood no. 2 I enquired of a priv. sec. and here is the truth. Watson was asked on what days he would be in town and would come to see me. He named two or three of which one was Derby Day. The private sec. asked if he had any preference and he said "no" and that is how the appointment was made.

So just tell your friend who speaks with indignation that he is a silly ass and had better go to bath and that he wants his head washed or whatever other phrases are most familiar to those who go to the Derby.

I shall be away Sept. 26 for a week and also on Sept. 5 for a week. George gets back from Canada about Sept 19 in time to go off on deer stalking visits so he will be good for a chaperon in September, but if you will tell me your dates I shall try to arrange a chaperon for you.

Fallodon
31 July 1910

Are you still having a bad time? I fear so, but then you know that I always take the gloomiest possible view of what it must be like to be the wife of an officer with high military command in time of peace. "Pray for me" was what Dorothy wrote of herself to more than one friend when I went into office in 1905. I even find some comfort in the thought that she has been spared it.

I have been home since Saturday morning and alone, and have enjoyed the place and the season, which means amongst other things that I have eaten quantities of fresh strawberries and raspberries. The squirrels are in great form but they have taken to raiding the strawberry beds and make them a sad sight. Also there have been catastrophes amongst my young ducks, but I haven't got to 48 years of age without knowing that one can have no pleasures of this sort without worries and disappointments.

I have been reading some Gibbon as always after the Session and delighting in the large composure of the style and the flavour of sentences such as describe how in the heat of ecclesiastical controversy writers lose sight of the profane virtues of sincerity and moderation etc., etc.

It is after midnight and I am only writing to tell you that I have been thinking of you.

I have just been reading two or three of Dorothy's letters written to me in this month in 1903: every now and then I find something written to me which makes me feel it is worth having lived and which makes me feel very grateful. Don't think, however, that I am not grateful also to some living friends, both because she liked them and because they have been kind to me since.

Fallodon
3 September 1910

I delighted in your long letter with its numbered paragraphs— you have an excellent pen with which to delight your friends. But I have been away on a shooting visit at the E. Tennants, where there is not only shooting, but fishing, bridge, billiards and a covered lawn tennis court: the result is that not only had I no time to write letters there but am in sad arrears now…

Fallodon
4 December 1910

I am glad you are feeling young and well and I am sure you are looking it. (This isn't quite my usual style I think, but no matter.)

I am divided between joy at the thought that the election will so soon be over and depression at the thought of the speeches that are still before me. But what if the election opens the door of my cage and I fly out?

George is here with me, having never seen an election since 1880. He thinks my speeches sensible on the whole. But they are getting very stale speeches and I feel inclined to stop in the middle and say to him "is that the 6th or only the 5th time you have heard me compare the Referendum[1] to a Pig in a Poke?"

The gardener would insist on sending a Sunday paper into the house this afternoon, a thing which I never countenance, and I see that Auburn's Charlie is well in, at which I am pleased.

You needn't worry about politics—the result of all this is going to be a reasonable settlement of several things, unless the Tories get it all their own way at the polls, in which case they won't settle reasonably—nor perhaps would our people if they got it too much their own way.

What a blessed day Sunday is at election time!

There are such extraordinary nice marks of squirrel feet on my blotting papers.

Fallodon
26 December 1910

I find your initials in a book that has come by post this morning. I see it is just the book that I shall like to read after tea, but I write now, because I have put off writing for so long that I daren't put it off any more. I have been through the furnace of an election once more. It was a short nightmare this time. I heard one or two of my colleagues, one only this time I think, shriek rather loudly while he was suffering from it, but I hope we shall all meet with our nerves steadied by the Christmas holidays and our temper soothed by plum pudding. Arthur Balfour looks as if he didn't eat enough plum pudding. I thought he got rather wild in

---

1 A proposal by Lord Lansdowne on 21 November that when the Lords twice rejected a bill passed by the Commons, a national referendum should be called to resolve the question. Then on November 27, Garvin proposed in the *Observer* a referendum on Tariff Reform. This was accepted, with some misgivings, by the Unionist leadership. This is likely the referendum to which Grey refers. Balfour then proposed one on the issue of Home Rule.

the election. Elections consist of saying that the proposals of the other fellow mean something which he says they do not mean. This time the election was particularly ironical, because two sets of men who had spent the autumn in amicable discussion finding out how well they got on personally and what points of agreement they had, spent the election in denouncing each other.

I am weary at the thought of another spell of office: all last year I kept loosening the straps thinking that I might soon put the burden down: now I have to buckle it closer without having put it down at all. But one must take life as it comes; it is of no use to plan, for things so often turn out contrary to what was expected, as if God resented our planning and reserved that for himself. So don't you worry about the prospect of life at Bell Hall.

I saw a middle aged looking man and a young one walking together in front of me on the platform at Kings Cross the other day and had just time to notice that the older man walked with more direct firmness and decision than the younger, when I saw that the older man was Neville: the other was I gather Sir George Abercromby,[1] whom I have met as a boy at Stratton, but I had no time to remake his acquaintance. I hope he is properly devoted to Neville.

George and I are having a placid Christmas here; we play draw-bridge[2] with each other from dinner till midnight. Shall we still be doing that when he is 80 and I am 84? And will you come to stay with us then? I shall have three bath chairs so that we can all go out together.

I suppose the rascal is with you: my love and best wishes to you all.

---

1 Abercromby (1886–1964), a Scottish baronet and distant relative of Grey by marriage, served as Lyttelton's aide de camp while the latter was Commander-in-Chief in Ireland.
2 a version of contract bridge for two players.

3 Queen Anne's Gate
31 January 1911

A very miserable thing has happened. George has been hurt by a lion in East Africa.[1] Alfred Pease is with him and has sent me two cables—the first says "am hopeful," the second "no immediate danger." As the second is dated Nairobi it is clear that he has been conveyed safely to the hospital there to which the first cable said he was being taken.

I don't know the nature of the injuries: I suppose blood poisoning is the danger and there are long days of anxiety ahead.

If George is taken away it will be the breaking up of the only bit of home I have made afresh in these last five years.

P.S. I don't want Neville to put off coming here—the news may be better before the 7th and I had been looking forward to Neville's coming.

My brother Charlie arrives in London on the 4th.

---

1 George Grey (1866–1911) served twenty years in Africa, initially commanding troops in Rhodesia against the Matabele and Mashona. He rose to the rank of colonel, but resigned his commission to serve as manager of the Zambesi Exploring Company in Southern Rhodesia. He then led exploring and prospecting parties in Northern Rhodesia and the Congo, locating, among other discoveries, the great mineral belt of Katanga. He resigned as manager of Katanga Concessions when Belgium annexed the territory in 1906. He was called by the natives "Bwana M'kubwa," the Great Chief. After some years traveling and big game hunting, he was appointed Commissioner in Swaziland. Rights had been sold indiscriminately by tribal chiefs, and Grey's work consisted chiefly of adjudicating and reconciling rival claims. He had the difficult task, in his words, "of the preservation for all time of native rights without prejudicing the progress of European industry and civilization." Lord Selborne wrote of him, "I have never met a man with whom it was a greater pleasure and satisfaction to work than George Grey...I doubt if in the whole history of the Empire any Englishman has ever performed a more tiresome and intricate piece of administrative work than the disentanglement of European and native rights in Swaziland by George Grey. The position was a nightmare. Every acre of land in Swaziland had been 'conceded' by the Swazi chief to some white man for grazing, for tillage, for forestry purposes, and for the exploitation of minerals... Within two years George Grey had reduced chaos to order... It is a very difficult thing in a country like South Africa to gain the absolute confidence of the native and to retain the absolute confidence of the white man, but George Grey did this with more success than any other man I ever met."

In January 1911 Grey, now director of Tanganyika Concession, Ltd., went lion-hunting with Sir Alfred Pease and other members of the Pease family in Kitanga in East Africa, south of the Mua Hills. To Pease's horror, Grey galloped after a pair of lions being trailed by the party. The rear lion charged downhill from a hundred yards. Grey dismounted and fired twice, at twenty-five and five yards, but the lion reached him and mauled him before being killed by the others. Grey was taken to a hospital in Nairobi where he died of septicemia on February 3, 1911.

3 Queen Anne's Gate
6 Feb 1911

It is very bad and I can't work or read with attention to anything outside George and my trouble. I don't see trouble differently and I have the same thoughts about sorrow and suffering that I have had since Dorothy died. But I feel as if strength of spirit had ebbed away or been spent and I haven't enough left to stand up against this.

Charlie arrived on Saturday and he feels very rightly and understandingly and I can talk to him. We are going to Fallodon alone tonight.

George was such a rare person and he was making his home more and more at Fallodon and he was looking forward to increasing happiness there.

I can't tell you what I feel: it is desolating.

3 Queen Anne's Gate
15 Feb. 1911

Certainly come to tea on the 3rd. I have put it down in my book. I hunger to see you—the number of friends who knew and loved both Dorothy and George is not so very many, though each had many friends who loved them especially well.

I can think of nothing else but these two: in time I suppose the grief will blend and the less be merged into the greater, but just now they seem separate and my thoughts go from one loss to the other.

Hilda has proposed a Waldstein evening[1] and I am going to dine with her and Arthur alone on Monday, which I shall love doing.

---

1 She would be playing Beethoven's Piano Sonata no. 21 in C major, opus 53.

My brother Charlie is here: George's death has gone deep into him: the six days at Fallodon did us good and I am doing my work again but drearily, very drearily.

P.S. I am so dreading the letters which must come from Alfred Pease with all the details which can give only pain: the first letters no doubt with hopes, now of no avail. From the moment I heard of the accident only two things seemed to matter—would he get well and was he in pain? The cable said "not in great pain" and could not answer the other question.

I hear Nairobi hospital is well equipped and Alfred Pease is not only a devoted friend but an excellent nurse so I am sure all was done that could be done.[1]

3 Queen Anne's Gate
27 February 1911

I am longing to see you and am keeping 5 o'clock and onwards here free for you on Friday. My youngest brother is with me— we have on Saturday and today got the letters about George and know now for the first time all that happened and how he died.

There is much that is comforting: he had no unrelieved acute pain and no distress of mind except the apprehension of being crippled for life.

If blood poisoning did not set in they thought his life would not be in danger and latterly they thought the left arm would be saved, though they feared that one or both hands would be more or less crippled.

He slept well every night—the last day he dozed a good deal, but they were not in alarm till about 6 o'clock—he rallied a little

---

1 Alfred Pease (1852–1939) was a member of a prominent Quaker mining, textile-manufacturing, and banking family from Yorkshire. He served as a Liberal M.P. from 1885 to 1892 and 1896 to 1902, but resigned after the collapse of his family's businesses and settled in Africa, where he gained a reputation as an outstanding big-game hunter. Pease had a falling-out with Asquith and never returned to politics. His younger brother Jack was a Cabinet Minister from 1910 to 1916 and his sister Ella was one of Dorothy's closest friends.

at 7 and they were easier; at 8:40 he died. There was no pain in the end—he just breathed more and more gently until the last breath.

But reading all the details has just knocked me flat again for the time.

3 Queen Anne's Gate
15 March 1911

Will you come to luncheon or to tea on Saturday?

Were you quarreling with your sister so that your brother had to change his place and sit between you in the middle of the Bach mass?

30 March 1911

You seem to be disappearing into space—it is reported by Kate that the telephone says you aren't coming to 3 QAG at all: I suppose the telephone knows: it sometimes gets correct information, though it never carries conviction to me. However assuming this to be true I have asked the F. Buxtons to take refuge with me April 3–5.

Let me know your next dates, when you know them: my servants will be at Fallodon on a holiday after the 5th til May but in May the house will be in full blast again.

I don't know the address of Bell Hall so send this to the last place you told me of in London.

3 April 1911
Dear Katharine Nauseated

I am going to Fallodon on Thursday night.

Wednesday evening I could give you supper—that is the only time. Can you come then?

You mind all the things you write of because you are nicer than they are. We have to pay in this life even for our own nice qualities.

I went Saturday evening to Cottage and had a very good Sunday there—the birds sang me into a good mood and I am feeling less tired today than I have done for weeks—in fact I believe I am rather well.

The Francis Buxtons stay with me till Wednesday and I have had a very nice dinner alone with May Buxton this evening. Now I am back at the H. of C.

3 Queen Anne's Gate
14 April 1911

I was amused at having to hand you over to that little M.P. whose name I don't know but whom I suppose to be one of our whips or the private secretary of Mckinnon Wood, the F. O. Undersecretary.[1] I found Charlie M. on the Govt. bench and sent him off to you.

I am much taken with the idea of your getting up a combination amongst my friends to not care for me and so see what the effect is on me. You make me wonder whether I go through life taking a great deal more than I give: it sounds very unfair and I don't like being unfair. But I don't think I ask for more than I try to give.

Alfred Pease is due tomorrow and I hope to get to the Casseley[2] on Monday evening or Tuesday morning.

---

1 Grey apparently didn't know the Liberal whips by sight. Thomas McKinnon Wood (1855–1927), Scottish businessman, son of a shipping magnate, M.P. for St. Rollux division of Glasgow, protégé of Asquith and the Tennant family, was Grey's second Parliamentary Under-Secretary, succeeding Edmond Fitzmaurice, Lansdowne's younger brother. Fitzmaurice had been elevated to the Lords on receiving the appointment, as traditionally the Under-Secretary represented the government in the House in which the Foreign Secretary didn't have a seat, normally the Commons. Having both representatives in the lower House was a significant departure, though less intended as slap at the Lords than to give Grey some relief and permit early escapes on weekends. The appointment was also a concession to Liberal businessmen, who felt their interests overlooked by the Foreign Office.
2 the river Cassley in Sutherland, Scotland

London on Good Friday seems very peaceful as far as I can judge from inside the house, for I have been working all the morning. I am now waiting for the dining room to be thrown open as a sign that my lunch is there.

After luncheon I think I shall walk and look at the outside of the first house we had in London—17 Hereford Square. I haven't seen it since 1886.

It is very easy to live in the past altogether. Not for you yet perhaps, and certainly not for Margot, who is coming to tea with me.

P.S. Viscount Morley O.M came to lunch yesterday and we talked some business and some pleasanter things than business and then walked off together to our respective offices.

PO Rosehall, Sutherland
21 April 1911

Thank you very much for the address for a head stone. I want to put a sentence on it. Do you think simply this would do?

George Grey

"Trusted, followed, honoured and beloved by all who knew him."

My talks with Alfred Pease were comforting: they just confirmed everything that was comforting in his letters.

I hope to stay here till the end of next week. I have had four days fishing—extraordinarily good—2 salmon in the four days on a 15-foot rod and not very large flies.

But oh dear! how glorious it would have seemed a few years ago and how little difference it makes now! Perhaps that means one has more hold on the deeper things of life and death. Thank you very much for your sympathy and kindness to us.

I am sure you cast very well: you look as if you would, and I am so sorry you got no pole—very likely they were not in the water.

Don't send your letters to the F.O: I have everything opened that goes there: it is the only way and I trust Priv. Secs. absolutely. Indeed one cannot do otherwise.

My address is 3 Queen Anne's Gate, London S.W. (till out of office) and things are forwarded just as quickly from there.

Itchen Abbas
25 June 1911

I am very much amused that you have written to me about having forgotten the banquet: it is the sort of thing I should have done—both the forgetting and the writing—and I know exactly what has gone on inside you.

You must have had a good day for the Review—sun and ripple to give life to the water—but too cold to be quite perfect.

I shall be back tomorrow morning and shall be in to luncheon. I wrote to ask Auburn and her husband to dine on Monday—dinner is at 7 and we shall have old Birrell in gala opera uniform and perhaps shaved.

I have written to Mrs. Lawton for places in her gallery for you and the rascal (whom in writing to Mrs. L. I call your daughter) on Wednesday and Thursday.

Fallodon
5 August 1911

You have written me a splendid letter: you are very full of life and I rejoice in your vivid expression of it. I met Yeats at lunch at 10 Downing Street, but Margot was between us and he and I had no talk to each other. But I don't know that we should have had much to say to each other.

I have never read any Nietsche [sic]: I imagine it is to be strained, unwholesome and unnecessary, but I don't know what it is. I believe he put an end to his own life.

Morocco is getting better.[1] The Prussians are tiresome, cynical people. They think the time has come for them to get something, and they will get something, but not as much as they thought. My colleagues have been very good and it hasn't been necessary for me to say a word outside the F.O., but I had had a lot of work in it.[2] At one time it became very interesting, but I hope it will get dull enough to let me stay at Fallodon after Parliament rises.

What a state people have worked themselves up into over the Parliament Bill! Two years hence the Bill will be detested by the Liberal Party and be the sheet anchor of the Tories. From our party point of view it is a very short-sighted bill.[3]

I go back to London on Sunday night: I have moved the servants here and have gone to Haldane in London. My sister Jane and niece Joan (her daughter) came today and stay for a month.

---

1 At the height of the Agadir Crisis, July 24, Grey had warned McKenna, First Lord of the Admiralty, of the possibility of a German attack on Britain. The Imperial Fleet was on maneuvers off the coast of Norway, and "as we are dealing with people who recognize no law except that of force between nations,...mobilization for maneuvers at full strength could be used if desired for attack." [*British Documents on the Origins of the War,* VII, p. 625]. After the French sent troops to Fez to restore order and uphold the authority of the Sultan at the end of April, Germany had demanded all of the French Congo as compensation for this violation of the Algeciras agreement. At the end of July, Germany modified its demands to territory south of the Alima river, defusing the crisis temporarily. The French still thought the claims excessive, and fresh demands from Berlin at the beginning of September again heightened tensions. These were withdrawn on September 16, and remaining differences were resolved on October 22. Grey, as usual, tried to steer a middle course between his Foreign Office officials and Cabinet critics.

2 This is a reference to Lloyd George's Mansion House speech on July 21. Coming from a "Germanophile" and leading Radical, the Chancellor of the Exchequer's warning to Germany (and to France) not to exclude Britain from negotiations over Morocco had a salutary effect on Berlin, in Grey's view.

3 As noted, the bill was what Grey referred to disparagingly as "the C-B proposal." It abolished the right of the Lords to reject money bills and to vote down bills passed by the Commons more than twice. Grey still wanted to reform the upper house, retaining 50 of the 623 peers eligible to sit in it, with the remainder elected by counties. Unlike the previous year, he did not threaten to resign over the issue. The bill was "short-sighted" because it still required the Commons to pass three times legislation rejected by the Lords. The Parliament Bill was accepted by the Lords on August 10 after a bitter and protracted fight, and only under the threat of the creation of Liberal peers in sufficient numbers to offset the four-fifths Conservative majority in the House. On July 24 Asquith had been howled down in the Commons by Tory die-hards. They fell silent when Grey, flushed with anger, rose. Glaring at the Conservative back benches, he said, "If arguments are not to be listened to from the Prime Minister, there is not one of us who will attempt to take his place."

They live with one servant in Oxford and I take some pleasure in giving them a month of good time now. Also I can flirt a little with the niece, age 10.[1]

I am missing George very much here. I opened one or two of his boxes and found many things carefully designated or chosen by him for African travel: all these must go to Charlie as I am no traveller. So I settled to wait till Charlie came home before I unpacked things.

I don't know why I showed you that letter in London: it was an impulse, but I am glad I did show it to you and it was a relief to me to do it. I will show you a letter of Dorothy to me, when next you stay with me.

Is there any chance of your coming to Fallodon this autumn and if so about when would it be? I have three visits of my own— shooting visits but otherwise shall be at Fallodon till end of October.

People also are beginning to fix dates for coming here—so if you can come please let me know.

P.S. Pamela Glenconner, lately Tennant, née Wyndham (isn't it rather tiresome of women to change their surnames so often?)[2] has sent me this photograph saying it is the one you liked; so I sent it to you. I am feeding my old chiloe wigeon, dead since. I think I look rather touching.

---

1 Jane (1868–1949), Grey's middle sister, married an Oxford clergyman from a literary Huguenot family, Charles Everett Cambridge de Coetlogon. Joan married Joycelen Salter, a vice-admiral during the Second World War.
2 Eddy had recently been created Baron Glenconner after losing his seat in the December 1910 election. Pamela would change her name one more time.

Fallodon

2 September 1911

So you are going to Farnham and will not come to Fallodon! Verily then the come-along-bishop is revenged on me.[1]

I have been here a week—a brand snatched from the burning.[2] Tomorrow night I go to London—to 28 Queen Anne's Gate.[3] I could give you luncheon at the Ritz on Tuesday at 1:30. Wednesday I shall (m. v.)[4] return here. The 9th I go to Balmoral.

I am sad about Charlie Buxton's death—it will be desolating for his sister Phyllis and it will plough poor Sydney up, though he has a lot left to him.[5]

I have a party here—2 sisters, 1 brother-in-law, 2 nephews and 1 niece.[6] I like to see them happy and it is a convenient sort of party that I can leave at any moment when Morocco brings me to London, and that entertains itself when I have a busy day here with F.O. work. I have a new motor car—a sort of drawing room on wheels: very luxurious. However as you won't come to Fallodon you can't go in it. Nevertheless it isn't a good year for Fallodon. I live on the verge of going to London every day and am "disturbed by work."[7]

---

1 Edward Talbot (1844–1934), Bishop of Winchester, one of whose residences was Farnham Castle, Surrey. He was Katharine's cousin, the son of her father's sister, the cousin as well of one of Katharine's brother-in-laws, Sir Reginald Talbot, and a brother-in-law in his own right, having married one of Neville's sisters.

2 The reference is to John Wesley's characterization of himself.

3 As on other occasions, Grey presumably didn't want to bring servants down with him, preferring to stay with Haldane.

4 *Morocco voulant* or *Morocco volonté:* Morocco willing

5 Charles Sydney Buxton (1884–1911) died on August 31. He was serving as private secretary to his father, who was President of the Board of Trade.

6 This would likely have included, along with Jane and Joan, Constance and Edward Curtis and their sons Peter and Gerald, who lived just 16 miles from Fallodon, at Acton House, Felton, Northumberland. Alice Graves and her husband, the humorist C. L. Graves, were separated. She lived at Oulton Lodge, Aylsham, Norfolk, he at the Atheneum in London. (Graves was an editor at *Punch* for many years, collaborated on several books with E. V. Lucas, wrote biographies of Sir George Grove and Alexander Macmillan, and published two volumes of light verse.)

7 Negotiations were continuing between France and Germany as to exactly how much of the former's Congo territory would be offered to Berlin in exchange for recognizing the French abrogation of the Algeciras treaty

Fallodon
18 September 1911

I shall (m.v.) not be in London this week, but on the 25th and 30th and Oct. 1. I shall be in London for the day only each time. Will you be there any of those days?

I heard what Wilhelm Uncouth said to the French and much other bombastic stuff besides.[1]

The Winston Churchills have been here for a Saturday and I like it: they are so exceedingly nice to each other. Morocco killed a little party of three who were coming here ten days ago. I had to put them all off and go to London. So I haven't done much entertaining. You seem to be hanging about the South a good deal and favouring a lot of people without coming near me, but it has been a bad year anyhow for me. Nevertheless if you come this way, let me know. I am away Sept 25 to Oct 3, but the house is full Oct 6–11, but otherwise I might be here and should be delighted to see you. Next year perhaps may be a better year for me and for you as regards Fallodon visits.

Things are really very nice here: … of seven delightfully tame partridges that I have reared I am afraid the whole seven are ladies: if so they will presently be discontented: but otherwise I have had no troubles. I fear this is too good to last. I have been here very little and that is tiresome.

Have you been reading anything? I have settled down to Clarissa. I get very impatient with her virtue, but there is some witching about Richardson's writing that compels one to read on.

---

1 The Kaiser said he intended to clear the French out of Morocco "by fair means or foul." (L. Cecil, *Wilhelm II*, v. 2 (Chapel Hill, 1996), 164.) He also claimed he could over-run France "whenever he liked." (*British Documents* VII, 451, 453.) Typically, the Kaiser at various times was both more bellicose and more moderate than his Foreign Minister Kiderlen Waechter.

Nuneham Park, Oxford[1]
27 September 1911

They have been very anxious about Francis Buxton, but they hope the danger is over and there is no reason why he should not recover completely. It is intestinal trouble that can be cured.[2]

I enjoyed our meeting in London very much. It put me into a good mood to see you and talk with you and I am sorry you aren't staying here.

I have no time to write for the time that I do not give to shooting, bridge, and sleep must be given to F.O. work. I cannot but enjoy the clever luxury of this house, though I should not be suited to live the life of it.[3]

3 Queen Anne's Gate
8 December 1911

Could you come to supper 8:15 on Monday or Tuesday? I really think I shall be more at leisure on either of those evenings.

P.S. It was exasperating to me to have last evening spoilt and I am afraid I wasn't nice about it. I sent a private secretary to attend to you, but he found you flown.

Fallodon
29 December 1911

I am so glad to have the Bailey book,[4] and to have it from your hand. Some of the things I must have read in the Litt: Suppl: of the Times, but things read so much better in a book and these of J. B. are worth having in a book.

---

1 The home of Colonial Secretary Lewis Harcourt

2 Francis Buxton (1847–1911), Sydney's cousin, was a former M.P., Public Works commissioner, and London School Board member. He died six weeks later, on November 14.

3 Built for Harcourt's ancestor the first Earl of Harcourt in 1756, the house had been extensively remodeled by "Lulu" and his American wife, the niece of J. P. Morgan.

4 John Bailey, *Poets and Poetry: Being Articles Reprinted from the Literary Supplement of 'The Times'* (Clarendon Press, 1911).

I sat down today and read the article—it is now the chapter—on Wordsworth's creed and went entirely with it.[1] J. M. is tenderly but faithfully dealt with in that chapter. Do you know it?

I have been here alone: I am sure more than ever that when I go out of office I shall not go in again. Of course I have been thinking very much about past things and that makes my work seem irrelevant even when I am doing it.

But I wish time would go on quickly—the loss of George is still so fresh that it hurts when I am alone and at leisure.

I hope you will come here next year: it is long since you have been.

Fallodon
19 January 1912

You have sent me a very good and interesting letter: it sounds dull to call it "wholesome" also, but it is that, though nothing you say or write is dull.

What you say about being able to enjoy solitude and yet not being meant to be lonely is interesting and true: it is also true that I couldn't care for (I should shrink from) the companionship of anyone who couldn't enjoy solitude.

You are frighteningly penetrating in your insight.

What you say about public life and its claims and my place in it I do not accept so unreservedly. I see some truth in what you say, but there is a lot more to be said. I am full of a curious pre-sentiment that I am very near some great change in my life: put roughly the feeling is that I shant live out the year. Last night after I was in bed and just dropping off to sleep I felt as if I might just pass off in sleep: it seemed so natural. But perhaps it is only that I am soon going out of office or that this long spell in office has begun to affect my liver. However don't think that I am morbid:

---

1 "Wordsworth's Creed," the "central doctrine" of which is that nature will have a "formative and corrective influence" on all "who will make the needful self-surrender."

I like these feeling and I don't get morbid at all and I haven't been alone for nearly 3 weeks. Last week I put in some days at the F.O; then I went to Glen;[1] then I came here and have had one sister and niece and yesterday a sister and brother-in-law in addition staying, with whom I played bridge after dinner.

Now as to yourself. You want to begin to die a bit after May 10: in a sense you will begin to live: there is a great part of us that can't live while we are in office. At least there is in people who are really alive and not machines. For instance I do really with a live and deep part of me want to see more of Auburn and of Charlie M. too, but in London and office I am just a machine and I cannot make time, partly because even when there would be time I haven't energy to make it and I feel so deadened. I wish she would publish her pômes and then I should know where to find them; I still have her Abbey sonnet by heart, but nothing else.

You ask about my London house: the facts are as follows.

I go back into it about February 5: I leave it for good on March 3 and it becomes a club. Between Feb. 5 and March 3 I must find another house if I can: if I can't there are at least two other houses in Queen Anne's Gate to which I can go temporarily as a guest, while I continue to search for a house.[2] It shall certainly be a desideratum (do you like this word? I don't, but I use words I don't like when I am writing about dull things) in a new house that there shall be a room that you can come to, which means I suppose two rooms: one for you and one for Camel's Hair[3]—and then there is Neville sometimes also.

The window here is being almost indecently open (I don't quite know why I say "indecently." I suppose I only mean "excessive"): there has been no ice on my ponds and I haven't seen a snowflake; though I found a slight sprinkling of fallen snow on the moors

---

1 The home of the Tennants (since 1911 the Glenconners) near Innerleithen, Scotland.
2 28, Haldane's, and 34, the Glenconners'
3 presumably Katharine's maid

to which I took my lunch today. The papers tell of severe weather and snow, but it has overlooked Fallodon.

3 Queen Anne's Gate
8 February 1912

I don't promise not to resign if I have a real difference of opinion about anything, but the rumour you have heard is sheer invention.

There is another worse rumour. It is that as a favour to me Haldane has given the army contract for supply of stone to the lessee of my quarry.

There are some stone quarries in the parish of Embleton but I neither own nor have any pecuniary interest in them and know nothing about their affairs. Thus are reputations made and destroyed: so it ever was and in this life will be.

It is time I had a holiday but I shant force freedom unnecessarily.

3 Queen Anne's Gate
18 February 1912

I suppose my real feeling about the garter was that I was very pleased at being offered it, but shrank from having it.[1] It will make life a little more conspicuous and more complicated: and it gives me a feeling of being still deeper in.

I do love to be in the country and free to go out and look at the sun and be out for the day without having to work early before I go out and late after I come in to make up for having spent a day out of doors. It is more than six years since I have done that, for even when J. M. has taken my work I have kept in touch with some things and he has only had for a fortnight—one fortnight

---

1 King George V had just made Grey a Knight of the Garter. Asquith may have proposed the honour as a rebuff to Grey's critics. He wrote: "I only send you a line to assure you that, after nearly four years of what is called power, this is the one thing which, in a personal sense, has given me deep and abiding pleasure."(Trevelyan, 186.)

in over 6 years. However women are always in office in their own houses, so you may not sympathize.

I am sure your rascal looked very nice at the ball—I hope it was a real and not a sham water lily in her hair—please tell me for certain—and also when you are likely to be here.

I have this house til May.

3 Queen Anne's Gate
6 March 1912

It does me good to see Neville in these troublesome times. He is so unworried. I haven't time to write much. We are all living under too much pressure—the Govt., Parliament, employers and employed.[1] The industry and wealth of this great country has been built up under increasing pressure, which is becoming too much for human nature. That is the underlying cause of all these troubles. The only remedy will be to take things more easily, but that means a painful shrinking of trade and population

Fallodon
8 April 1912

I have had 5 days and 4 nights here and am going back to London tonight, but with the intention of going away for a fortnight on April 14 to fish at Rosehall. A certain Viscount Morley of Blackburn (Order of Merit) will step into the F.O. in my absence and is much looking forward to it. My callous body has kept well—all its machinery goes on and I have nothing to say to a doctor, but I have a mental and spiritual yearning for freedom

---

1 The Haldane Mission to Berlin between Feb. 8 and 12 had not been a success, as Grey and the F.O. anticipated. Germany again refused to consider altering its naval program unless Britain acceded to a "political agreement"—a pledge of neutrality in any European war, regardless of its origin. The Balkans looked restive. The F.O. heard rumors of a military alliance between Serbia, Montenegro, Bulgaria, and Greece that portended a war against Turkey. Then on March 1, the nation's miners went on strike, after the failure of negotiations brokered by the government. About 850,000 men came out, idling an additional 1.3 million in other industries. The strike would end only after the passage of a minimum wage bill at the end of the month.

from work, which all but renders me incapable of doing work: in other words though I am not ill, I want a holiday very badly.

This coal strike is the beginning of a revolution. We shall I suppose make it an orderly and gradual revolution, but labour intends to have a larger share and has laid hold of power. Power has passed from the King to the nobles, from the nobles to the middle class and through them to the House of Commons and now it is passing from the House of Commons to the Trades Unions.

It will have to be recognized that the millions of men employed in great industries have a stake in those industries and must share in the control of them. The days when the owner said "this industry is mine; I alone must control it and be master in my own house" are passing away. The owners still say that, but it has ceased to be real because they cannot act upon it. The Unions may of course like blind Samson with his arms around the pillars, pull down the house on themselves and everybody else; if they push things too far and the owners are too unyielding there will be civil war; but I think the good temper and spirit of compromise that is inherent in English character will save us from catastrophe. Mistakes will be made and suffering will result, but we shall all learn by experience. The coal strike seems to be coming to an end, but there are strikes of railway men, transport workers and shipping ahead of us—perhaps all three together and perhaps the miners soon again.

Trade booms, wealth increases, labour is less well off than 10 yrs ago:[1] labour is now organized and conscious of its power and it will insist upon a larger share of remuneration. There are unpleasant years before us; we shall work through to something better, though we who have been used to more than 500 pounds a year may not think it better.

---

1 Wages in industry rose nearly 6% between 1902 and 1912 and would go up almost another 4% before the war.(B. Mitchell, *European Historical Statistics* (London, 1978), 72.)

The only thing that makes me doubt, is whether, if I were God, I should not say "this boasted civilization that has defiled beautiful country, made hideous cities be built up and is being maintained by ghastly competition and pressure, makes men swarm together and multiply horribly, is so abominable that I will sweep it all away." If God does think that then the industrial countries will perish in catastrophe, because they have made the country hideous and life intolerable. And I can't say that this would seem unreasonable to me, for I see 999 people out of 1000 living a life that I should hate—only they don't seem to hate it, but I am not sure that God doesn't hate it.

I don't know why I have written all this. I didn't intend to and I don't think you will like it. This has been the windiest Easter that ever I had—warm but very windy and today the wind was too bad; it tore off young sycamore leaves and the buds of flowers thereof and strewed them on the ground—Nature does enjoy royal waste and profusion.

Albert, his wife and his daughter Evelyn are alone at Howick and twice I bicycled over to tea there and stayed to dine—playing billiards with Albert and bicycling back to Fallodon at midnight. It is so much better to bicycle than to drive. One gets in at midnight, warm and invigorated and having had communion with the night. We should all be so much happier if we could get nowhere except by the use of our own legs, though of course being used to trains and motors we should think we were miserable without these whirlabouts.

The news is that my brother Charlie will be home in June for six months and I am rejoiced in this; my brother Alec and his wife also come home next month til October and I and the sisters have to consider what is right and possible to do with them. Alec and his wife are the family problem.[1]

---

1 Alexander Henry Grey (1870–1914) may have suffered brain damage as a child after being struck by a cricket ball. Nonetheless he went on to become a minister and served as vicar of St. Jude's in Arima, Trinidad. In 1900 he married the daughter of a clergyman, Ethel Mabel Gertrude Huggins.

Let me know when you will be in London—I shall be at Rosehall April 15 to May 1, then with Haldane for a few days while my household gets into 24 Sloane Gardens.

P.S. I have again enjoyed the familiar sound of the wind here: it must be six years since I told you it was as if my mother were in the room, but it seems like yesterday. Since Dorothy died I think I have had little sense of time.

Rosehall, Sutherland
22 April 1912

It is a very solemn thing that your official career is ending and I am sorry for you.[1] It isn't so very long since I met you at Bombay in a very early stage of your official career: time all runs together in my head since Dorothy died—only three times did I come to Rosehall with her and five times now have I come alone and yet the five times seem the exceptional and unfamiliar.

It is a good thing that you are going to travel this year: it will break the contrast of the change of life (I use this phrase in the general not in the Sir Almroth Wright sense)[2] and you will find lots of interest in the travel and the people you meet, and the Rascal's pleasure will be pleasant to you.

I shall be in 24 Sloan Gardens the week of May 6: you must come to lunch there one day to see it. Why not come on Wednesday May 8?

It is so warm here that one feels inclined to bathe:[3] I am getting no fish because the water is so low, but I bask in the sun and I think I shall come back fresh and restored. I shall be back in London before the end of the month...

They had no children.
1 Neville Lyttelton had just resigned as Commander-in-Chief in Ireland, a post he'd held since 1906.
2 Wright (1861–1947) was a bacteriologist who developed an anti-typhoid fever vaccination, and occasionally wrote on social questions, such as women's suffrage.
3 swim

The account of the sinking of the Titanic, when 150 feet of her stood up on end is the most awful thing I ever read and the circumstances are most miserable—wives and children saved while husbands and fathers have to stay and be drowned; and all the men saved have to explain how they came to be saved, so that it was awkward for a man to be saved. Just think of being in a raft and having to tell drowning people around you that there was no more room! It is very miserable.

I wish I had been there and given up my place on a boat or a raft to a married man and so died: it would have pleased me to end that way and I am not afraid of a water death, though an abject coward about some other sorts of death and about all physical pain.

Could you believe what a title this note paper supplied by the shop—the only shop I believe between Lairg and Lochinver—has? It is called "Scottish Silver Liver-Faced Stationery."

Itchen Abbas
16 June 1912

How are you and when are you coming back? If by June 27 will you come with me to the Handel performance that day at 2:30? I have two tickets, one for you and one for me.

The news about me is that I have seen one of the Irish plays and wept at the end of it.[1]

Don't stay away forever and send me a line to 24 Sloane Gardens, S.W. to say when you will come back.

---

1 Possibly Yeats's *The Countess Cathleen,* revived a year earlier at the Abbey Theatre, Dublin. At the end of the play the countess, though she had sold her soul to the devil, is redeemed because she did so to save her tenants from starvation.

24, Sloane Gardens, S.W.
5 July 1912

Dear Katharine Rested,
On Monday I am engaged for lunch and dinner.

Tomorrow (Sat.) I go to a Trustees meeting at the British Museum—Bloomsbury at 12. I could come to Cumberland Place and lunch there or take you to lunch as soon as my Trustees meeting is over. I shall call on the chance, unless you telephone here (4449 Victoria is I believe the beastly number) before 10:30.

Of course I spoke to Seely[1] and Haldane about Chelsea[2] when I saw the vacancy. Haldane has played up like a brick and I believe it is all right.[3]

2 August 1912

The man who has your gratitude is but one degree less proud than the man who has your love.

I am very relieved that you are now safely Chelsead: it is such a safe permanent thing and dignified too.

I am sorry I can't ever become an old soldier to be looked after by you.

I am with Haldane till Aug. 7 (except Sat. and Sunday when I am at my Cottage.) On Aug. 7 I go to Fallodon and on the 12th to the Glen for four days and then back to Fallodon.

Fallodon
24 August 1912

I went to see Hilda this week: of course she looks frail but she had no signs of being ill and was in a comfortable shelter looking at the sea. I thought it must be tiresome for her not to be allowed

1 J. E. B. Seely (1868–1947) was Secretary of State for War, having recently succeeded Haldane.
2 The Royal Hospital, Chelsea, London, a retirement home for veterans.
3 Neville was duly appointed governor of the hospital, a handsome sinecure.

to walk and go about, but except for that it seemed a comfortable and not unhappy life, and there are nice people about who come to see her.

I have only been a few days here, having been at Glen shooting and at my sisters on the Coquet occasionally. Tomorrow I go to London for a bit.

Two sisters, 1 nephew and 1 niece are here.

I am very dull inside just now: chiefly I think because I cannot get any shooting or fishing without doing my work under pressure, early in the morning and late at night or in the motor car: it seems very incongruous to do any work in knickerbockers, but I have to. And today there is the parish and district flower show and that dullens me.

Hilda said you were with the "come-along-Katharine bishop" so I send this to Farnham... I don't suppose you will stay there forever. Also it is said that you sail somewhere next week, so evidently you won't come to Fallodon, but some day you will come when I am out of office and we will have a nice time.

28 Queen Anne's Gate
21 September 1912

I was in Scotland when your letter reached me and had no time to write before you sailed. Now I am having a very busy time and am off tonight to meet the Russian M.F.A. at Balmoral[1] and I shall have 3 or 4 days at Fallodon before I plunge into the vortex of the Session.

I took the Bartons to see Hilda at Howick last Tuesday. She looked really better and she likes Howick. I think it suits her. I

---

1 Discussions between Sergey Sazonov and Grey focused on Persia, the Foreign Secretary emphasizing Britain's opposition to the return of the Shah and its objection to the shelling of Muslim shrines by Russian troops. Sazonov pressed Grey on what measures Britain would take to assist Russia in the event of war with Germany. Grey, of course, was evasive. But he found Sazonov "very amiable" and felt the meetings went well. The Foreign Minister offered no intimation that the Balkan states were about to declare war on Turkey.

went to tea also alone one day in the week before. That the news of her is good as far as I can judge is what I really have to tell you.

For the rest I am full of work and in consequence "dull inside," but lots more of news would out if you were here to talk to.

I shall be back in London by Oct. 7.

24 Sloane Gardens
16 December 1912

Thank you for your letter: I often wonder what Dorothy would have been thinking of it, but it looks so different inside from what it does outside. It would have meant for the time the destruction of all home life—seven years of home almost all destroyed. I remember George in 1892–5, seeing the misery at home in those years of office compared to the happiness of the years before, saying he wished it was over: and I shrink from what it would be now for anyone who had to live with me at home. In the office and in the F.O. work I am good, but I take it out of people who speak to me in the lobbies of the House of Commons—<u>they</u> are all camel's hairs.

I asked you to come to luncheon on Mon. and you said you were pretty sure you were engaged and could not, but would look when you got home and I said "very well, if you can't come Mon. let me know what day you can come": hearing no more I asked my sister and a friend to lunch on Mon. I got back from my weekend at 11 this morning, but what with Peace delegates and F.O. work could not get to 24 S.G until 1:30—there I found your letter—too late!

Mrs. Creighton comes to lunch on Wednesday—will you come then: it is my only day. Brute that I feel, I would love to see you.

24 Sloan Square
18 December 1912

You are quite right—"miser" is too strong a word, but it is one of my bitter memories that in 1892–5 my unhappiness and groaning in office made Dorothy sometimes unhappy. And I am afraid I should have been doing the same now—for of course I am harder driven now than then. As it is I am doing my work well, as far as when overworked one can do anything well, but being a bear outside it and making an enemy of everyone not connected with my work who comes near me. I told one colleague yesterday, who was tiresome, that I was very near killing either myself or him. This week besides the real work there are Delegate luncheon and a funeral service and Queen Alexandra wants to see me, etc., etc.

I wish you were settled in your house—I don't forget that you are having a bad time too, and it is shameful of me to dump my complaints on you; but it is some relief.

24 Sloane Square
29 January 1913

I am engaged for dinner tonight. Feb 1 is my Dorothy and George week: I feel very resentful that I cannot go away quietly for it and I shall just keep my evenings as much to myself as I can. Will you come to supper with me here at 8:15 on the 3rd, 5th, or 6th...? I should like that.

33 Eccleston Square, S.W.
16 June 1913

Certainly I approve of the tent. I enclose a cheque for 10 pounds that it may be thought of as my tent.

If there is a surplus you can spend it on giving the tent some extra thing.

This is to be Marconi week.[1] Next week is Poincaré week.[2] And they are all Balkan weeks still.[3]

33 Eccleston Square
4 July 1913

I heard this afternoon that Hermione had an operation for appendicitis this morning but that all was well. I do hope it is so: I am so sorry for your anxiety. I am just going away till Monday and feel inclined to ask whether it would be any good if I stayed in London. I could always come to you if I could be of any use.

I am going to Cottage for tonight and on to the Sydney Buxtons on Saturday at Newtimber... You must not trouble to write: I am telling the servants here to get news from your servants and let me know it tomorrow.

And your anxiety about Alfred is still present.[4]

P.S. Since I wrote this we have spoken on the telephone, but as it needs no answer, I send it.

---

1 The House was to vote on two amendments in the wake of the scandal. The first accepted the expressions of regret by two of the three implicated ministers (Alexander Murray, the Master of Elibank, had left the government) and exonerated them; the Unionist amendments did not accept their apologies, and would have resulted in their resignations if passed. Lloyd George, Sir Rufus Isaacs, and Murray had purchased shares of the American Marconi company in April 1912. They did this five weeks after the British company had been selected, pending ratification by Parliament, to construct a wireless network linking the Empire. The two companies were separate entities and the trio didn't wind up profiting from the transaction. However, Isaacs and Lloyd George had failed to disclose the purchase during a debate in the House in October 1912.
2 The President of the Republic arrived on June 24. He was given a warm reception and did not press Grey to convert the Entente into a defensive alliance, as had been expected.
3 The Ambassadors' Conference, which had convened in London in December 1912 was a great diplomatic success for the Foreign Secretary. But Serbia, having lost Albania and been denied access to the sea, refused to honor a pre-war agreement with Bulgaria about the division of Macedonia. On June 26, Bulgarian forces attacked the Serbian and Greek armies in Macedonia. The Treaty of London had just been signed on May 30, but Grey correctly anticipated further trouble.
4 Alfred Lyttelton had been struck in the stomach by a cricket ball. An abscess developed. Surgery was unsuccessful and he died in a nursing home the following day.

Itchen Abbas
5 July 1913

I have got a telegram saying that Hermione is going on very well but that Alfred is dead. He had had the best of his life, but he had much to live for still and his life was a great joy to you and to numbers of friends. I grieve with you and Neville. There was glory and radiance about Alfred to an uncommon degree and though I met him comparatively seldom I have many touching memories that I shall harvest as one does, when people who have been anything in one's life go out of it.

I wish you could see Cottage some day: it is so peaceful. I am free for luncheon on Thursday or Friday next week—or on Monday next the 7th; if you would like to come to lunch send a line to 33 Eccleston Sq.

Fallodon
18 October 1913

I liked your letter very much: you said many nice things in it and you shall clear your chest of the things you didn't get off it, when I come to London. I move my servants up on the 27th, but I shall be there for some days in this coming week.

I have been alone here for 3 days. Most wonderful days of sun and warmth and colour; and I have been twice to the sea and lunched there. These are the first days I have had alone at Fallodon since February and I read a lot of letters that Dorothy and I wrote to each other in 1896 and 1897: they included the West Indian letters, when we were separated there, and they are extraordinarily nice, especially hers to me; and for some time I just went back to what I was in the first months and years after she died and I ceased to live in the present at all. At such times I can't understand how it is possible for me to be alive without her; and such new life as I have made in the last 8 years seems to disappear altogether. But though I am filled with indescribable longing, it doesn't bring any impulse to what is called "commit suicide." I do have that impulse sometimes, but it is always hives or suffering from gout that gives me that and it is a distinct thing. I doubt whether great grief or great emotion of any kind impels to suicide—anything that is great has some quality of patience or something that keeps it wholesome.

I am amused at you saying you felt like a mother to me—I rather like it.

Fallodon
6 December 1913

I see the sad news in today's paper. I knew Spencer Lyttelton very little—we often had a word at Brooke's, but that was all: it will be very hard for you and Neville and the others coming so soon after Alfred's death.[1]

Is life to be nothing from now onwards but repeated sorrows either to ourselves or our friends? It has been like that for some years.

Fallodon
13 January 1914

I am to be in London all next week. I have private political dinners to go to on most nights, but if you call at home I would come to lunch some day, not Mon.

I had some sisters and offspring here for Christmas and the new year and liked them.

I have been alone now for some days and have enjoyed that too and am in high revolt against office and London. I should like

---

1 Spencer Lyttelton, the sixth child and fourth son of the 4th Baron Lyttelton, was the only rich member of the family, having an income from property in New Zealand endowed him by his god-father and great uncle, Lord Spencer, after he had been dismissed from positions in the Navy and the Royal Scots Fusillers. There followed a brief stint as one of Gladstone's private secretaries, but Lyttelton was addicted to gambling, led an idle life and died poor, the family scapegrace.

just for once, for a year or two in my life, to live in places and do things that I don't detest. Your life has been harder than mine, but then you couldn't help it and I could. And it doesn't depress, hurt, and anger you horribly to wake up on London. And you don't yearn for Bell Hall as I do for Cottage or Fallodon.

So don't take any high line with me or I shall throw things at you.

Brooks's, St. James's St.
5 February 1914

I found your letter when I got home late last night. I am going to Fallodon tonight. I may not be there again till July. I come back Monday.

The ancle [sic] is much better, but still a long way from sound. I am having Swedish massage and the swelling is vastly diminished, but I have snapped and torn musells [sic] and ligaments.

P.S. I am glad to get just the end of the week at home, but I have only got even that by interfering with Cabinets and I fear getting myself disapproved of.

33 Eccleston Square
22 February 1914

Today being Sunday I have looked up the address of the Selborne Society[1] and have ordered six boxes suitable for tits, 2 for starlings, 2 for robins and 2 for spotted flycatchers to be sent to you. If the bill is sent to you it will be contrary to my instructions to the Society, so please send that to me.

There is great charm about music in your room at Chelsea and I thought your voice sounded very well and when Neville's voice

1 Founded in 1895 to commemorate the eighteenth-century naturalist and ornithologist Gilbert White, author of *The Natural History and Antiquities of Selborne* (Hampshire) (1789).

sounded reading aloud I said in my naughtiness "of such is the K. of H."[1]

Luncheon here on Thursday the 16th at 1:30 if you and Neville, either or both can come.

P.S. I am glad the Auburn's spirit is not dinted by electioneering.[2] I am sure she has serene spaces to which she can retire, where elections and clothes don't count.

33 Eccleston Square
26 March 1914

So sorry I couldn't lunch today and forgot to telephone. If this crisis[3] is over I go away on Tuesday night for a fortnight and shall be at Cottage Saturday to Monday and have a man lunching with me on Mon. and am engaged to dine out.

Would you and Neville be able to lunch on Saturday at 1:30. I would like to see Neville and hear what he thinks about the Army. I am inwardly boiling with indignation at this stupid prejudiced attempt to dictate policy to us and break us—for that is what it really is; and if it goes on I shall be for taking the hottest Election upon who is to govern in this country that has ever been in our time.[4] I haven't made this sort of speech yet, but I've got it in me and I don't know whether even Neville would soothe me.

---

1 Kingdom of Heaven
2 Having been appointed to the Cabinet as Chancellor of the Duchy of Lancaster earlier in the month, Masterman was obliged to seek re-election. He lost twice in by-elections.
3 The "Curragh Mutiny." On March 20, Brigadier General Hubert Gough and 60 of his officers threatened to resign if ordered north to suppress an uprising by Ulster Volunteers, as the Third Home Rule Bill was being debated in the House. Intelligence had arrived that the Volunteers were preparing to raid Carrickfergus and other armories. The Cabinet approved a statement that the incident had been a misunderstanding, but two paragraphs were added by the War Minister, J. E. B. Seely, in which it was stated that the government did not intend to "crush opposition to Home Rule." The addendum was disavowed by Asquith during two days of heated debate in the House, March 23 and 25.
4 Grey by this time had come to believe that the government should not proceed with Home Rule—as this would now entail the use of force—until it had received a mandate from the electorate. Unlike most of the Cabinet, he favored "Home Rule within Home Rule" for Ulster, rather than its temporary exclusion.

P.S. French[1] is a trump and I love him, and some of the others are splendid, but the political lot[2] make me ready to sound the tocsin.

Bridgeton, Morayshire
12 April 1914

I send you a salmon from Rosehall. I only had the fishing there till the 8th and then came here and by Wednesday I must be back in London. I cut two days off my fortnight that I look forward to and live for from one year to another and even then I see that the House and Press cackled because I didn't cut 5 days more off it in order to stay for the last day of a debate in which I couldn't by the rules of the House speak any more.[3] God help them!

I am enjoying these days more than ordinary cold-blooded, duty-chilled, goody-goody people in black coats can imagine and am feeling well in a sense that is unknown in towns and makes towns seem a crime—thank you very much nevertheless for your letter about my speech.

May is going to be the really critical month of decision in the Irish question and my time of trial as to whether I can help things or not will come then—if I live through the visit to Paris in April.[4]

I am staying at a farm house with Glenconner (né Eddie Tennant) and Jack (his brother) and we fish all day waist-deep in the Spey, and my hands feel like files and I am awfully well.

---

1 Sir John French, then Field Marshall and Chief of the Imperial General Staff. He was pressured by Generals Roberts, Robertson, and Wilson to persuade the government not to use the Army in Ulster. He resisted, but threatened to resign if Gough were not reinstated. (Gough maintained he would have obeyed a direct order to march north.) French himself resigned the following month, along with Seely.
2 Chiefly, Sir Henry Wilson, friend and ally of the Conservative leaders.
3 on the Home Rule Bill
4 He had reluctantly agreed to accompany the King. The Foreign Secretary knew he would be pressured to tighten the Entente with Russia, and was asked to authorize naval conversations between the two countries.

I hope you are having pleasant days too—as far as it is possible for a woman to have pleasant days—and that in your next incarnation you will be born a man and like salmon fishing.

Fallodon
18 April 1914

I didn't mean the salmon to taste of olives nor the letter I wrote after sending it, which probably crossed yours.

I'm afraid I was irritable at lunch: for over 8 years I have been leading a life that does violence to all my natural feelings and I'm broken in spirit and temper: but perhaps I shall recover after a few weeks out of office.

I am here just for the weekend and return to London tomorrow night and then go alas! to Paris.

P.S. I hope you have got this weather and are getting well: it is your gallantry in going at so many fences that knocks you up—and you mustn't feel it a shortcoming that you don't take all the fences you see.

28 Queen Anne's Gate
4 September 1914

Except for 2½ hours drive on Sunday afternoons I haven't been out of London since the last Sunday in July and I see no prospect of getting away.

It is a terrible time. The Germans seem to have taken us back to the time of the Huns. I have just heard that my nephew is reported "missing" and we may never know what has happened to him.[1] He may have been wounded and left on the field when

---

1 Cecil Graves (1892–1957) was educated at Gresham and Sandhurst. Cut off from the retreat after Mons, his company was surrounded and forced to surrender. Identified as Grey's nephew, he suffered a punishing captivity, including periods of solitary confinement, until transferred to the Netherlands as part of a prisoner exchange. After retiring from the army in 1925, he served as Deputy Director and then Joint-Director of the BBC. Graves inherited Fallodon on Grey's death, but sold it in 1945.

our force was retiring before those fearful odds. It is terrible for my sister—I have just telegraphed and written to her.

P.S. I am staying here indefinitely. You and Neville might come to lunch some day. What day next week would suit you?[1]

28 Queen Anne's Gate
17 September 1914

My brother Charlie has been wounded, fighting Germans in East Africa: he is going on very well in hospital at Kisumu[2] but they have amputated his left arm above the elbow. I hope when he is well enough he will now come home, but I am miserable about it.

Let me know when you get back to the Royal Hospital.

33 Eccleston Square
9 October 1914

…My nephew is safe—a prisoner. My brother Charlie takes his remaining arm back to his regiment soon in East Africa to continue fighting.

33 Eccleston Square
2 December 1914

I am to lunch with Lady Rothschild tomorrow and as it has taken about 4 weeks to find a day I must keep that time for her. Otherwise I should have enjoyed meeting your General. I will come to lunch at Chelsea Friday.

I didn't get away from the F. O. til 7:35 this evening so there was no opportunity for moonlighting.

---

1 Two-thirds of a page has been cut from this letter, following the third sentence of the postscript.
2 Kenya

Fallodon
24 December 1914

I had to lunch out on Tuesday and escaped that evening. According to telephone messages, that was the time you suggested coming. I suggested another time on Monday, but they said you were not back.

My machinery was almost ceasing to work and I have handed over to Haldane for a few days and came early. Even the Generals at the front have had a few days off in turn.

I slept 10 hours last night and after one day here it is hard to believe there is war, though the Germans might raid and burn Fallodon any day.

When do you come back to London?

33 Eccleston Square
22 March 1915

I will come to dine on Thursday if I am in London. I am just hanging on till I can get an opportunity to go away for a week: it was to have come Thursday three weeks ago: it hasn't come yet and I am faintly hoping it may be next Thursday, but it probably won't.

Acton House, Felton, Northumberland
21 June 1915
dictated to Constance Curtis

I am not to go back to work till about July 10. The oculist has been down from London to examine my eyes and is now exceedingly hopeful of saving my sight permanently so that I shall be able to read to the end of my life, but he insists upon my not reading or writing for another three weeks, and after that saving my eyes as much as possible and wearing dark glasses for some 18 months, and continuing at intervals certain treatment which he prescribes, I am to be made safe.[1]

So I had your letter read to me and I am dictating an answer. I had not seen Fallodon in June for 19 years and have had 3 weeks there. Several things which we had planted from 20 to 30 years ago I have now for the first time seen in flower. As to these plays to which you say that Charlie says that I go so often—the facts I believe to be as follows. Since he came home he has taken me to Peter Pan. I have taken him to Rosy Rapture. Ella and Monty Pease have taken us both to Peg o' My Heart and that's the total of my play-going in six months—an average of one play in 2 months.[2] Assuming that I keep up this average and go to one play in the next 2 months, which play would you like to go to?

The war grows more disheartening every day like something which is approaching a climax of catastrophe. I hear that in one annual family gathering in Germany there were present a year ago 13 men of military age; this year there is one left—all the rest have been killed.

I do feel for Hilda's anxiety.[3]

---

1 This news was more cheering than what he had been told earlier. After having problems playing squash, he consulted an oculist in February 1914. He was advised to stop smoking, which he did. Though he was pleased how easy this was after thirty-three years, it didn't help. In May he was told by two doctors that he was suffering from severe degeneration of the retina and choroid in each eye, and would lose the ability to read. Eventually he would only be able to distinguish light from dark. They advised him to give up his work and rest his eyes for six months. He declined, not wanting to abandon his colleagues during the Irish crisis, but made arrangements to see a specialist at a clinic in Germany. Then the war intervened.

2 *Peter Pan* was first staged in 1904. *Rosy Rapture, the Pride of the Beauty Chorus,* a burlesque also written by J. M. Barrie, opened in March 1915 to mixed reviews. It was series of skits satirizing different types of stage plays. *Peg o' My Heart,* by J. H. Manners, based on the lyrics of a popular American song, ran in New York for a year and a half before opening in London. It's about the adventures of a girl from an Irish fishing village obliged by her grandfather's will to go to London and become a lady.

3 Arthur Grenfell was serving in France as an officer in the Buckinghampshire Yeomanry, his Territorial regiment. Grenfell was later a major in the 9th Lancers and ended the war as a lieutenant-colonel in the Royal Flying Corps. He was wounded twice and mentioned in dispatches three times. Two brothers enlisted and were killed.

33 Eccleston Square
11 July 1915

Thank you for your very touching and sympathetic letter on my return.

I never felt the burden of sheer duty so heavily as on this voluntary return to London and work.

33 Eccleston Square
4 August 1915

I see the news of Gilbert Talbot's death and grieve for you all.[1] It is hard to be alive in this time through which we are passing.

33 Eccleston Square
18 August 1915

I will come to dine on the 14th and we can arrange another quiet time then, though I feel so ground down with work that I have little help to give and am just craving for some relief from my own particular burden.

I am going to Cottage Friday evening, work permitting.

13 September 1915

I am glad you are in the country; I had a few beautiful days at Glen, which was all I expect to be able to get and then came back here in time for the worst Zeppelin raid, which was hellish, though it wasn't near me.

I am writing to Emily Drover (address Itchen Abbas Chesford, Hants) to say that you will perhaps go to see the Cottage and will write to her if you do. She can then be at home and open it for you and give you tea if you like.

---

1 Talbot was the son of Katharine Lyttelton's sister Margaret and Major-General Sir Reginald Talbot.

Itchen Abbas
7 May 1916

...I am here for the usual 24 hours. The country is most beautiful, and having dined at 4:30 yesterday afternoon, I had a whole evening free to walk and sit about till the birds stopped singing. How many other rich people in England do you suppose had that luxury?

I return to London this evening

33 Eccleston Square
23 June 1916

This was once intended as the title of a book: "Six months in a main drain and we never saw the end." I will now call it "Bell Hall or six months in a main drain and we never saw the end."

I grieve for your cottage. 20 hours is generally all I can get at mine, i.e., Saturday evening till Sunday afternoon, and my bicycle there hasn't been mounted for a year.

Here is my Sunday at Cottage as a rule: 1. F.O. work (3/4 done, 1/4 left undone). 2. a short walk. 3. One garden job done; 4. Three garden jobs left undone. 5. at 4:30 walk to Winchester carrying F.O. pouch and take train to London. 6. Arrive in London so crushed spiritually to say D-mn. 7. Spend evening doing F.O. work that has come on Sunday.

33 Eccleston Square
9 July 1916

In April 1915 I wrote to the Pres. of the Lib Assoc. to say I could not stand for Parliament again because of my eyes. So now one Sec. of State had to turn out of the H of C at once, it had to be me.

There is the long and short of it and I believe the whole of it.[1]

---

1 The Foreign Secretary had just been ennobled. Asquith, taking over the War Office after Kitchener's death, discovered that no more than four Secretaries of State were permitted to serve in the

33 Eccleston Square
23 August 1916

I am filled with concern and anxiety for you and those who depend on you. You have lived a very gallant and chivalrous life, working for others and now you have got to rest for a little and let others do their own jobs and work for you. If you will do that you will soon be well and able to help them again: if you don't you may become an invalid for a long time, not able to help and perhaps even a burden to others. Very likely they won't do their own jobs as well without your help, but it will be good for them to try for a little.

I am sure God intends us to use our brains as well as our feelings about our duties and it is clear to my brain that your paramount duty for the moment is to submit at all costs to the discipline of rest—because to you it is a discipline and not a luxury.

You know that you press things upon me that I can only accept as discipline—work of course is one and then spare time to be made and spent in walking London streets and doing Muller's exercises: so now I press on you what I consider is to you the repugnant discipline of rest and self-indulgence. Do be sensible—the penalty of not being sensible may be so heavy for you and those who love you.

P.S. Remember that your real form of self-indulgence is doing duties and responding to claims; it is the most insidious form of self-indulgence and most difficult to rest from.

Commons at the same time, and Grey, his eyesight failing, was an obvious candidate to be transferred to the Upper House. The King offered the Foreign Secretary an earldom, but Grey's cousin Albert objected to there being two Earl Greys, and so he became Viscount Grey of Fallodon. On at least two occasions during the previous year he had tried to resign, but Asquith had pressed him to remain, telling him that it would "be universally interpreted as a German triumph."

33 Eccleston Square
23 October 1916

…I hope Arthur Grenfell's wound is not a cause of anxiety: if it be not dangerous it must be a relief to Hilda that he is out of the fighting.

According to casualty lists it is only about 1 in 3 of the officers hit who are killed, but recently with the exception of Arthur Grenfell everyone I know and care for who has been hit has been killed.

27 October 1916

I did have a pang the other day when I stayed at Maythorn and saw a man put on white flannels to play lawn tennis and reflected that I should never put on white flannels again because I can no longer see a moving ball: but I walked off alone amongst trees, which I can still see and which I like better than most people (not friends) and most games.

Fallodon
11 January 1917

There is at present no telegraph here but a post of sorts and your letter of the 8th got here today. I am so glad you had such a happy family party at Bell Hall—your letter reads happily as if it came from a wholesome collection of humanity.

In the first 4 days after I got here I felt well except that I could get no appetite. I went out alone with a gun, perspired under the weight of what I shot and stocked my larder. But 11 such inhuman years as I have had—for to me they have been inhuman—are not so easily dismissed.[1] I said before I left London that now the strain was over the breakdown would come and so it has been. My trouble has never been, in the ordinary sense of the word, indigestion, and now it has been something much worse than that and I have been laid up since Christmas. But I am to get quite well in time. I was really better this week and may be able to take a little solid food next week When not in pain I am more happy than I believed possible in the thought that I am out of office and out of London. I get out a little most days—this week every day; but I cannot do much—I mayn't even have beef tea yet and live as I began life mainly on milk—diluted however now with barley water. Don't prescribe for me—I have had excellent and careful opinions from 2 good doctors and 1 surgeon and they all agree, and I agree with them, that I shall get perfectly well in time.

I haven't been up to much reading and often when I am up to it, I get so extraordinarily happy in thinking of the wonder of leisure that I just lie and think of it—as an animal basks in the sun. It is incredible, inexpressible—it is like having died and gone to Heaven.

One sister or another has been staying her to look after me—my sister Jane is here now.

---

1 The failures of the Dardanelles and Mesopotamian campaigns, and then of the Somme offensive, along with the Irish rising at Easter, had eroded confidence in the government, as had Asquith's equivocations on conscription. He was described by colleagues as "ill and frail" with "hands shaking," exercising little control over debates and looking bored. There was growing pressure to replace the large Coalition Cabinet and unwieldy War Committee with a smaller and more efficient War Council. The moving spirits were Edwin Carson, Max Aitken, and Lloyd George, with Bonar Law a somewhat reluctant accomplice. Asquith agreed to create a new War Council, but insisted on presiding over it, and turned down a compromise proposed by Law on November 25. Six days later, Lloyd George presented the P.M. with a virtual ultimatum and then resigned on December 4th. The Munitions Minister offered to serve alongside Asquith as head of the War Council, but the P.M. rejected this, as well as the suggestion that they both continue in office under Law or Balfour. A full-throated attack on him in the *Times* on the 4th had stiffened Asquith's resistance. The P.M. resigned on the 5th, perhaps hoping Law and Lloyd George would be unable to form governments, but more likely wishing to retire with dignity. Grey, with the rest of the Liberals in the Cabinet, resolved to go out with Asquith. Balfour succeeded him as Foreign Secretary, like "a powerful graceful cat walking delicately and unsoiled across a rather muddy street," said Churchill. (Churchill, *Great Contemporaries,* 249; cited by Jenkins, 461) Ironically, it had been Balfour, First Lord of the Admiralty, whom Lloyd George had most wished to remove from the Cabinet. No prominent Liberal, including Churchill, was invited to join the new government.

Fallodon
5 February 1917

As I had intended I am now going through papers and this first week of February I am looking through some of Dorothy's papers, which are as she left them. It is poignant work—I untie knots which her fingers tied and touch things that have never been touched since she touched them.

Amongst her private letters I found this. How it got here I don't know, but you may like to have it now

I got well enough to be alone some time ago, so my sisters are at their respective homes and I am alone. I am now comfortable—no sickness and hardly ever pain or even discomfort, but I am not fit for a day's work yet. After 5 o'clock I do little but read gently and rest on the sofa. It is comfortable but there is so much to be done and enjoyed with a library inside and one's own house and home and I feel that my weakness wastes it. On coming outside I see whole vistas of enjoyment if the war were over and if I were sure of money enough to live here. It is a beautiful world outside of towns and much to be enjoyed when there is peace and health but what I care for most is on the other side and I am ready to go there, when I can honourably do so.

After sparing Fallodon all January the frost has at last come north and my ponds are frozen. There is some snow but not enough to make the fields pure white. The weather is an absorbing interest for me; to see the days lengthening and the great earth slowly but daily tilting England more towards the sun; the enormous sweep of seasons. I believe men will never get right till they get united by some sort of admiration and reverence for the great elemental works of God and think less of their own artifices. I am told to avoid work and worry at any rate till after Easter and I accept that readily as I don't believe talking can affect the war at all: for the moment nothing matters in the war except what is done on land and sea. So I have just put all I had available with the War Loan and remain a spectator. It seems to me a horrid anxious time and I wish I could feel sure that in the real difference between Lloyd George and me he was right and I was wrong. There is nothing for it now but for this govt. to have the best chance the country can give it.

Brora, Sutherland
7 April 1917

I am glad the salmon was useful. If I get plenty I will send another: and what is the address of the Mastermans and Arthur Grenfells and any others whom you think would like salmon?

I come south after Easter: tomorrow I go to Rosehall Sutherland

I am much refreshed: stronger in body and no longer tired in brain; I can sit in a chair now quite bright without going to sleep. If it were not for anxiety about the war I should be happy.

Acton House, Felton, Northumberland
6 May 1917

Thank you for your letter. I knew you would mind the destruction of Fallodon. Everything had been kept in the place in which Dorothy put it—it had all been spring-cleaned when I was away and I was to have gone into it the day after it was burnt.

I am ashamed of minding it as much as I do as at this time, when so many others are suffering still sadder things.

There isn't much bedroom furniture left, though many things were got out of the first floor. Nearly everything was saved out of the ground floor by the devotion and courage of servants and neighbors. The kitchen wing remains and the statues—all the rest of the building is destroyed, except the outer walls and not all of them remain.

I am staying with my sister here to get insurance and other miserable business settled.

Itchen Abbas
1 June 1917

Your letter arrived here today. The satisfactory thing about digging and manual work is that you see the result and are sure there is a result and that the result is more or less what you intended. In all brain work and in committees and parliaments and governments you so often get a result that you did not intend or are not sure that there is any result. God settles the results quite independently from our intentions. For instance the Prussians planned this war and brought it about and God evidently intended the war to produce tremendous results in the world, but they are not at all the results that the Prussians intended, nor at present even those which the Allies contemplated. The Russian Revolution is one of the biggest results so far.

But in manual labour God generally lets the results be what we intended, and if we plant potatoes they grow, though no doubt God varies the crop by arranging the weather. And at each stage of manual labour the result is evident and definite; when you have ploughed a field you see that it is ploughed and looks quite different to what it did before.

I would gladly have come to your Rascal's house party yesterday if I had been in London; but I have only been there twice and for one day only each time.

I knew how it would be when once the lid was taken off, or rather when the cage door was opened.

I cannot bear London or any big city: the last 11 years of office have become like an horrid dream: the whole thing was so alien to me that I cannot believe I ever lived that life; and London when I was in it the other day was like a strange place.

I have had wonderful days here: they make me long terribly to have Dorothy with me; but when I think of all the sad and awful things public and private I should have to tell her, if she came back, the war and all its horrors and the grief it has brought to friends' homes, and then the other griefs: think what a tale it would be as she asked how her various friends were—the Birrells, the Pauls, Francis Buxton. Your years have had troubles enough, but the account of you would be comparatively cheerful of the friends. I think I would give the best account of Mrs. Creighton—her great sorrow had come before Dorothy died and since then each of her daughters have married.[1]

And now of course the burning of Fallodon would be added to the tale. Well when I think of all this I feel it selfish and cruel to wish Dorothy back, though I long for it so. It is better to wish that I should go to her.

No one can now live in the rooms she made at Fallodon or alter them or decorate them after I am dead—that at any rate is safe, but I can never have a home that will be a home as Fallodon was: the old red brick cannot be reproduced; I can with the furniture that is saved make the inside of some of the rooms in a new home sufficiently like the old rooms to remind me perpetually that they are not the same. That is what I suppose I shall do after the war; till then there can be no building. There were 5 servants bedrooms in the kitchen wing: 3 of those are being turned into 2 bedrooms—one for myself and one for Charlie if he comes home: the three upper servants are staying and they and an odd boy will run the show and I shall live in the shadow of the ruin; but the garden and familiar country will be there. The housekeeper's room will be my sitting room: the books and surplus furniture have gone to a warehouse in Newcastle.

I know nothing about what is happening in the war, but I read the newspaper every day with anxiety and interest. I am sure I can do no good by talking: and I am disposed to think Lloyd George is doing well, considering all the difficulties he has to face; but

---

1 Two of Louise Creighton's four daughters, Beatrice and Lucia, never married, and her youngest and favorite son Oswin, serving as a chaplain, would be killed near Arras on April 9, 1918. The Birrells lost a son, Paul suffered a nervous breakdown, and Francis Buxton had died in November 1911.

I admit I have little else but his own speeches to go by, except something I heard from a good and unbiased opinion last month.

I shall have to go to Northumberland to my sister's house in about 10 days to deal with fire insurance matters...and may see you as I pass through London.

My love to Neville. I am sure he does splendidly. I was thinking of hiring myself out—under a nom provisoire—to avoid public comment—to some farmer for harvest time.

P.S. My pen has run away with me and you had better not attempt to read this letter till you are at leisure. There is nothing in it.

Itchen Abbas
3 July 1917

My nephew Adrian Graves is just home on leave for 10 days: he was in the Messimes fight and has been recommended for his work in it: he was hit 3 times and only grazed each time; at any rate he remained on duty. He comes here for a night this week: I feel prostrate with admiration of him. It is also a great relief that at last one of those I most care for should not have been killed when hit.

P.S. I haven't read the Mesopotamian report yet, but I see from paragraphs and articles in the papers what the drift of it is. I am deeply sorry for Hardinge, who I think has had very bad luck in being let in for it at all.

As to responsibility there, I know what I think about that.[1]

---

1 Along with General John Nixon, Commander of the Northern Army in India, who planned the campaign and over-ruled his field commander, Hardinge, the Viceroy, was made a scapegoat for the failure of General Charles Townsend's advance on Bagdad and the surrender of his division at Kut. Balfour refused to accept Hardinge's resignation and motions condemning him in both Houses failed.

Fallodon
20 July 1917

The best strawberry in flavour is British Green: it won't grow here, but in some places it does well.

I will send you runners of President and Garibaldi (also called Vicomtesse Hericart de Thirry, but I find Garibaldi easier to pronounce). These each have mint in flavour. For a late strawberry, try Givons Late Prolific (this name always gives me a vision of an immense sow lying on her side and suckling an innumerable progeny—a sight that is perhaps not unknown at Bell Hall), Laxton's Latest (not "Latest of All"), and Waterloo, but of these I have not runners.

I passed through London in the latter part of last week and stayed two days at 34 QAG[1] where I met Birrell looking to my great delight shaggy and well. When you were travelling from Bell Hall to London, I was on the train going north.

I am now settled in here with all I need in the way of space, but it is very curiously arranged. My meal room is the old housekeeper's room…under my bedroom and close to the kitchen and there I also write and read after dark. I have two sitting rooms both very comfortable but oddly placed—one is George's horn room, now very well furnished, light and airy with a fine view of the back yard…

I have really every comfort that one man needs for living alone and if it were not for the memory and comparison with the old house, I should have no reason to be sad. The destroyed part was so much Dorothy's that its destruction is in a sense a fitting consequence of her death and my feeling about it is getting to seem part of my feeling for her. But it is very sad nevertheless for its own sake. I have begun to do work in the form of writing, but I don't know what will come of it.[2] It is very pleasant to work at

---

1 The Glenconners'.
2 presumably the precursor of *Twenty-Five Years* or the lost autobiography.

leisure in work of one's own choice, not under pressure. I have never done it before.

My three faithfuls, Alice, Lavinia, and Barbara anticipate all my wants and comforts and I am served in the spirit in which Algernon Falconer (I think that was his name, but nearly all my books are warehoused and I cannot confirm by reference) was served, before he married, in Gryll Grange.[1] He lived in a tower in the New Forest.

Fallodon
11 October 1917

Your letter of reproach arrived yesterday. You have every right to reproach me, but my fault is not very deep; it is the fault not of intention but of daily procrastination. Your former letter came just before I went south. I carried it about intending to answer it and your letter of the 1st found me with the other one back in my writing table here.

You asked about Albert. I saw him twice after they brought him to Howick: once for half an hour lying in the sun in the garden and once for only a few minutes in his room.

It was a great privilege to see him—he was very splendid: meeting death not only with courage but with enthusiasm, just as he had met every great adventure in life. I couldn't always share his optimism and enthusiasm about particular things in life but I was filled with admiration for it now. The hope of what is to come after death is infinite and justifies all optimism. There are two things here that stir me with unbounded hope and admiration—one is individual human love and the other is the exceeding beauty of the world; and these lead naturally to infinite hope in future things. About all else—the Colonies, the British Empire etc. etc.

1 The final novel by Thomas Love Peacock (1785–1866), published in 1861. Falconer has seven female servants and no males. Dorothy Grey preferred female servants in the house. Pamela Glenconner was even more insistent about having no butler or footmen.

my admiration is severely limited by criticism. But Albert's spirit of meeting death seemed to me to consecrate all the enthusiasm of his life.

I saw Alice Grey at Howick Grange just before I went south. She spoke naturally of ordinary things, but her face was full of grief and suffering. One can't love much without suffering much, if one survives the other. I gather she was splendid in all the last days with Albert, keeping herself attuned to his spirit, though she knew all that his death would mean for her. The courage that there is in love is sublime. Charlie Howick and his sister seemed to me very good too, so steady and sane and thoughtful. No one could have been better accompanied and comforted than Albert up to the water's edge.

I forget when it was that I last wrote to you, but I will give you my news for a month back. After the funeral at Howick I went to Vernon Watney's deer forest.[1] I have never cared to shoot at stags—I don't know why—so I walked on the mountain tops with him for three days and saw him stalk. It is splendid country and I enjoyed it; then I spent two days with Haldane at Cloan—then a week here—then a Sunday with my sister and brother-in-law near Henley; there I hired a bicycle and bicycled to Nuneham, for Harcourt's shoot, where Johnson of the H. of C. came to valet and load for me. I like being at Nuneham. Thence I bicycled to the home of a friend—Herbert Leon[2] —at Brill in Buckinghamshire and spent a Sunday there. He has been there for 20 years and I had never gone there yet and had promised to go as soon as I was out of office, and liked that very much. Thence a cross-country journey by train to Cottage, where I stayed a whole

---

1 Watney (?–1928) was a naturalist and antiquarian who wrote about West Oxfordshire. His *Cornbury* and the *Forest of Wychwood* (1910) is considered a minor classic. Grey later called him his "most intimate friend," but no correspondence appears to have survived and he is not mentioned by any of Grey's biographers.

2 Leon (1850–1926) was a wealthy Jewish financier, former M.P., and leading supporter of the Liberal Party. He purchased and developed Bletchley Park, the estate that would later house British counter-intelligence operations during World War II.

week alone, except that I bicycled to Blackmoor on Saturday, taking my things for the night on the bicycle, stayed the night with the Selbornes, and bicycled back to Cottage in storms of intense wind and rain on Sunday morning and planted bulbs in sunshine in the afternoon.

On the morning of the 8th I lunched with A.J.B.[1] in London, dined at Brooks's with Bongy[2] and one of my late Priv. Secs. and came here by night.

Now you are back in London I will let you know when I next come South, though it may not be for a long time.

I am very sorry to learn that Hermione has been ill—you have anxiety, but it is less I hope than if she were in the trenches or the Flying Corps. Frank Pember's son has been killed and he has no other son left—that is the greatest sorrow that the war has brought to my friends this year.[3]

P.S. I am writing in the summer house where you once found me writing my fishing book:[4] it is a day of cloudless sky and the sun fills the summer house.

Fallodon
16 January 1918

Twice lately I have had to pay a flying visit to London: the first time I actually myself established a connection by telephone and asked for you, but you had not returned to town. Yesterday Pamela I understand communicated with you. I am sorry to have missed you and will have another shot if I come up again. The telephone seems to me more evil than ever. One of my efforts resulted in my hearing distinctly the whole of a conversation

---

1 Balfour

2 Maurice Bonham Carter (1880–1960), Asquith's son-in-law and former private secretary.

3 Francis Pember (1862–1954), a friend from Balliol, was then Warden of All Souls College. He would go on to serve as Vice Chancellor of Oxford University from 1926 to 1929.

4 *Fly Fishing* (1899)

between two other people and I failed entirely to establish any communication of my own.

I hear from more than one source that you have spoken of my going to Washington. How much do you know of that old story?[1]

It is fine but not comfortable to be looking on at the close of an epoch. I feel deep in me that the civilization of the Victorian epoch ought to disappear. I think I always knew this subconsciously, but I took things as I found them and for 30 years spoke of progress as an enlargement of the Victorian industrial age: as if anything could be good that led to telephones and cinematographs and large cities and the Daily Mail. I have nevertheless gone back to the NER board, which I like. I cannot bear the continuance of the war, but it has to be till the Germans cease to hope for victory.

Fallodon
17 January 1918

I forgot to congratulate you and Neville on the honour that Hermione has conferred upon you by being knighted. (I understand she has some order of the b.e.[2] for war service. I don't suppose it to be equal to her merit, but I hope it is considered a pleasant recognition of her work.)

---

1 In May, 1917, Balfour, the Foreign Secretary, wished to appoint Grey as Ambassador to replace Cecil Spring-Rice. But the War Council felt he was too "pacifist" and Grey himself demurred. He left open the possibly of serving as an envoy after the war, and in the fall of 1919 was dispatched to Washington as special Ambassador to promote the League of Nations and closer Anglo-American relations.
2 Order of the British Empire, established the previous June.

P.S. Did you know that John has a paragraph about Dorothy in his book?[1] I saw it quoted in a local paper here and wrote to thank him.

Fallodon
19 January 1918

I hoped that Hermione had been Damed. Dame Hermione of the British Empire! How grand that would sound! But titles don't matter: she is splendid as plain Hermione.

The Victorian age has made its contribution to history—that will remain. "There shall never be one lost good."[2] But industrial England is an ugly thing and reads the Daily Mail and runs to cinematographs, and every human civilization in turn has decayed and perished. Statesman cannot arrest the progress of great forces; when these forces are on the upgrade statesmen make reputations and get credit; when the forces are on the downgrade the statesmen are blamed, but "God fulfills himself in many ways lest one good custom should corrupt the world"[3] and He alone knows what it has been in the power of statesmen to do.

I haven't yet read John's book, except that extract about Dorothy. I look forward to reading the book, but for the moment I have other books on hand and I cannot read more than a limited amount by artificial light.

Now that I am alone and have leisure to think I realize as I could not do before the cumulative effect of being without Dorothy and without George and of those eleven awful years in

---

1 *Recollections*, v. 2 (1917). Morley wrote of her: "She was a woman of truly remarkable character both intellectual and moral, with uncommon and original traits—but all of them pointing towards high thought and feelings, and an independent life stripped of artificial trappings." Of Grey himself, he wrote, in a diary excerpt from 1908, "Grey followed… in that curiously high, simple, semi-detached style, which, combined, as it always is in him, with a clean-cut mastery of all the facts of his case, makes him one of the most impressive personalities in Parliament… He is a remarkable figure, wholly free of every trace of Theatre."
2 From the poem "Abt Vogler" (1864) by Robert Browning
3 From "The Passing of Arthur" in Tennyson's *Idylls of the King* (1835, revised 1842)

office. I see life as a great happiness and yet feel full of sad experience, moving toward the stillness of my rest.

Hearing from you reminded me that I had not for a long time thought of Auburn's sonnet on Westminster Abbey and at supper I recalled it: at first I could not remember the first three lines, but they came back to me before I finished supper and I have it all perfectly again.

Fallodon
21 January 1918

I am sorry for your meat trouble. Meat is scarce here and I live on game which I shoot myself weekly to save the beef and mutton supply, but I haven't enough game except to relieve the local situation. It is a bad woodcock year or I would live on them. I once went out on three occasions for a total bag of one rabbit.

But for the moment bacon is less scarce in the township of Fallodon because one of the shepherds has killed a very large pig, so I am sending you a bit by parcels post.

P.S. Rabbits are few here and I have no one except one woodman to catch them or I would send rabbits to friends.

Fallodon
24 January 1918

I fear from your postcard you are expecting a whole side of bacon and will be woefully disappointed with the 2 lbs (more or less) that I sent.

My cook hearing that a neighboring pig had been killed bought what she thought reasonable for my household use: I being touched by your meat difficulties and also by those of my sister Jane in Oxfordshire thought I would spare a piece for each of you—hence my little effort.

I can't imagine that this is contrary to any food regulation, but next time you fear I may be breaking one please don't put it in a postcard that will be read in at least the local offices here. I believe my house supplies are most moderate, but postcards in the country are a fertile source of gossip.

Fallodon
28 January 1918

I had no notion who Mrs. Guest was and no book of reference here and didn't see any account in the paper, so I did not realize till your letter came that anything had happened that concerned you. I am very sorry for you all. Suicide itself does not shock me, but the thought of the distress that has probably preceded it is pathetic and it must be very distressing to near relations and friends, if it is caused by trouble that could have passed. Then indeed it is grief and a waste, and not release.

The relief to my sister and to my nephew of his being in Holland is unspeakable: letters are coming from him and he has come through this horrible ordeal of nearly 3 ½ years of German prison camps splendidly.[1] I honor both of my nephews more than I can say. The younger one after doing instruction at home is soon to go out again. It is only by wonderful escapes that he is alive and I fear that he cannot escape forever. He has done so well too—M.C.[2] + bar + normal stripe.

Rosehall, Sutherland
10 April 1918

Thank you for your letter. My nephew died splendidly. He held the Germans off a hill with his machine guns for a whole day. He was wounded and continued on duty, then wounded

---

1 Cecil Graves was interned in the Netherlands as part of a prisoner exchange. When the Germans discovered he was Grey's nephew, he was treated harshly, and spent some time in solitary confinement.(C. R. Graves, "Cecil George Graves," unpublished reminiscence.)
2 Military Cross. Created in 1914, it honored "an act or acts of exemplary gallantry during active operations against the enemy."

again and, unable to walk, was being carried by a sergeant when he was shot through the head and killed instantly.

I felt sure he would not continue to escape when he went back to the front this last time. Now his mother has to suffer. I had arranged to take over the money charge of him and give him his Oxford course, which he desired, after the war and had thus begun to feel him to be a sort of son. That is all over as much else in my life is over.

I am here with Frank Pember till next week when I shall probably get to Fallodon.

P.S. A salmon will start by rail addressed to Hagley station for you tomorrow, and will arrive, if not abstracted on the way, on Saturday or possibly Monday.

Fallodon
31 Jan 1919 (dictated)

I've got your card and would certainly come to the party if I had been in London, but I shall be here on the 4th and for some time to come. I think with great satisfaction of this engagement and congratulate you all very much.[1] I cannot see to chose wedding presents and shall be grateful if you will choose one for Hermione or let her do it for herself with the cheque which I send.

Brora, Sutherland
8 March 1919

I am sending you a salmon. Please return the basket to me here. I was here when Hermione's wedding took place and was sorry to be out of reach. I hear it was a very beautiful wedding. I am very much in favour of happy marriages and I like to think of

---

1 Hermione Lyttelton was engaged to Lionel Hitchens (1874–1940), a member of Milner's "Kindergarten." They were married later in the year.

this one. Writing is a labour for me and I cannot see what I write. I do not care for having things sent to me, so I am increasingly withdrawn from current life, but I like the life here. We are a party of four.

Fallodon
6 June 1919

You will have no difficulty about tickets for Robert Cecil's meeting on June 13th if you will write to the Secretary, League of Nations Union, 22 Buckingham Gate S. W. 1, saying how many tickets you want.

I did not go to Norway, but I had to go to Newcastle to take the chair for an Albert Grey memorial lecture by Bryce on the 27th. I shall only be one night in London on June 13 and go to Cottage the next day, but I will let you know when next I have any time in London.

I am not without hope that Wright's treatment may succeed. His glasses enable me to read distinct print or writing, but there is no definite improvement in my sight yet.

I am glad you have noticed how glorious the month of May has been and how splendid the weather.

Rain is badly wanted now for the crops.

Fallodon
15 August 1919

I get to 34 Queen Anne's Gate early Wednesday morning. What time can I come to see you that day? Not luncheon, because Lloyd George wants to see me and luncheon is often his hour and I may have to lunch there.

Sent a line on Tuesday to 34 QAG so that I may get it early on Wed. I had a shot at you on the telephone when I made a lightning visit to London the other day, but the telephone said you were both out of town.

Rosehall, Sutherland
20 February 1920

Wright's treatment consisted solely in the use of his glasses. I have not got any improvement in my sight yet from the use of them, but they are an immense boon to me as without them I can neither read nor write. As long therefore as I can replace the glasses if I lose or break those I have, I get all that I want. It is said Wright's brother is to carry on his work.

So much for your question. Now as to weather. In this Riviera climate there has been no rain to speak of for weeks and weeks. It is the driest April I have ever seen. The sun shines perpetually and I bask in it, caressed by light zephyrs. The river is a thread: even Charlie gets few fish and I have got only 1 since March 24, but I was away all that week on railway and other business.

Dorothy and I always found that we could not get the Fallodon feeling for two days or so: we used to think about that and regret it. No doubt it was on that experience that she spoke to you. On the other hand I think we got Cottage feeling in a day.

Brora, Sutherland
16 March 1920

I note what you say about interest in public work, but you must remember that for 32 years I was in the thick of public work and that of the last 11 years of them I was so hard worked that what I craved in friendship was a little change and relief.

Even this week I am spending 4 days away from here on railway business and for the rest, impaired sight which makes reading, writing, and even ordinary things like eating a strain and labour is in itself a considerable occupation as well as preoccupation.

227

Brora, Sutherland
25 March 1920

You will have inferred from my last letter that I cannot come to the Passion music. I should have loved it had I been within reach. I gather that I wrote Bellshill by mistake for Bell Hall. Bellshill is the name of the house my mother lived in latterly almost 10 miles from Fallodon.

The physical effort of writing with my nose in the paper (I don't mean that I actually write with my nose and not with a pen) interferes with my brain and I make mistakes; and the labour of reading hinders revision.

Some day I hope to come to Bell Hall. I should like it, but after this fishing I must be at Fallodon for a bit and then at Cottage. The rest of the party is gone to the river and I am going for a walk in the moor.

Itchen Abbas
11 July 1920

I have been in London very little and only when R. Cecil has insisted on my coming up to make a speech or when NER business has brought me up... I have to make two speeches this week, but shall only be up for one night and the time is full of business there...

I get very weary of not being able to see properly and I find London more than ever depressing: in the country I get some sense of satisfaction and congenial surroundings and there are pleasant smells and sounds.

Fallodon
26 Oct 1920 (dictated)

I was glad to get your letter. My eyes are no better, but also no worse. I can read a book in good print to myself by artificial light nearly as fast as a person with average sight could read it aloud; in daylight I cannot read so fast. The result is that I get through little in amount. It is more laborious but also much less tedious than being read aloud to, and I am independent of assistance. This I owe to Wright's glasses, without which I can't read a word.

Opal Whiteley's Diary will be liked with enthusiasm by some people, others will be indifferent and others will resent it as an inanity.[1] I belong to the first lot. To me it seems that it should not be read as the work of a man, woman or child, but of an exceptional being who is in the nature of a wood-elf, or a child of nature if you like to call it so, who has the feeling for nature in a more intense degree than we have—possibly because it is lacking in some of the human and divine elements with which we are complicated. This makes it exceptional and remarkable, and to people like me exceedingly interesting.

Charlie and I are still living here and as I can only write with my nose on the paper, I can't write and smoke at the same time, and as I am smoking at the moment, Charlie is writing to my dictation.

I don't know what is going to happen to everybody—expenditure is going up and we have, I think, reached the limits of taxation. Retrenchment in expenditure will lead to a great row[2] but continuous [sic] of the present expenditure will lead to collapse. In other words, we have got to get through in one way or another a period of discomfort and national suffering which may produce catastrophe. Happily, though this seems to be the logic of our present situation, public affairs seldom produce what seem to be their logical consequences. So I hope possibly to begin the rebuilding of a small Fallodon next year.

---

1 The diary was allegedly written by Whiteley (1897–1992), a girl from a small town in Oregon, when she was six. A self-taught naturalist, the child prodigy achieved fame as a public lecturer by age twelve. She called herself "the Sunshire Fairy" and claimed to be the daughter of Henri d'Orléans.
2 "catastrophe" crossed out

Please give my love to Neville. I hope to see you when I am in London some time next month. As to age, I note that the united ages of Neville and you are now 135 years. Charlie and I at present are together only 105. But next year I shall get into my 60th year. I think I was born about 50 years too late. Had I been born 50 years sooner, sport would have been better and cheaper, politics would have been more manageable, I should not have spent the first part of my life in the decline of one epoch and lived into the painful transition stage in which we now are, there would have been no crowned teeth and I should have kept my sight unimpaired to the end of life. But it is too late to alter all this now and I am glad I got through the first 50 years of my life without realising that I had better have been born sooner.

P.S. [in Grey's handwriting] Charlie's comment is that this letter is like a chapter of the book of Job.

Howick
2 January 1921

I never answered the letter you wrote me after Glenconner died. It is almost like the break up of a home to me and I had much affection for him.

We get more bare as we get older. And now I am just sending this line to thank you for your letter and to send you my best wishes for all of you in the new year.

I have no news of myself: I am well but sight no better and life in consequence laborious and ineffective.

Charlie (brother) and I are here for this Sunday.

Rosehall, Sutherland
27 April 1921

Since I wrote that presumptuous letter offering a salmon we have had summer weather here and drought and the fishing has failed. So I have had no salmon to send.

Having things to do at Fallodon I am going there tomorrow, and my nephew Cecil Graves goes south too as the fishing here is hopeless.

I am becoming more and more of a recluse, having no house in which to entertain people, but I must be in London occasionally in May and shall hope to see you then.

Brooks's, St. James St.
19 May 1921

I have got your own letter and also that from you and your two signatories. The latter I will answer in time: it is most difficult to draw up written replies to these requests and I appreciate the suggestion in that no reply is absolutely necessary.

In these 4 ½ years of freedom and retirement my mind travels to conclusions which do not lend themselves to political action and would seem strange to all of you. You urge that there is a personal quality or difference from the common in me that would make me invaluable in politics: I have come to think that I am so different in my sense of values and outlook that I am not suited to politics at all.

I don't see much in the papers, but the story of the man who broke his oar and kept on rowing is familiar to me. He considered, however, that he was helping the boat to go in the right direction. You all of you want me to row in a direction in which I do not really believe. I will explain more when I see you.

I am so sorry to hear of money troubles: they are indeed widespread and inevitable. Everybody, except war profiteers, is hit in degree, but I know that for people like you, with fixed incomes, no pre-war margin, and others more or less dependent on you it must be particularly hard. I know your courage will never falter, but I wish it had been not so tried.

I have a busy morning and might be rather late as I have eye treatment (I am trying a new kind) at 12:30 and it lasts ¾ of an hour: but I shall look in here before it to see if there is a message...

Itchen Abbas
14 July 1921

The Dryden lines are new to me. They are very apropos and I am glad to have seen them.

I am spending my last days of this summer here and go north on the 20th to Newcastle for railway business and then on to Fallodon. This is the 32nd summer of Cottage (it was built in 1890) and of these Cottage summers I shall now have had 16 alone—exactly half, and after this the balance will grow on the alone side.

Brooks's Club, St. James
26 November 1921

You have written me a very nice letter and I have liked it very much. We didn't mean to make any announcement yet, because we haven't settled when we can marry and so we don't want an avalanche of letters and the things that such an announcement brings.[1] But 6 months ago I told Pamela that when she felt free to

---

1 Lyttelton apparently chose not to keep the letter in which Grey told her the news of his engagement. He had informed Louise Creighton around the same time. "For some years as I supposed people knew I have had a very delightful and intimate friendship with Pamela Glenconner. It did not impair my close friendship with her husband and I was equally in the confidence of them both. A few months ago I told her that when the time came and she could marry again, I should ask her to marry me. She said it was too soon yet and that she still had to make a home for her 3 sons and that was her first care. We agreed therefore to go on seeing each other frequently but to make no change at present. And so things remain... I do very much wish I had told you before." (E. Grey to L. Creighton, 8 November 1921, Bodleian.) But three days later he clarified the situation In a postscript dated November 11: "I think the best course is that we should let it be understood that there is an engagement but that nothing is imminent." He added, "I hope you will always be sure that I shall prize your friendship and be always grateful to you for all you have done for me." Pamela and Edward were married in a private ceremony at Wilsford on June 4, 1922. The only witnesses were Christopher Tennant and Grey's youngest sister Constance Curtis. "We told no one else beforehand as we wanted to have it quite quietly without wedding presents, spectators and photographers: and in this we succeeded."(E. Grey to L. Creighton, 5 June 1922.)

marry again I wanted her. Since then I have had increasing happiness; it gets better and better and now I am living on a higher plane of spirits than I have been on for many years…

It doesn't of course mean any break with the memories and affections of past years. But it is true that for some time and especially just lately, when I am living at Fallodon and Pamela is in the south, it does mean that when I come south I spend all the time I can with her, and have seen little of other people.

I am going back to Fallodon at the end of the month and today we are going to Maytham till Monday.[1]

P.S. Maytham Nov 28

I liked especially the way in which you bring Dorothy and Eddie in, and so did Pamela, to whom I showed it.

Fallodon
18 February 1923

Thank you for your letter. Cottage is gone and all the little things that had gathered there in 33 years are burnt. No one was in it at the time and bedding had been left to air before a fire.

And now Pamela is ill: apparently her heart has been gradually developing trouble for several years.[2] The doctors assure me that there is no cause for anxiety, but that rest for some months is imperative: at present she may not see visitors. I am going back to London tomorrow. We had 7 months of real happiness and now life is clouded by health.

---

1 the home of Jack and May Tennant
2 She had arterial sclerosis, and would die of it on November 18, 1928.

Fallodon
7 December 1923

A line to congratulate you and Neville and the 3 gallant daughters on Charlie M.'s success. I am so glad for him.[1]

I am sorry that when we had got an honest man as P.M. in Baldwin he should have done such a stupid thing as to precipitate an election and go in for protection, which I believe would ruin the country politically and economically.[2] Not half the returns have got here yet but it looks as if Baldwin had thrown away his party's majority and his own position.[3]

Pamela sends her congratulations too; she is delighted with the success of Lucy's husband, and was so pleased to meet Hermione at Oldham.

Fallodon
19 August 1924 (dictated to Pamela)

I have a vast amount of work on hand, among other things I am writing my memoirs of the Foreign Office. Until this is done I am making as few promises as possible of any other work, but will consider, when I am a little freer, whether I can say yes to what you ask. Pamela and I are here till September—and are having a fairly quiet time, and a very happy one. I hope you are having the same.

My best wishes to Auburn and Charlie Masterman.

P.S. [from Pamela] I add just a line to say how nice Hermione wrote to me from Overstrand; and I hope to see her when I shall be visiting Stephen in Norfolk on the 2nd of September; who

---

1 Masterman was returned to the House as MP for Manchester Rusholme in the General Election of 6 December 1923.
2 Baldwin need not have called an election for another four years, but expected a mandate that would strengthen his position within the party.
3 The Conservatives lost 86 seats. Though they retained 258, they were now outnumbered by the combined Opposition, the Liberals winning 158 seats and Labour 191. Ramsay MacDonald became Prime Minister.

I am glad to say is making very good progress.[1] I did so much enjoy meeting her at dinner with the Selbornes in the summer, and saw such a reminding look of what I remember in you sister Margaret's[2] face long ago, at Isel in Cumberland, when I was a child in the nursery; and her visits to us were a joy and delight—of music and stories; and sayings such as "de Vines and de Veeze" and other such! There she seemed to be again—in Hermione's face.

Edward is very well, and we have had lovely days—and his work makes great headway. It is going to be an important book.

Fallodon
11 January 1925

It is distressing to say I can't give a lecture, but my one discourse on open air, mostly birds, has been give so often that I cannot do it any more with reporters present. The things I have to tell are so well known to all people who know about birds that it makes me ridiculous to have it reported again and again.

Just now I am striving to get my political book finished before the middle of March, when I go for 10 days salmon fishing, and I must keep the time free from other things. I might do what you want next year, if I am more free, but I do not feel that I have a new lecture on any subject in me.

I took Pamela as far as Paris, where she stayed 4 days at the Embassy last month: thence she went on to Villiers to spend some 8 weeks with her Stephen, who has to spend the autumn and winter months there as a precaution. I meet her at Wilsford in a few days now.

Except for railway work I have been here for the last 3 weeks and not in Switzerland at all. Now that my sight has failed so

---

1 Stephen Tennant (1906–1987), Pamela's youngest child, had been diagnosed with incipient tuberculosis.
2 Margaret Mary Stuart-Wortley Talbot (1841–1937), Katharine's eldest sister.

much I find life very tedious except here and at Wilsford, where I know the surroundings. The other exception is salmon fishing—the one sport that I can still do after a fashion.

Charlie is still in Africa, exploring and leading the life he loves, but we expect him home this summer.

Love to Neville.

Fallodon
22 May 1925

I am glad the salmon arrived. I have just had 9 days of fishing with Jack Tennant on the Spey and am now on my way to rejoin Pamela at Wilsford.

I could not be at Milner's funeral; I would have gone to the memorial service, but I was far away. You can generally rely on statements about my movements in the papers to be wrong.

Milner was a fine straight figure in public life; his work was over, like that of many others who have spent their strength in the public service and reached old age. There was nothing to be wished at last but a peaceful end, and that I hope he had.

We have no home in town now and except when railway work demands it, I do not come there. My failure of sight adds to the discomfort and misery of living in London.

Fallodon
6 September 1925

I have read Princess Lichnowsky's[1] letter with much interest and appreciation. The impression I got when I saw her in London in 1924 (I did not know she had been there this year) was that she was one of the people into whose soul the iron of war had

---

1 Mechtilde Lichnowsky (1879–1958), novelist and poet and wife of the former German Ambassador Karl Max Lichnowsky.

entered very deeply. What she says about her lizards reminds me of the lines

"As a lizard with the shade

Of a trembling leaf

Thou with sorrow art dismayed."[1]

My bad sight would have disqualified me from being on the Land Commission: I can read only a little and with great effort (except in Braille) and to have columns of newspapers and reports read aloud would take endless time and even then not keep me in touch with huge complicated problems, as I used to be.

But the Land Commission won't solve even the mines problem. There have been enquiries enough into that and all is known about it. The problem before us is how to face the hold up of the community, which the extremists will force. The trouble in the coal mines is only one pretext for doing that; I shall be surprised if another pretext is not found before the Commission has completed its enquiry.

We are here till Christopher's wedding; his engagement promises as good a prospect of real happiness as any human prospect can afford.[2]

We have no home in London now: Pamela was ordered in March to spend her time quietly in the country and has been entirely at Wilsford or here. I spend a night at Christopher's flat when I have railway or other work in London, but it is always a great rush. When I come there for any time I will let you know.

Pamela is building a small house in Smith Square, having sold her home in Buckingham Street; if as the doctors expect she gets well, we shall be in London more next year.

---

1 from a song by Shelley: "Rarely, rarely comest thou, Sprit of Delight."
2 Christopher Grey Tennant (1899–1983) and his wife, the former Pamela Paget, divorced in 1935.

Delvyr Lodge, Orton, Morayshire
12 March 1927

Pamela has had to go to the Riviera with her boy where I paid her a visit, but railway and other things prevent me from being away for long at a time.

Fallodon
9 September 1928

What you say of Vernon Watney is very true. He was a man of very rare quality. People often said that they found him reserved and difficult to know; but for his friends he had a rare and peculiar gift for intimacy, confidence, and affections. He was my most intimate friend and his death is a great grief and loss to me. With Haldane too another chapter of very close association with my life has had "finis" written to it.

My brother Charlie has been gored by a buffalo in Africa and has a hole in his chest and a collapsed lung. He is at Kigoma[1] and we hope he will be well enough to start for home in a month or two; but for the great sturdiness of his nature he must have been killed and he very nearly was killed.

I can only read a newspaper enough to keep in touch with one or two big things, but Pamela tells me that Lucy is standing for Parliament in the Salisbury division. This is very interesting, and we are full of good will.[2]

Fallodon
21 October 1928

Thank you very much for your letter. I feel that I can hardly take in all that Charlie's death means: the last brother is gone.

---

1 Tanzania, then Tanganika.
2 Lucy Masterman lost the election, coming in second in the poll.

Both he and George were wonderful men; both were fearless and this has brought the life of each here to an end.

It is just like going through the loss of George over again; for Charlie had occupied George's place and made his home here, when he was in England.

Vernon Watney's death too makes a gap in my life that can never be filled: he had rare qualities and very warm affections and a peculiar gift of intimate friendship. Indeed outside the family he was my most intimate friend.

P.S. Pamela and I have been here for over 2 months; we come south at the end of the month.

Fallodon
30 November 1928

Thank you for your sympathy. There is no life left in me and I shall stay here till some life comes back to enable me to do my work.[1]

The inside of every room in this new home was arranged by Pamela and will always speak of her, as the old house spoke of Dorothy till it was destroyed by fire 11 years ago.

My sister Alice has come with me for a week or two as she did 23 years ago: she helped me then and will help me now. I have had wonderful letters from Pamela's friends about her, and Alice reads them to me, for my sight is not equal to much reading.

---

1 Pamela Grey died November 18, 1928. Edward had caught an express south that was stopped especially for him. Christopher Tennant told him of Pamela's death in the railway carriage at King's Cross. "He heard the tragic news calmly. But then the pent-up emotion of his long vigil became too much for him and he broke down for a minute. Then he made his way towards the motor-car which bore him to Wiltshire to his dead wife." (*Daily Mail,* 20 November 1928.) According to the obituarist in the *Morning Post,* Pamela "was the incarnation of faith, hope, and charity... Her feet were set on the Mystic Way from childhood, and she...found other-worldly messages in birds and flowers and in the sayings and doings of poor folk... No more rare and beautiful spirit has lived in this age of ebbing faith, and even those who knew her ever so little were happier for the knowledge." (*Morning Post,* 20 November 1928)

If as I think the faith that Pamela had about the other side is true, she at any rate is happy and is spared all what those who still live have or may have to go through.

Fallodon
29 December 1928

I was glad to get your letter. I grieve that I was the cause of your friend missing that visit to Wilsford. I never feel that people ought to think of me as "poor." I have had happiness in life beyond the common lot—if it is not arrogant to judge the common lot. Is not the estimate that people form of what I have lost in itself a measure of what I have had?

I shall begin to take up non-public work next month—such as the railway, which is a duty and is the only thing for which I am paid and thereby under special obligation to do or to give up. And I shall go for a short visit to Frank Pember and to my sister in Shropshire in the course of the month, if all goes well.

But a health problem has to be faced. I have never been really well for nearly 2 years and I have had seven attacks of illness this year, 2 of them in the last four weeks and I must have the whole thing talked out with Sir J. T. Walker, who is one of the great experts in my sort of trouble.

P.S. Thank you for your very kind suggestion about a room in your house. I will not forget it, if I am in need.

My best wishes to you and Neville and to all yours for the new year.

Fallodon
7 February 1929

You have sometimes asked me to make a sign when I come to London. If all goes well I shall be there for one day only to attend a railway committee at 3 on Thurs the 14th. If you have no large party may I come to lunch that day?

P.S. I hope Neville is well. Even I, though I am so much younger than he is, have become aware that age is liable to many infirmities.

Dane End, Ware, Herts.
10 March 1929

I should have enjoyed hearing the music with you, but I must go to Fallodon to attend to business there as soon as I can and I cannot be in London on the days you name.

Christopher's wife is very ill with pneumonia after having had a baby last month. The signs now are that the worst is over and the doctors think she will pull through. Christopher is showing all his splendid qualities of clear head, courage, strength and tenderness, but he has been through an awful time and there is still anxiety.

I was with Jack Tennant on the Spey for a week: he was in bed for a few days with a bronchial attack, but was recovered when I left. Fishing was poor.

Fallodon
4 December 1929

After such a blatant mistake in my letter to you, I ought never to write letters again. I am ordering Springy's life to be sent to you and when I next come to see you I will inscribe it for you.[1]

Many thanks for copying out the lines.

I dined at the club last night and alas! heard 2 more recent books praised in a way that made me long to read them.

---

1 *The Letters and Friendships of Cecil Spring Rice,* edited by Stephen Gwynn. A contemporary of Grey's at Balliol, Spring Rice (1859–1918) served in Embassies in Washington, Berlin, and St. Petersburg before being named Minister to Persia in 1906. After serving as Minister to Sweden from 1908–1913, he was named Ambassador to the U.S. He was close to Grey and wrote him copiously and candidly from his three posts, even offering occasional advice—something no ambassador would normally do.

Fallodon
2 January 1932

You have been often in my thoughts and I write to enquire about you and where you were. I hear you are resting in a nursing home and it is doubtful whether I ought to write to you: in any case you must not spoil your rest by a reply.

I have little news of myself. I feed my birds still, but I cannot read: happily being older I can rest in a chair in a way that would have been intolerable in youth. My sister Jane and her daughter are here for a week and I am very glad to have them here.

The world is so troubled and I do not see light through the troubles so that I am half-hearted about sending optimistic wishes for 1932: I hope it may find us better at the end of it. There was an interesting forecast in a talk on the wireless last night. I do not know if you may listen to the wireless yet. I hope you do not find the rest irksome and that you will benefit from it.

My best wishes are with you. I shall get news of you from a daughter.

Fallodon
4 January 1932

Please tell Hilda when you would like me to come. I shall love to see you. I had made enquiries about you. As a result of these I did not like to break in with a letter to you direct; but Hilda already has a message for you. Now that you have written, though I am not sure that you had Hilda's permission, I write direct.

I hope you do not find the rest irksome. You have a really good retrospect to look back upon. I do not believe that you have any sins of commission at all and such a high standard of life and duty maintained that there can be hardly any sins of omission. When you appear before a tribunal that knows everything, you will be surprised to be told how good you are.

Empire Hotel, Bath
15 January 1933

I enjoyed my visit to you yesterday. My sister has just sent me Margot's article on herself in the Sunday Times. It suggested to me that some people find their greatest happiness in such glimpses as they can get of "central peace subsisting in the heart of endless agitation."[1] Margot finds it in "endless agitation."

---

1 from Book III of William Wordsworth's "The Excursion."

APPENDIX

Sex and the Foreign Secretary

"They married and lived happily ever after" ends the common novel. "Did they? What extraordinary people!" is the comment of common sense.

Mandell Creighton

The first biography of Grey in over forty years makes some new and startling allegations about the Foreign Secretary's private life: he may have fathered several illegitimate children. Grey's tastes were apparently eclectic. One woman he impregnated was the daughter of a London estate agent, another a Maid-of-Honour to Queen Alexandra.

The first of these claims surfaced in 2003, in an article in *Family Tree Magazine*. The irony of Grey having produced a "German Love-Child" was appreciated by the editors of the *Journal of Liberal History*, which reprinted the story.[1]

Briefly, in 1893 Grey was supposed to have had sex with a young woman named Florence Annie Slee, whose father owned a surveying company and estate agency. When she became

---

1 H-J. Heller, "Sir Edward Grey's German Love-Child," *Family Tree Magazine* (v. 19, n. 12) (October 2003), 29–31. *Journal of Liberal History* 46 (Spring 2005), 12–14.

pregnant, Grey arranged a sham marriage between her and his youngest brother Charles, who was twenty. This was conducted in an unlicensed chapel, by a hard-up clergyman eager for the marriage fee. Thus it wasn't recorded in the General Register, but the family received some sort of certificate. The pregnant young woman was then sent off to Germany in the company of her governess and piano teacher, both German women in their mid-thirties, armed with the certificate and a generous subsidy from Grey, and delivered her baby in Bremen. She was sent back to England after several months, and the two German "aunts," Sophie List and Dora Thomas, raised the little girl on the island of Borkum. Charlie Grey went off to Africa to join his brother George. The girl was told that her English parents had died of tropical fever on the Dark Continent. Her son, the article's author, believes that she learned the truth on a trip back to London when she was twenty, but she never spoke a word about her parentage or her English relatives. The two "aunts" also kept mum.

The documentary evidence consists of a German birth certificate and a baptism certificate, both of which list the father as Charles Grey, "*Offizier in Englischen Diensten.*" The fraudulent marriage certificate had convinced a Saxon bureaucrat and a pastor, and the "aunts" were able to raise the girl as a respectable, upper-middle-class English orphan.[1]

There are several problems with the story, the chief being that there is no evidence Grey ever met Florence Slee. Not only his social position, but his busy life at the time—he was Under-Secretary of State for Foreign Affairs and left each weekend for Itchen Abbas—would have made such a relationship unlikely.[2] It

---

1 Another bit of evidence consists of a photo in profile of the article's author, Hans-Joachim Heller, revealing "the Edward Grey nose." Next to it is a photo of Charles Grey, also in profile, with a very different physiognomy. Also, the guest house the "aunts" purchased in Borkum, later converted to a kindergarten by their ward, was named "Constance," after Edward's youngest sister, Heller claims. It was she, he believes, who negotiated with them and dispensed the final settlement, and they regarded her as their benefactress.

2 Inundated with work, he normally read despatches and letters at the Foreign Office all morning and worked in an office in the cellar of the Commons after lunch. He and Dorothy had taken a

is difficult to imagine the circumstances under which they might have met.[1] What social event could they both have been attending? Did Grey accost the unchaperoned middle-class girl on the street? Where would they have had sex? There is, of course, the added difficulty that given everything we know about Grey's character and Dorothy's, such a liaison, behind her back, is improbable. Grey worshiped his wife, they were inseparable, and both valued candor above all other virtues.

There is an alternative explanation. Before she returned to London, Florence Slee entrusted to Fraulein Thomas and Fraulein List two small photographs that they eventually passed along to her daughter, Winifred. One was of herself and the other was of a young man who Hans-Joachim Heller originally assumed was Charles Grey. Further investigation revealed that it was of Ernest Upcott Story, Florence's brother-in-law, the husband of her older sister Kate, and a stock-broker in London.[2] It is certainly odd that Florence would bring with her to Germany and leave to her daughter a photograph of her brother-in-law—and none of her parents or siblings. Was Story the father of the child? This would certainly explain the urgency of the situation, the need for absolute secrecy, and the willingness to spend great sums of money. The English had a particular horror of sexual relations between a man and his wife's sister. It was regarded as little better than

---

house on Grosvenor Road, largely for its proximity to Waterloo station, and nearly every Saturday morning the couple would leave before dawn and catch the 6:00 train to Itchen Abbas. The extramarital affair would have to have taken place in late May or early June of 1893. Parliament was in session continuously from early spring, and the routine seldom varied. It is difficult to trace the movements of the Greys with certainty, but there's no evidence Dorothy left London for Fallodon during this period.

1 Today there are no doubt occasional couplings between estate agents (realtors in the U.S.) and clients in unoccupied homes. It's highly unlikely a single woman in 1893 would have been showing homes, and in any case the Greys were not in the market for a new house, so an encounter with Florence in her father's office is also unlikely.

2 The Storys appear to have had at least two sons, Aubrey Ernest Story, born in 1891, and Ernest Upcott Story, Jr., who served as a 2nd Lieutenant with the Royal Defence Corps in the First World War.

incest, even after the wife had died.[1] At best, such an adulterous relationship was a double betrayal—of sister and wife.

Ernest Story, unlike Edward Grey, would have had many opportunities to get to know Florence, to win her confidence, and perhaps her love. It is not hard to imagine an impulsive coupling. He may have whispered that she would not get pregnant; he would take precautions.

The rest of the scenario could have unfolded as Heller speculates. Charles Grey was not an uncommon name.[2] A Charles Grey, or someone using that name, could have gone through a sham marriage with Florence at an unregistered chapel. The attempt to link this individual to the Fallodon Greys may have been a later inspiration. Not only was it gratifying to the "aunts," but it better covered the tracks of Ernest Story. Charles Grey is identified on the birth and baptism certificates as an English officer. Edward Grey's brother was not. There were 11 Greys on the active list for the second half of 1893, including a C. W. Grey.

There is an additional consideration. Winifred moved to Berlin with her husband in 1938, and, after the Second World War, she and her two young sons were trapped in the Soviet zone. Life was extremely difficult for civilians in the occupied east long after the German surrender, and from the winter of 1946 Winifred received food parcels from the British Red Cross. In 1947, she was granted permission to visit friends in the British sector and hoped to be able to remain there.[3] If she had been informed on her fateful trip to London in 1914 that her father was the Foreign Secretary, or even Charles Grey, she may well have kept silent about it for some years, as she was admonished. Certainly during the Great War, when Grey was being demonized in the

---

1 Lord Lyndhurst's Marriage Act of 1835 explicitly prohibited a widower from marrying the sister of his deceased wife. From 1842 to 1907, bills legalizing the practice were repeatedly voted down.
2 There are presently twenty-six listed in the UK telephone directory, along with two Charlie Greys.
3 Testimonial from M. B. Jowett, Staff Commandant, British Red Cross Society, Berlin, 25 June 1947, and note by H-A Heller on reverse of the copy.

German press, there would have been no incentive to disclose that she was his daughter. Once the war was over, though, one would think she might have revealed the relationship to close friends or family. Lord Grey was a distinguished elder statesman; she would have been connected to the British aristocracy. But especially in the bitter years after World War II, when she was scrounging for food and trying desperately to escape from the Soviet occupation zone, Winifred would have had every incentive to reveal the secret to British authorities, and to enlist their help to verify it. On the other hand, if she had learned in 1914 that her real father was her uncle, she would have had no wish to mention this to anyone.

Michael Waterhouse also relates a "family legend amongst a minor branch of the Lascalles family," that a boy raised by one Rowley Lascalles, the son of a chaplain, was another love-child of Grey's. The sole evidence is a listing in the census of 1911 of an "Edward Grey," residing in the household as a "visitor" with "private means." He had been formerly listed as "Edmund Lascelles," a son.[1] But surely if the Lascalles family, which included the Ambassador to Germany from 1895 to 1908, Frank, had taken upon themselves the responsibility of raising in secret the Foreign Secretary's son, the last thing one would expect them to do would be to call the child, or permit the child to call himself, "Edward Grey."

The story of still another illegitimate child, though more detailed, is no less speculative. This time, Grey might possibly have met the alleged inamorata: she was, Waterhouse suspects, Violet Vivian, a Maid-of-Honour to the Queen Mother. As with Florence Slee, however, there is no evidence the two ever came into contact. The story is based entirely on information that was

---

1 Waterhouse, 47.

told by her parents to a woman named Dorothy May Nelson, born, probably, in 1911. She had been adopted, her parents said, and though her original name had been registered as Janet Lincoln, she was actually the child of Sir Edward Grey and "a well-born Englishwoman with royal connections."[1] She was not given this information until 1945, and then only because she was about to name her own daughter Janet. When Dorothy Nelson eventually checked her birth certificate, it listed her mother as Mary Della Lincoln of Washington, D.C., leading Waterhouse to suspect that Grey's friend Teddy Roosevelt assisted in the business. According to Dorothy's daughter Janice Babbitt, the adoption record remains sealed.[2] As with Winifred Heller, Waterhouse relies heavily on "the extraordinary physical resemblance" to make the case for Grey's paternity.

Violet Vivian is the suspect on the grounds that both in 1910 and 1911 she traveled to Canada, and that her brother got divorced, hardly persuasive evidence. Vivian, moreover, never married, and it would have been a serious breech of etiquette for a man in Grey's social class to have had sex with an unmarried upper-class woman—not to mention the risk that she would have been running. Grey was a widower. If he was enamored of the Maid-of-Honour, why didn't he begin a relationship with her—of which there would more than likely have been some record? As his letters to Katharine Lyttelton and other confidantes reveal, Grey abhorred Court life and dreaded his visits to Windsor and Balmoral, and a Maid of Honour seems almost as far a reach for Grey as an estate agent's daughter. In either case, random sex with someone he didn't know well seems completely out of character.

Nonetheless, impulsive couplings between unlikely partners happen, and rumors about these brief affairs cannot be entirely

---

1 M. Waterhouse, 256–7.
2 Telephone conversation with Janice Babbitt, 13 May 2013.

ruled out.[1] The fact that Dorothy Nelson's adoptive parents were told that her real father was Grey and were admonished not to tell anyone counts for something.

The fact that all of Grey's correspondence was destroyed shortly after his death, most likely by his oldest sister, and his journal and autobiography a few years later, must inevitably raise suspicions that something illicit was being concealed.

There is also the curious report by, of all people, Harry Cust. He had just dined at 10 Downing Street with Asquith, Kitchener, Balfour, and Grey, he told his nephew in May, 1916. "Sounds wonderful, doesn't it? But Grey was so totally absorbed in his idol Wordsworth having had an illegitimate daughter in France when he was twenty-two that he could talk of nothing else: the First Lord of the Admiralty [Balfour] was shocked, the Prime Minister delighted, and the Minister for War had never heard of Wordsworth."[2]

There may possibly have been personal reasons why Grey's interest was piqued. Twenty-first century readers are likely to be more impressed by his confession, once again as reported by Marie Lowndes, that when, "after many years of marriage," Dorothy offered to have sex with him, he turned her down.[3] Did she suspect he was having an affair, and act out of jealousy?[4] While this is possible, women mature sexually later than men, and Dorothy may have felt desires she hadn't experienced previously. Her

---

1 As Marie Lowndes wrote apropos of George Eliot, "The longer I live the more I feel how little one really knows of one's friends' lives, especially in that all-important matter of sex, and if that is true now, when people are so unconventional and speak so freely to those they care for, think what it must have been in a day when reticence was the absolute rule."(S. Lowndes (ed.), *Diaries and Letters of Marie Belloc Lowndes* (London, 1971), 100.) Also, newspaper editors were respectful of reputations, and the private lives of Grey and his Cabinet colleagues were not investigated and publicized as they would be today. Those of Asquith, Haldane, Harcourt, Lloyd George, and Morley, among others, would have made interesting reading.

2 R. Storrs, *Orientations* (London, 1943), 33.

3 M. Lownes, *A Passing World* (London, 1948), 175.

4 This is the supposition of her grandniece. (C. Chance, *The Widdrington Women* (Andover, 2010), 185.)

feelings about children may also have mellowed; she may no longer have been terrified at the prospect of giving birth.

As for Edward's motives, many will be convinced, with Waterhouse, that this is conclusive proof he indeed had a mistress and wished to continue to "compartmentalize" his life. But apart from the problem as to why Pamela would tell the story to her friend if she herself had been Edward's lover at the time (and she's the only real candidate)[1], there is the possibility that Grey in fact believed, as was reported to Lowndes, that both he and Dorothy were "happy and satisfied with the life they had agreed on leading."[2] Sexual intimacy with his wife, he may have been convinced, would fray the bond between them rather than strengthen it. Grey was not impotent: Pamela became pregnant in 1922 or 1923. But he may have had low testosterone levels and have become habituated to occasionally relieving himself through masturbation—regarding it perhaps as something like urination or defecation.

For many, merely the fact that his was a *marriage blanc* is sufficient evidence that he must have had affairs: what Dorothy denied him, he would have sought elsewhere. For Heller, he was "a jolly, sociable and sporting man" and "it was rumored he had love affairs in London."[3] For Waterhouse, "Grey was a handsome, healthy, active man in the prime of his life... Living alone in London was asking for trouble."[4]

But the past is truly a foreign country, and it's always a mistake to lightly project back our own tastes and values. The second half of the 1880s saw a widespread questioning of conventional

---

1 Neither Heller nor Waterhouse suggest that the affair with Florence Slee was anything more than a one-night stand. Of course if their relationship had already become intimate, Pamela may have been relieved she was not, in a sense, betraying the sister-wife, and pleased that she had Edward to herself.

2 Lownes, *Ibid.*

3 Heller, *Journal of Liberal History,* 13.

4 Waterhouse, 43.

ideas about the relationship between men and women, and about male biological imperatives. Paradoxically, the very fact that the Greys were enlightened late-Victorians, with advanced views on "the woman question," helps explain their willingness to live as brother and sister.

This is not to deny that the couple may have been influenced as well by traditional nineteenth-century attitudes toward sex: that women in the upper classes had little or no sexual drive and regarded intercourse as an unwelcome imposition,[1] and that the act was physically and emotionally enervating for both partners.

There is also the fact that the "honeymoon" consisted of two weeks at Fallodon, in the company of Edward's mother and siblings.[2] There can have been little privacy for the inexperienced newlyweds. Sex may have been not much more pleasurable for Edward than for Dorothy.

But around the time of the Greys' marriage, there seemed to some enlightened English couples the prospect that, as Mill and other advanced liberals had hoped, marriage would be based on intellectual and emotional affinities and its bestial physical side would diminish in importance.

Edward and Dorothy were married in October 1885. In February of that year the couple's favorite novelist published *Diana of the Crossways*.[3] Diana would be celebrated as the prototype of "the New Woman," but she was based on a woman who

---

1 In the much-quoted analysis of Dr. William Acton, the leading authority on sex in the second half of the 19th century, "a modest woman seldom desires any sexual gratification for herself. She submits to her husband's embraces, but principally to gratify him; and were it not for the desire of maternity, would far rather be relieved from his attention." (W. Acton, *The Function and Disorders of the Reproductive Organs in Childhood, Youth, Adult Age, and Advanced Life* (London, 1875), 143.)
2 *Dorothy Grey,* 21.
3 Part of it, twenty-six of forty-three chapters, had been serialized in seven installments in the *Fortnightly Review* the previous year. (L. Stevenson, *The Ordeal of George Meredith* (New York, 1953), 257.)

had died seven years earlier at age sixty-nine, Caroline Norton.[1] Meredith, however, made one significant change in her fascinating story: his heroine was chaste. She marries to escape the attentions of her admirers, then refuses to sleep with her husband. The reader is not meant to sympathize with him.

Dorothy was enthralled by the book. "It's the only novel I ever liked well enough to read over again," she told a friend.[2] She later wrote, "It seems to me that a great part of what understanding of humans I have has been got through George Meredith. He lets in such a light on the workings of things."[3]

What undoubtedly endeared Diana to her was the combination of chastity and recklessness, frigidity and passion, self-denial and willfulness. Dorothy no doubt sympathized also with Diana's love of nature and her frustration at being unable to escape London, trapped in West End drawing rooms by her career as a novelist of Society. Edward was quite unlike Diana's husband August Warwick, but the convictions of Meredith's heroine may have reinforced her distaste for physical intimacy.

In the weeks after their honeymoon, Dorothy may well have fastened onto a second model, her namesake, the sister—and muse and chronicler—of Edward's beloved William Wordsworth.

---

1 Mrs. Norton had already appeared in novels by Disraeli (*Endymion*) and Dickens (*Pickwick Papers*), and had herself published two autobiographical novels (*The Wife* and *Woman's Reward*) half a century earlier. Celebrated for her vivacity, wit, and beauty, she had been involved in acrimonious public battles with her husband, first over the custody of their children after they separated and then over her income. The granddaughter of Richard Brinsley Sheridan, Norton was a prolific and successful author and had also received an inheritance from her mother. Under English law, her earnings became the property of Mr. Norton, and he had the right to deny her access to her children. Still more scandalous were the divorce proceedings initiated by her husband in 1836, claiming that the Prime Minster, Lord Melbourne, was his wife's lover. (The charges were dismissed, but Melbourne, who had already had more than his share of scandal—he had once before been named as co-respondent in a divorce suit and his wife had carried on a notorious affair with Byron—promptly dropped Mrs. Norton.) To compound her notoriety, Caroline Norton was also accused of leaking to the *Times* the information that the Peel government had reversed itself on the Corn Laws, a secret she had allegedly learned from her supposed lover Sidney Herbert, and which caused the government to fall. In fact, the information was supplied by Lord Aberdeen and she and Herbert were probably not lovers.
2 *Dorothy Grey*, 139.
3 *Ibid.*, 144.

Their relationship may well have been an inspiration for the couple. The year after the Greys married, the first biography of Dorothy Wordsworth appeared, and though it is not mentioned in what little correspondence between the Greys survives, it is likely they read it.[1] In her enthusiasm for the countryside and in her powers of observation, Dorothy Wordsworth was a direct inspiration for the poet—and Edward must have been impressed by the similarities with his Dorothy, and noted approvingly the strength of the bond between them.

Five months after *Diana* appeared came the titillating revelations of "The Maiden Tribute of Modern Babylon." Girls as young as thirteen were procured from London and the provinces for the gratification of wealthy debauchees at West End brothels.[2] W. T. Stead, the author of the series and the editor of the *Pall Mall Gazette*, in which it was published, was born and raised in Embleton, about two miles from Fallodon,[3] but another Northumbrian, a relative of Grey's, had already focused the atten-

---

1 Edmund Lee, *Dorothy Wordsworth: The Story of a Sister's Love* (London, 1886). The book was issued at the conclusion of the publication of the definitive eight-volume edition of Wordsworth's works (1882–1886), edited by W. A. Knight, and was followed three years later by Knight's three-volume life of the poet. Though twentieth century critics naturally searched high and low for signs of incest, there's no evidence of this, though as children the brother and sister did like to lie down side-by-side outdoors, pretending they were in their coffins.

2 *Pall Mall Gazette*, 4, 6, 7, 8, 10 July 1888. What made the story so sensational—and led to its author's arrest—was that he himself had purchased a thirteen-year-old girl from Marylebone for the purpose of sexual intercourse. The class element was not neglected: readers were reminded that it was "the daughters of the people" who were offered each night "as dainty morsels to minister to the passions of the rich."(J. Walkowitz, *City of Dreadful Delight* (Chicago, 1992), 97–8.)

3 He had succeeded the virginal John Morley at the PMG and would himself be succeeded, after an interval, by the inveterate rake Harry Cust, neither of whom would have touched the story. The son of a Congregationalist minister, Stead soon demonstrated great ability as a writer and publicist, achieving national recognition in 1876 for a series of articles on the massacres of Bulgarian peasants by Ottoman troops. "The honour of Bulgarian virgins," the crusading journalist had proclaimed, "is in the custody of the English voter."(E. Bristow, *Vice and Vigilance* (Dublin, 1977), 108.) Gladstone took up the cry, and the English voter had responded. Now it was English virgins whose honor was menaced. Stead's revelations were followed by riots in the paper's offices, as would-be buyers swarmed in for copies; no newsagent would distribute the issues. Within weeks, mass meetings were held throughout England, a demonstration in Hyde Park drawing nearly a quarter of a million, and a petition bearing 393,000 signatures was presented to Parliament, which hastily passed a major piece of social legislation that had been stalled for years, the Criminal Law Amendment Act. This raised the age of consent from 13 to 16 and strengthened the ability of the courts and police to protect girls from procurers and seducers.

tion of educated men and women on the distasteful subject of prostitution.[1] Josephine Butler's great crusade (her words) had directly inspired what came to be called the social purity movement. It was the double standard of the Contagious Diseases Acts that infuriated repealers: men were not targeted for inspection, nor were soldiers confined to their barracks or sailors to their ships if they were infected.[2] Both the "libertarian" and "interventionist" opponents of the Acts[3] believed that men ought to—and could be induced to—control their sexual passion and become as pure as women. "The essence of the great work which we propose to ourselves," wrote Butler, "is to Christianize public opinion, until, both in theory and practice, it shall recognize the fundamental truth that the essence of right and wrong is in no way dependent upon sex, and shall demand of men precisely the same chastity as it demands of women.[4]

"Men will rise to any standard you set for them," declared Jane Ellice Hopkins, founder of the White Cross League and the most famous of the moral purity campaigners.[5] While she had her

---

1 Josephine Butler's grandfather was the younger brother of Edward's great-great grandfather, the first Earl Grey. Butler's interest in prostitutes had a tragic origin. The wife of an Oxford tutor who had become vice-principal of Cheltenham College, she had watched in horror as her five-year-old daughter Eva plunged to her death at her parents' feet when the balcony onto which she had rushed out to wave goodbye to them collapsed. "I became possessed with an irresistible urge to go forth and find some pain keener than my own, to meet with people more unhappy than myself," she wrote. (J. Walkowitz, *Prostitution and Victorian Society* (New York, 1980), 116.) She had failed to catch her daughter, but she would rescue fallen women.

2 The Contagious Diseases Acts of 1864, 1867, and 1869 authorized state inspection of prostitutes in sixteen garrisons and ports to protect soldiers and sailors from venereal disease; women found to be infected were then quarantined. To its proponents it seemed a sound, modern, scientific approach to a problem affecting the security of the nation and Empire.

3 The former objected primarily to the arbitrary arrest and examination of women suspected of being prostitutes; this violated their civil rights and smacked of the corrupt and tyrannical *police de moeurs* on the continent. The "interventionists," while they shared the indignation at the targeting of prostitutes and not their clients, wanted the government to intervene more actively to suppress vice. Not only should procurers and brothel owners be vigorously pursued, but the owners of establishments that incited men's lusts should also be prosecuted—including music hall owners and publishers. The split was institutionalized when the Personal Rights Association was founded by defectors from the Ladies National Association for the Repeal of the CD Acts in 1871.(Bristow, 81.)

4 J. Butler, *Social Purity* (London, 1879), 12. See the eight-point Declaration published by Butler in the *Daily News* in January 1870 1869.(J. Butler, *Personal Reminiscences of a Great Crusade* (London, 1911), 9–10.)

5 Bristow, 99.

greatest success with working-class men,[1] there were some takers in the upper ranks.[2]

With cynical shrugs or with outrage, the link between upper- and middle-class marriage and prostitution had long been acknowledged. "But most thro' midnight streets I hear/ How the youthful Harlot's curse/ Blasts the new born Infant's tear/ And blights with plagues the Marriage hearse," wrote William Blake in 1794. So the interest in prostitution reawakened by Stead revived the marriage question as well. Did marriage depend on prostitution? Did it enable middle-class women to retain their virtue while their future husbands were able to resort to prostitutes until they had completed their education and professional training and were earning an income permitting them to marry? If so, as Louise Creighton wrote, prostitutes should be honored for their self-sacrifice.[3] Was marriage itself a form of prostitution, in which women provided for their husband's sexual needs in exchange for shopping money?

Inspired by the furor over the *Pall Mall Gazette's* revelations, a group of middle-class Londoners launched a discussion group they had been considering for some time, the Men and Women's

---

1 One observer, who had heard all the great British and American revivalist preachers, wrote, "We never heard an address more calculated to meet an audience of common men than hers; and we never saw an audience more deeply moved. In diction and argument it was beautiful and powerful; but in fervour and pathos it was unbelievable."(R. M. Barrett, *Ellice Hopkins: A Memoir* (London, 1907), 14.) "Beneath the power of the Cross of Christ," Hopkins wrote, "I have seen four hundred rough, world-hardened men weeping and sobbing like children over their sins," she wrote.(Barrett, 19.) Her charisma is all the more remarkable as she was physically unprepossessing, unlike the beautiful, ethereal Butler. Hopkins was the daughter of a Cambridge geologist and mathematician, to whom she was devoted ("he made it possible for her to realise the Divine Fatherhood of God," she wrote), and began by organizing Bible classes.(Barrett, 10.) She moved into rescue work, but found greater satisfaction—and greater success—in addressing and advising men. She converted hundreds of men in the villages around Cambridge, brazenly entering pubs and preaching the gospel of moral purity.
2 The Anglican Church Congress established the Church of England Purity Society in 1883 under the leadership of the Archbishop of Canterbury, Edward Benson.(Bristow, 100–1.) It was inspired by Hopkins' eloquence and merged with the White Cross League eight years later.
3 L. Creighton, *The Social Disease and How to Fight It: A Rejoinder* (London, 1914), 33.

Club, one of the few organizations to admit both sexes.[1] Its chief organizer was Karl Pearson, son of a Quaker solicitor and the recently appointed Goldsmid Professor of Applied Mathematics and Mechanics at University College London. Even Pearson, a Darwinian repelled by the religiosity of the purity campaign and the "unscientific" feminism of Wollstonecraft and Mill—and a supporter of the CD Acts—still felt that men should be encouraged to restrain their passions.[2] "Surely the happiest state of the individual," he wrote, "is to disregard sex and not to be conscious in...friendship...of the likeness or difference of sex at all."[3] Club member Maria Sharpe, who he was eventually to marry, agreed: men "did not realize that women married men for their minds" and they exchanged vows with "no desire for children and repulsion toward the exercise of the sex function."[4] Two other women circulated papers arguing for self-control on the part of men.[5]

Edward himself did not of course sign the pledge of Ellice Hopkins's White Cross League, nor did he apply for membership in the Men and Women's Club.[6] But both of the Creightons embraced the moral purity movement, and the subject was likely to have come up in conversation. Louise was deeply stirred by Ellice Hopkins' pamphlets when she read them at Embleton. "I

---

1 Even opponents of the CD Acts were segregated by sex: there was an all-male National Association for the Repeal of the CD Acts and a Ladies National Association. Members of the Men and Women's Club were carefully selected; bohemians were not admitted. The men were educated at Oxford and Cambridge and mostly professionals, lawyers, doctors, academics. Papers were read to the group each month and discussed. Records were carefully preserved for posterity.

2 Wollstonecraft, like Mill, argued on utilitarian as well as moral grounds for the emancipation of women, which would be achieved by educating them as men were educated. Men would benefit, as well as women, if they were regarded as rational creatures.

3 Walkowitz, *City*, 153.

4 *Ibid.*

5 Their health was at stake. The act of "coition on the part of the man," wrote one, was "a violent action, bordering on convulsions and causing great exhaustion."(Kathleen Mills, "Checks to Population," quoted by Walkowitz, *City*, 158.) Women were freer, another member claimed, in so far as they had liberated themselves from sexual passion and that as society evolved, "moral strength" replacing physical strength, men would follow suit.(Henrietta Muller, "The Other Side of the Question," in *Ibid.*, 151–2.)

6 Hopkins' converts signed after five minutes of intensive prayer, vowing "to fulfill the command, 'keep THYSELF pure.'" and "to maintain the law of purity as equally binding upon men and women."(J. E. Hopkins, *The White Cross Army*, x.) On the purity campaigners, see Bristow, 94–121.

must do something to raise the moral standard amongst the people," she vowed, and commenced rescue work.[1] When Hopkins founded the National Union of Working Women in 1888—not a union at all, but a middle-class organization dedicated to improving the lives of working class women—Creighton became its first president.

Louise Creighton eventually weighed in on the question in a long pamphlet of her own. "The degradation of numberless women and the suffering and disease which follows" are a direct result of the weakness of men and the double standard "which exacts purity for women and condones incontinence in men."[2] She was responding to a pamphlet by Christabel Pankhurst, which had launched the battle cry "Votes for Women, Chastity for Men," for even radical suffragettes endorsed the purity campaign.[3] Creighton deplored the "spirit of antagonism" in Pankhurst's approach. Chastity was more difficult for men than for women: their passions were stronger and were fostered by their upbringing. Girls were encouraged to be coquettes, boys to be "domineering and self-assertive."[4] But she was convinced a higher moral order was attainable, and the double standard eliminated.[5] Mandell Creighton also signed on, helping to found and becoming first president of the Council for the Public Morality, established to combat "organized temptations to immorality."[6] The Council was run by the veteran purity campaigner William Coote, long-

---

1 L. Creighton (J. Covert, ed.), *Memoirs of a Victorian Woman*, 66. Rescue work involved confronting prostitutes and attempting to convince them to give up their trade, a difficult and sometimes dangerous form of philanthropy. Gladstone was the most famous practitioner.
2 Creighton, *Social Disease*, 2.
3 There were of course a few voices calling for "free love"—a risky prospect for non-aristocratic women before effective birth control. Inevitably, there was a society advocating the sexual emancipation of women, with its own journal (the Legitimation League; it published *Adult*), where libertarians and anarchists mingled uneasily.(L. Bland, *Banishing the Beast: Sexuality and the Early Feminists* (New York, 1995), 156.)
4 Creighton, *Social Disease*, 63.
5 *Ibid.*, 76. The solution was education, though ultimately self-mastery could only be gained "by seeking the grace of God and trusting His strength."
6 L. Creighton, *Life and Letters of Mandell Creighton*, v. 2 (London, 1904), 386.

time secretary of Stead's National Vigilance Association. Louise Creighton praised him highly in her pamphlet.

Creighton, the father of six who shocked his pupils at Embleton by kissing and hugging his wife in public, certainly did not advocate abstinence from sex in marriage. But the letter he wrote Dorothy on learning of her engagement eloquently seconded the exalted and decidedly uncarnal conception of marriage she had formed. "Yes," he wrote, "you have found out what I have tried to lead you to discover,

> that the joy of life lies in self-knowledge, and that love is the one key to that knowledge... Love...comes on suddenly, abruptly, it is overwhelming, and complete: it has to pass on to something less dazzling but more permanent, less splendid but more useful—to the large-eyed steadfast love that will bear the wear and tear of common life. "They married and lived happily ever after" ends the common novel. "Did they? What extraordinary people!" is the comment of common sense. Marriage is the beginning, not the end of real life...
>
> One thing only let me say, the truth of which I have profoundly felt, and feel more and more day by day: the love which does not increase in both [partners] the love of God—that does not blend with our highest feelings of reverence and quicken them and sweep us upward, humbled yet satisfied with our humility—the love which does not do this falls short of that completeness which is the guarantee of its eternity.[1]

In the summer of 1888, the marriage question was hotly debated for a full month in the pages of the *Daily Telegraph*. The

1 M. Creighton to D. Grey, 2 September 1885, in L. Creighton (ed.), *Counsel for the Young* (London, 1905), 59–60. Dorothy is identified in the book as "A. B."

paper received some 27,000 responses to the query "Is Marriage a Failure?"[1]

The question posed by the *Daily Telegraph* was inspired by an article published in the *Westminster Review* the month before by the Scottish feminist Mona Caird, who had been rejected for membership in the Men and Women's Club.[2] The article con-

---

1 H. Quilter, *Is Marriage a Failure?* (London, 1888), 2. Two decades earlier, in July of 1868, the *Daily Telegraph* had asked its readers to respond to the query "Marriage or Celibacy?" On this occasion it received over 5,000 replies, publishing a total of 270. (*The Daily Telegraph* was the first mass circulation newspaper, selling 150,000 copies a day by the 1860s, more than the combined total of all of London's other morning papers.(J. Robson, "Marriage or Celibacy? A Victorian Dilemma," in J. Weiner, *Papers for the Millions: the New Journalism in Britain, 1850s to 1914* (Westport, CT, 1988), 189, 190.) The 1868 query was triggered by an earlier exposé of the white slave trade, this one involving European girls enticed to London and trapped in brothels. But the phrasing of the question also reflects the way in which the modern debate on marriage, begun by Olympe de Gouges and Mary Wolstonecraft in the early 1790s, had been deflected by the second, expanded edition of Malthus's *An Essay on the Principle of Population* (1803, the first appeared in 1798), in which he added "moral restraint"—delayed marriage, pre-marital abstinence, and, he hoped, some degree of marital continence—to the checks on population provided by vice (abortion and contraception) and misery (starvation and disease). Neo-Malthusians like J. S. Mill advocated birth control within marriage, but this was of course completely unacceptable for respectable couples. Anyone promoting this was subject to arrest, like Mill himself in 1823, and, notoriously, Annie Besant and Charles Bradlaugh fifty-four years later. For enlightened intellectuals Mill eventually held up as an ideal his own *marriage blanc,* and in the 1860s interest was stirred in celibacy. About 10% of English men and women remained unmarried, a high percentage even by European standards. A follower of Mill, the economist T. E. Cliffe Leslie, offered in 1863 a stout defense of the "old maid" and "old bachelor."("The Celibacy of the Nation" passionately argued that sexual abstinence was associated with the advance of civilization, and that it was "something quite fresh and modern." Spinsters and bachelors were selflessly postponing the Malthusian day of reckoning, when population would outstrip resources.(reprinted in T. Cliffe Leslie, *Essays in Political and Moral Philosophy* (Dublin, 1879), 14.) Both sets of letters to the *Daily Telegraph* offer a rare insight into middle-class marriages. (Quilter claims that no aristocrats and only one or two working class readers wrote in, though he reproduces letters from several.) Most of the letter-writers on both occasions described their own experiences, sometimes poignantly, blaming inflated expectations and the behavior of the opposite sex for involuntary celibacy and failed marriages. Many urged sensible changes in marriage law. Few, however, discussed the institution in a philosophical or historical light, to the despair of Mona Caird, who contributed a couple of letters.

2 The essay was much improved when published in book form eleven years later. Rejecting the idea of an unchanging "woman's nature" that makes marriage in its present form inevitable, the article cursorily surveys practices over several millennia. A peaceful matriarchal age was ended by a succession of hunting tribes who seized women in raids—the origin of the idea that women were men's property. The asceticism of early Christianity further devalued women, but the chivalric ideals of the Middle Ages promised an improvement. Unfortunately, Luther, Caird's bête noire, reversed the trend, along with "the commercial spirit." No more was there to be a spiritual union of husband and wife. Women were to be chaste before marriage, to protect their value, and be child-bearing machines afterwards. The wife is compared to a chained dog and a criminal in an iron cage. Great faith is placed in co-education to liberate women.(M. Caird, "Marriage," *Westminster Review* (v. 130, n. 2 (August 1888), 186–201.)

cludes with a plea for the self-ownership of women: an "acknowl-edgment of the right of the woman to *possess herself* body and soul, to give or withhold herself body and soul exactly as she wills," and hopes for the day "When man and woman in an equal union/Shall merge, and marriage be a true communion."[1] The Greys would have endorsed the couplet.

✑

Probably nothing did so much to stir debate on the marriage question in the 1880s as Ibsen's *A Doll's House*. "Nora's revolt is the end of a chapter in human history," wrote George Bernard Shaw. "The slam of the door behind her is more momentous than the cannon of Waterloo or Sedan."[2] *A Doll's House* is the ur-feminist drama, but it is not difficult, even a century and a quarter later, to see how shocking and exhilarating Nora's declarations sounded to contemporary audiences. Her husband Torvald wants to make love when the couple returns from a party in Act III. Nora, however, wants to discuss the relationship.[3]

The first English performance of the play (*Et Dukkehjen*, literally "The Dollhouse"), written and produced in 1879, was

---

1 *Ibid.*, 198, 201.
2 G. B. Shaw, *Our Theatres in the Nineties,* v. III, 131, cited by G. Ackerman, *Ibsen and the English Stage,* 1889–1903 (NY, 1987), 18. The stage directions require only that Nora close the door.
3 She tells Torvald that they've never spoken in earnest, and that he and her father have greatly wronged her—she was his doll, and then became her husband's. When he protests his love, she tells him that he has never loved her; he has only thought it pleasant to be in love with her. She has made nothing of her life and has not been happy. "I must try and educate myself," she tells him, after he promises that "playtime is over and lesson-time will begin," "and you are not the man to help me in that. I must do it for myself. And that is why I am going to leave you now." He reminds her of her sacred duties to her husband and children, but she replies that she "has other duties just as sacred: duties to myself." "Before all else you are a wife and mother," Torvald tells her. "I don't believe that any longer," Nora responds. " I believe that before all else I am a reasonable human being, just as you are—or, at all events, I must try and become one." The only explanation for her behavior is that she no longer loves him, Torvald declares. Nora admits this is true, and tells him her eyes were opened when he became enraged at her after her forgery was revealed. (She had forged her father's name on a promissory note to obtain money for her husband when he was ill.) She had hoped he would step forward and take the blame for the transgression, and defy Krogstad to blackmail him. When he tells her that no man would sacrifice his honor for the one he loves, she delivers her famous retort: "It is a thing hundreds of thousands of women have done"—altered to "millions" in late-20th and 21st century performances.

staged privately in 1885 or 1886 in a Bloomsbury lodging house, with Karl Marx's daughter Eleanor playing Nora.[1] The response in Scandinavia had been explosive. "People left the theatre night after night, pale with excitement, arguing, quarreling…" wrote Edmond Gosse. "The great statement and reply—'No man sacrifices his honor, even for one he loves.' 'Hundreds of thousands of women have done so!'—roused interminable discussions in countless family circles. The disputes were… so violent as to threaten the peace of households."[2] The reaction to the first stage performance in London was similar.[3] "A few of us collected outside the theatre breathless with excitement," recalled Edith Lees, Men and Women's Club member and future wife of Havelock Ellis. "We were restive and almost savage in our arguments. What did it mean?"[4] It was "less like a play than like a personal meeting—with people and issues that seized us and held us, and wouldn't let us go," wrote Elizabeth Robins, who would portray Mrs. Linden two years later. "Everyone in London had begun to talk about Ibsen that June."[5]

This is likely to have included the Greys, for though they don't discuss the play in surviving letters, Edward helped sponsor the first Ibsen festival in London (along with Henry James and Oscar Wilde)[6] and the couple soon became very close friends with Robins, the leading interpreter of Ibsen in England.

While it's impossible to say exactly what the Greys made of Ibsen, like *Diana*, like the discussion generated by the Stead and Caird articles, like the interest in the marriage question reflected in the

1 Ackerman, 37. G. B. Shaw played Krogstad.

2 E. Gosse, *Henrik Ibsen* (NY, 1912), 146, cited by Ackerman, 18.

3 It took place at the dingy Novelty Theatre on 7 June 1889, and starred the statuesque Janet Achurch as the doll-like Nora.

4 Walkowitz, *City,* 166. Maria Sharpe had already written an article on Ibsen in the *Westminster Review,* one of the first published in English on the playwright.

5 E. Robins, *Ibsen and the Actress* (London, 1928), 11; *Both Sides of the Curtain* (London, 1940), 195.

6 A. John, *Elizabeth Robins: Staging a Life* (London, 1995), 67. This took place at the Opéra Comique in 1893. Four plays were staged.

Daily Telegraph's correspondence and in the founding of the Men and Women's Club, *A Doll's House* would have reinforced a critical attitude toward the institution and the feeling that intelligent and moral couples owed it to themselves to redefine the relationship.

In choosing to live as brother and sister, the Grey's may well have believed they were embarked on something novel, even revolutionary, and something noble. They were pioneers of a new morality.

If changes were in the air in the late '80s, it is no surprise that other members of the upper classes continued to behave as their ancestors had, and as nearly everyone's descendants would a hundred years later.

In 1894, a year after Florence Slee gave birth to an illegitimate daughter, another English baby was born abroad, this time in France. The father was probably Roger Fry, the art critic and Bloomsberyite. The mother may have been Dorothy Grey's sister Ida—or possibly Dorothy and Ida's own mother, Cecilia Widdrington.[1] Dorothy had approved of the relationship between her rambunctious little sister and the earnest, but amusing Cambridge intellectual. Ida already had a dubious reputation, and Roger would be a steadying influence.

Five years later, Ida's reputation was considerably blacker. And Dorothy had severed relations with her.[2] But then, at age twen-

---

1 C. Chance, *The Widdrington Women and their Eminent Men* (Andover, Hampshire, 2010), 161–178. There are some problems with the chronology of the Widdringtons' trips to France. Also, if Ida had gotten pregnant, there would have been no reason Fry and she could not have gotten married. But it's possible he was no longer interested in the vivacious but superficial Ida, particularly if he'd been his prospective mother-in-law's lover—this would have made family gatherings a bit tense. And, if the baby were Cecilia's, she may have had no wish to pass it off as her husband's, as other women of her class did. The fact that Cecilia abruptly broke off her diary of Ida at the time when her daughter would have discovered she was pregnant also supports Chance's theory.
2 This followed from a disastrous stay in London with the Greys, during her second "season." Ida decided to model her behavior on the deplorable Margot Tennant, whom she met at one of Pamela Tennant's "Rosebud Dinner Parties" for debutantes. She plied Edward and Dorothy for gossip, flirted shamelessly with Haldane and Morley and other friends, and bantered, joked, sang, and made a spectacle of herself. Dorothy was mortified.(Chance, 122–3.)

ty-nine, Ida got engaged to Addison Baker-Cresswell, Master of the Percy Foxhounds, a Regency figure famous for wearing the tallest collars in London, and the wealthiest landowner in the county after the Duke of Northumberland. It would have been a brilliant match, if Addy—as he was known to all—had not been a dissolute wastrel, in the parlance of the day, and a notorious womanizer. He was also, as Cecilia noted, vain, unscrupulous, cruel, and overbearing—and an alcoholic. He was "a real bad lot," wrote Albert, Earl Grey, and added: "had D.G. not been so antagonistic to her merry sister who had a heart of gold, and if I may use perhaps a hard word, so selfish, a great deal of misery that now sits like a permanent cloud over the old home would have been averted."[1] Addy promptly resumed his bachelor habits after getting married, and three years later abandoned Ida for the wife of another man. Baker-Cresswell returned home repentant, deposited his illegitimate daughter with Ida, but then once again abandoned wife and family for extramarital romances, and left for good six years later. Lawyers for both sides advised against suing for divorce: each partner had far too much dirty linen.[2]

In 1921 Addy died of alcohol poisoning in a hotel room in New Forest, not far from Itchen Abbas. He just missed seeing the recrudescence of hedonism, materialism, and promiscuity of the '20s—for which Edward's step-children were to become the standard-bearers. He had lived, as he died, in close proximity to the Greys: Harehope House was just twelve miles from Fallodon. Cresswell-Baker enjoyed fishing, but of course Edward had given his brother-in-law a wide berth. After he and Dorothy attended Ida's wedding, there is no evidence the two ever met.

---

1 Albert Grey to Ella Pease, 17 June 1907. Durham University.
2 Chance, 187–198; 204–8.

INDEX

271